Contents

LANGUAGE IN
CHILDHOOD

First published in Great Britain in 1975 by
Elek Books Ltd., 54–58 Caledonian Road,
London N1 9RN

ISBN 0 236 31139 5

Printed in Great Britain by
Clarke, Doble & Brendon Ltd.,
Plymouth

Preface

This book has been written with two principal aims, the first of which is to extend published information, as distinct from discussion, about children's language learning. Although new studies of child speech have been reported in recent years, much has been written about only a few children, these being under three years old and mostly from the United States. It is hoped that a fresh study, this time from Britain and of children between three and seven years, is likely to interest not only linguists and psychologists but also those who teach and care for such children. The second aim is to look at existing notions of how children acquire language by considering what we mean when we speak of linguistic competence. During the last decade the influence of the work of linguists interested in the grammar of natural languages has been so strong that, while the forms of child speech have been examined with enthusiasm, the function of various forms has received scant attention. The consequences of the linguistic influence for theories of language acquisition have been to lessen interest in the nature of learning and to place quite heavy reliance on notions of a special innate language competence. While this is of considerable theoretical interest it also has implications for the education of young children.

The introductory chapter presents an account of different approaches to the study of language acquisition and outlines the author's viewpoint in conducting her investigations. The first of these is a study of the speech of her son at almost three years of age—a study that led to criticism of the notion of a special linguistic competence and to some attempt to describe modes of learning. The second is a study of the language skills of young schoolchildren which was intended to describe the development of their speech, to consider how literacy affects their knowledge of language, and to explore their competence in various tasks requiring discrimination and judgement of linguistic data. The implications of the findings are considered; and while no comprehensive, water-tight account of acquisition is proposed, a positive approach is made towards a more adequate theory of learning as an alternative to the unfolding of an innate competence.

All the work has been directed towards children with no apparent speech or language defects, although social disadvantage is considered. The selection of children for the first stages of the study was deliberately biased towards those who were expected to show a good command of language. It is hoped, nevertheless, that since a fairly full account of normal development is given, many who are interested in the development and education of handicapped children will find something to engage their attention.

The two studies were originally reported as *Learning to talk* and *Structure in the speech, reading and writing of young children,* these being unpublished theses for the degrees of M.A. and Ph.D. respectively in the University of Leeds. The author wishes to thank all those who have helped in the preparation of the book, to acknowledge the co-operation of the Chief Education Officer of the City of Leeds and that of the head-teachers and staff in the schools where the work was undertaken, and in particular to give very warm thanks to all the children who so willingly and cheerfully took part.

1 Language and Learning to Talk

LANGUAGE AND LEARNING

A year or two ago two children, aged nine and ten years respectively, were demonstrating their ability to give acceptable negative versions of statements such as *I like some sweets, I want some milk* and *I like dogs*. This involved using *do* as an auxiliary verb, together with *not* and the appropriate selection of a word to modify the object noun. This might be *some, any* or no word at all, depending on the context. The children readily gave forms which were regarded as grammatically correct in English and which therefore seemed to have been constructed by following rather a complex set of rules. Nevertheless, when asked by their mother 'How did you know how to do it?', one answered, 'We've learned it from you,' while the other said, We know it inside ourselves, in our minds. We don't just copy you.' To this the first replied that of course they didn't copy exactly, but they knew from listening how to do it themselves. During their performance they had become aware of regularity in their responses, but they were not aware of obeying any rules, nor did they know of ever having formally learned any relevant rules. Moreover they had produced their negative sentences without any immediate prior examples, for the instructions explained that a negative sentence was saying that something was not so, that words like *no, not* and *never* were added to a sentence to give an opposite meaning. After such instruction they had been asked to give the negative form of the first example. They proceeded to do so without difficulty, thereafter continuing with the rest of the sentences, yet the acquisition of their native tongue was a mystery to them, as indeed it is to anyone currently interested in children's language. Curiously, though, the children's spontaneous explanations expressed very clearly the main themes of academic discussions in recent years. Is there, or is there not, some form of given, possibly innate, knowledge underlying the processes of learning—a special language competence in fact? Furthermore what is the relationship between children's language and adults' language in learning?

This of course was a response to the form of the question. Until recently questions about the acquisition of language have largely been of the general form 'What can you do?' rather than 'How do you know how to do it?' Thus descriptions of child language focused on noting the acquisition of new items, of sound patterns, of vocabulary, and of markers of such features as word class, plurality, tense and mood; while ability to produce simple and complex sentences of increasing length was also of interest. From both small scale studies and larger samples some idea of the norms of development was obtained. But it has been increasingly recognised that the structure of languages is such that somehow the child has to learn not only an accumulation of items which he might conceivably attain by processes of imitation and association, but some basis for knowing what are and are not acceptable utterances when the possibilities of constructing both kinds by simple associations seem infinite. This notion of acceptable forms rests on the requirement that they should belong to the language system and be reliably interpreted within the language community (i.e. intuitively judged acceptable by a native speaker) not that they should conform to some standard criterion. To illustrate, a systematic use of 'was' with plural pronouns and 'were' with singular, as in 'he were' and 'they was', was found by the author to conform to the kind of rules used to describe standard English and to be totally acceptable within a dialect community in one part of a city; but it was not standard English nor was it approved by other speakers of English in the same city. The view that the speaker of a language possesses some implicit knowledge of its structure makes it as important to know what sense a child makes of language as it is to know what he can say, and in both cases the question of how he acquires his skill becomes important.

This shift in the orientation of investigation from normative studies became marked after the publication of Chomsky's *Syntactic Structures* in 1957 and his attack (1959) on Skinner's *Verbal Behavior*.* Essentially Skinner had attempted to give a functional description of language acquisition in terms of operant conditioning, whereas Chomsky pointed out that no theory of learning had accounted for the acquisition of the knowledge of the complex

* See References for full details.

systematic structure that was language, nor in his view could any theory of learning do so. The kind of structural system Chomsky had in mind was based on his work on syntax in English. He saw language as composed of sentences which had an underlying or deep structure as well as the simple linear surface form that might be spoken, written or analysed as a sequence of words or phrases. The simplest deep structures were those of simple assertions which could be intuitively analysed as composed of phrases functioning as subject and predicate, each of which could be separately further analysed. Thus a description of the deep structure of *The boy found a purse* would entail an analysis as shown in Figure 1·1. This demonstrates the underlying grammatical relations by

Figure 1.1

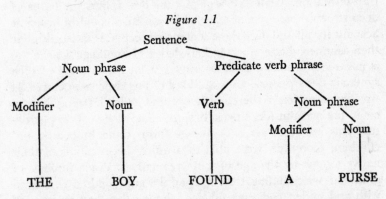

indicating how forms are functionally related. Thus the sentence comprises a noun phrase and a verb phrase functioning as subject and predicate. The verb phrase consists of a verb and a noun phrase functioning as main verb and direct object. The simple sentence *A purse was found by the boy* would require a similar analysis to indicate that the phrase *the boy* functioned as subject to the predicate *found a purse*, but an additional symbol would be required to indicate that the sentence has a passive form. In writing the grammatical rules that develop the various phrases into words in their proper order in the surface form of the sentence, certain additional transformation rules to yield the passive structure would be needed. In the 1957 version of his theory, Chomsky treated the passive entirely in terms of transformation rules applied to the same deep structure as the active, but in his 1965 theory he recognised that these rules were better regarded as based on a passive marker, as distinct from an active marker, associated with the *sentence* category of the deep structure. Other sentences in the language could also be formed by adding an appropriate marker, such as negative or interrogative, and using appropriate rules for developing the surface forms. Thus *The boy did not find a purse* and *Did the boy find a purse?* could be regarded as parallel transformations in that they also shared the same deep structure sentence. Yet other sentences could be formed by combining two or more simple sentences by embedding one in another. Thus *John came home* and *Mary came home* could be combined to form *John and Mary came home* if the deep structures of both were analysed and if appropriate conjunction and deletion rules were applied. Such rules again achieved a kind of transformation. Chomsky argued that descriptions in terms of deep structure and sets of transformation rules could in principle account for all and only those sentences acceptable in English. He then assumed that a working knowledge of the language such as is possessed by native speakers implies a tacit knowledge of such syntactic descriptions—a special kind of linguistic competence. It was the possession of this competence that he felt learning theories could not account for, especially since a knowledge of deep structure was involved, yet only surface forms could be heard; and children, moreover, were able to acquire the essentials of their native tongue by the age of fours years or so. While students of grammar were finding that both adults and children conversed with and understood each other as though they had an implicit knowledge of rules of syntax, students of phonology, following Jakobson (1956) were finding that there also seemed to be an implicit knowledge of similar kinds of rules (phonological rules) of sound patterning in language. This work strengthened the argument that language acquisition rested on the elaboration of competence rather than the accumulation of separately learned items. After the late 1950s earlier work was looked at in a new light. A comprehensive account of work relating to child language would itself make a large book. For interested readers a list of suggested further reading is given in the Bibliography at the end of this book.

The question in which the author is most interested is that which was addressed to the two children whose ideas introduced this chapter, namely 'How do children come to be able to understand language and talk as they do?' This question may be broken down into two subsidiary forms: 'What changes occur in what children can understand and say as they grow older?' and 'How do these changes come about?' The former question has been the principal focus of interest in research during the last decade, changes in the systematic use of various grammatical features such as markers of plurality, tense, interrogation and negation being most frequently explored. The general conclusions are that children's associations of words and parts of words in utterances are systematic rather than random, and are productive of new and appropriate combinations rather than being imitative or rote-learned. Children's utterances appear to be structured in some way from the start, and at a very early stage sentence patterning may be described in terms of sentence structures and transformation rules. Although these do not always correspond with adult forms, systematic shifts in children's structural systems eventually bring correspondence with adult language. Some workers have felt that the identification of patterns of change might in itself lead to an answer to the question of how the utterances come to be so structured, but little progress has been made on this front. A reading of a paper by Ervin (1964) which considers the problem soon reveals the reason. Change from one structural system to another is discussed in terms of processes like imitation and analogy, indicating that while the question of what the child can do might legitimately be discussed in terms of syntax and of language data alone, this is only one way of describing his activities. Behavioural descriptions are also important and it is only within a theoretical framework in which behavioural and linguistic descriptions can be satisfactorily related that some full account of the acquisition of language may be made.

At present there is no such adequate framework, but four broad theoretical approaches to the question of language learning can be identified in the literature. The first to be considered emphasises the nature of language as seen by linguists. In general the sentence structure of language has been described in terms of form (syntax), meaning (semantics) and function (pragmatics). Chomsky's work in elaborating a theory of the formal sentence structures of language has been associated with some fruitful work in linguistics and has proved a challenge to psychologists by specifying more clearly what is to be explained. Yet his comparison (1965) of the human learner with a grammatically programmed 'black box' or language acquisition device (L.A.D.), which could convert a rather messy and scrambled input of the kind of language samples heard by the learner into a knowledge of the grammar of the relevant language, was particularly empty. No human being, whether child or adult, sits passively processing heard sentences, for an essentially human characteristic is to explore the world, of which heard speech is an integral part, and actively to construct some regular and systematic understanding of it. It is precisely this point that has apparently been forgotten by McNeill (1966a) who has chosen to impose his own structural descriptions on samples of child speech, seemingly without any reference to what the children were doing in producing them and without any check on the child's intended meaning. He has then been forced to conclude that the child's own structuring of sentences is a mystery that can only be solved by resorting to some notion of innate linguistic competence, i.e. the innate possession of something like Chomsky's L.A.D. He almost manages to forget children altogether in his absorption with linguistics for at one point (on p. 38 in the cited work) he went so far as to suggest that a hypothetical example was as useful for his theory as the actual productions of children!

It may well be that the strategy of using theories of language to account for acquisition has been misconceived. It is important to notice that linguistic competence is an abstraction like intelligence—a summary statement about a way of behaving. In the case of the linguist it is the way he has been thinking about language, made possible by his ability to reflect on selected examples and use his analytic skills to infer systematic features. But the child's competence can be nothing like this, for such abstract thinking is not yet within his grasp. Thus the notion of a child's linguistic competence as being essentially a competence in dealing with the syntax of language as conceived by linguists may be totally in error. Syntactic descriptions may do no more than roughly reflect some other mode of construction. One approaches the use of linguistic theory as an explanatory mechanism in acquisition even more cautiously when it is realised that there is considerable discussion amongst linguists as to the appropriateness of Chomsky's theory of syntax as a theory of structure in language. Fillmore (1968) in particular has made telling points against it, criticising fundamental assumptions about the relationship between form and meaning. At this point it is possible at least to comment that two major criticisms of the linguistic approach must be that it demonstrates a possible mis-application of theory and a strong tendency to pay scant respect to either human nature or children's experience.

This last criticism may also be applied to most applications of theories of learning based on conditioning. These attempt to describe acquisition in terms of the formation of associations, between words as heard sound patterns or articulations, and between such words and referents; but the stimuli and responses are nearly always hypothetical as distinct from actual examples of speech. The most complex theoretical formulation of an account of learning is that given by Staats (1968), but he cannot account for the systematic changes in learning, the relatively sudden adoption of widespread use of plural forms by the two year old for example, or the systematic changes through sentences like *It no going* to *It not going* to *It's not going*, which are evident in the child's learning of negative and auxiliary verbal forms around the age of three years. Nor can he exclude in his account the possibility of the production of unacceptable and even meaningless utterances derived from the association of separately learned pairs containing a common element. For example, a child frequently used consecutive sentences of the form, *What's that? That's a car*, when looking at pictures, but he was never heard to say *What's that's a car*, in spite of the strength of the association. Furthermore association theory cannot exclude the possibility of a child's using noises which are not speech sounds but which happen to be associated with a referent. There is nothing to stop a child learning to use a whistling noise rather than the word 'kettle'. The whole complex business of attending to and selecting appropriate language forms is not accounted for.

Yet there are terms used in the psychology of learning which seem to be useful in considering language acquisition. *Generalisation* and *discrimination* readily come to mind. An interesting feature of these terms is that they are used in much the same way as in the natural language, having no very special theoretical status, although as processes they are explained in terms of differential reinforcement of responses. Lewis (1963) drew attention to children's over-inclusive use of early words, like 'dog' for several kinds of animal, and to their later more discriminating use. Investigations of the use of grammatical markers also show similar processes, and Braine (1963a) attempted to use these processes to explain the acquisition of syntax. He based his argument on a presumed ability to recognise patterns which allowed contextual generalisation, and carried out experiments (1963b, 1971) to find out whether adults could discover the 'syntax' of sets of sentences composed of nonsense syllables and structured according to arbitrary rules. Unfortunately in this he seems to have been exploring the competence of linguists rather than children, although his identification of similarities of patterning in children's two- and three-word utterances (1963a) was an important early step in the exploration of children's abilities. In general, however, approaches rooted in learning theory say much about what might be learned, but little about the learner, who is inevitably regarded as a passive reactor to environmental stimuli—this time as an empty black box because the theorists choose not to go so far as to put anything into it that might process information. Thus language or other stimuli go in and appropriate responses come out. Such theories may well summarise the findings of certain kinds of experiments, and they do have the merit of talking about aspects of actual behaviour, but they do not clarify what identifiable elements of behaviour may be appropriately classified as stimuli and responses in any particular explanation. The task of fully accounting for the acquisition of just one word like *can,* which has a complex sound pattern structure, bears different meanings in different contexts and belongs to different grammatical categories, presents enormous problems. Moreover, learning theories are designed to have general application to both human and animal behaviour so their usefulness is severely limited in describing or accounting for the novel and varied constructions which characterise so much of language acquisition and use. Perhaps a word should be said here, however, in favour of Skinner's work which is so often criticised to the point of rejection. His theory of operant conditioning has several merits. He did in fact observe his own child's speech, and therefore based his thinking on actual, as distinct from hypothetical, examples. He also considered utterances to be functional and therefore rooted in the rest of behaviour, and furthermore he suggested patterns of behaviour from which the child might produce certain kinds of novel constructions.

A further theoretical position merits some comment, namely the biological account of language in childhood. The fullest and most useful is presented by Lenneberg (1967), whose collection of observational and experimental data, describing the means whereby perception and production of speech are possible, together with his analysis of universal stages of development of language skills, is detailed and impressive. His comparison of normal with abnormal development is also extremely useful and interesting. But, although he paints such a full picture of the biological factors underlying the use of language, and shows how systematic behaviour is characteristic of all human skills, indicating the limitations and potentialities at various stages of development, he is unable to account for what actually happens in language acquisition. Although the normal human infant contains in his body all the developing structures whose functioning make the use of language possible, there can only be actualisation of this potential in so far as the child can make some sort of sense of the speech he hears. We need to know what goes on in the mind as well as in the body and brain of the child.

The three theoretical approaches mentioned so far all treat the child—if they treat him at all—as a passive subject to whom something happens as he learns. Yet this can only be a part of the story. Children are active, as any parent knows, and we cannot afford to neglect the question of what they do in their learning. Although there is no general theoretical formulation of a functional approach to language acquisition, many writers have emphasised the importance of considering what intentions and effects are associated with utterances. De Laguna (1927) adopted a restricted form of functional theory in taking the view that language should be regarded not solely as an abstract system, nor as a means of expression, whether of feelings or thoughts, but rather as a medium of co-operation between people. In her account, however, since she wrote before the full impact of structural linguistics was felt, she did not address herself to the problem of how a functional explanation might treat such proles as the use of phrase structures and transformations in sentence patterns. Skinner was being a functionalist when he was prepared to consider the effects of speech as a further stimulus and to consider the nature of reinforcement, but he would not have been happy to speak of intentions or effects as such within his theory. Yet many writers who have observed small children have adopted a functional categorisation of utterances. Thus Darwin (1872) analysed different kinds of crying in small babies as conveying information about pain, hunger and demand, and Lewis (1936) analysed early word and sentence utterances in terms of intended imperatives, denials, inquiries and comments. Most

B

observers see intentionality in communication developing early in the first year of life, and the implicit theme of their approaches is that comprehension and utterance have pay-off values within wider behavioural events. During the last few years there has been a reawakening of interest in functional descriptions in both linguistic and behavioural terms and a probing towards applying some sort of functional theory to the problem of acquisition. Stemmer (1971) has argued for an account of learning language structure in terms of classical conditioning, which he considers to be a suitable way of describing both the learning of word meaning and the learning of any appreciation of the context-sensitive functional equivalence of words and phrases. The latter he sees as the basis of understanding novel but appropriate sentence forms. Thus for him language ability rests on functional as well as formal categorisation. Although his treatment of meaning seems too slight as he does not explain what he would have to invoke to account for the leap from a listener's having a good chance of being correct to his effectively having a prior knowledge how to interpret an utterance, the emphasis on the relation between form and function is important. In a different vein, Halliday (1971) illustrated a functional analysis of the speech of a 19 month old child, an account which rested in the requirements of social interaction; while Brown (1968) has emphasised the importance of patterns of conversational exchange in language use and learning. Schlesinger (1971a), meanwhile, has challenged the basis of the linguistic argument for innate competence and argued strongly for an account of acquisition in terms of learning how to represent the semantic categories and relations of intended communications, and how to relate these systematically to the sound patterns of speech. Some evalution of these various positions will be found in the final chapter of this book.

It seems therefore that hitherto various theoretical approaches have been useful in clarifying problems relating to the question of language acquisition, but there is no overall frame of reference within which the question can be tackled fully. This is not really surprising when it is realised that such is the case in attempts to account for any form of what constitutes essentially human behaviour. The author's own work was undertaken within a frame of reference which was at first implicit rather than explicit, but which became clearer as time went on, so that it might now be helpful to attempt to formulate it as a whole. Two important areas of experience strongly influenced this development. Earlier study within the discipline of geography had led to a clear recognition that not only was the life and work of men influenced by the interaction between their biological nature and the kind of territory in which they lived, but that it was a product of their individual and joint efforts to impose some sort of systematic building upon the land, upon social groupings, upon economic effort and upon activity in science and the arts. Witness the immense irrigation systems of Egypt and the Sind, the growth of towns, the development of integrated systems of manufacturing, trade and transport, and the growth of various scientific and artistic cultures. It was in the nature of man to impose systems on whatever he encountered and to reconstruct them in the face of change, whether in his own skills, in social interaction or in the physical environment. Experience in parenthood led to a recognition that, in learning to talk, children were essentially taking part in this working life of mankind. Within the limitations of their immaturity they were working to make some functional sense of what they encountered, and this involved attending to adults and older children who tried to communicate with them and with each other. To this end the infants did not passively accept all that came to them in a haphazard way but, whether consciously or not, took a hand in the patterning of their behaviour and attempted systematically to control the action of others. With this recognition came also the awareness that as a parent the author was also working to understand the child's system of communication. The early stages of acquisition undoubtedly involve a dual process, the child coming to understand and produce the adult forms while the adult tries to acquire the child's—at least to the extent of comprehension and even sometimes of production!

With this sort of experience behind her the author came to study language acquisition in the context of work in the discipline of psychology. The nearest approaches to some overall theoretical formulation which made sense in the light of experience were found from two sources, though neither of these had been applied to natural language learning. The first approach, which has its adherents in the fields of clinical psychology and the study of personality, is that derived from Kelly's theory of personal constructs and which is outlined and discussed clearly by Bannister and Fransella (1971). Although the theory was intended to focus on psychotherapeutic interaction it may be more widely useful as a consequence of the intention to include theorists within the range of application, for it purports to cover the processes of making sense of experience. Basically each person is regarded as being able to recognise replication of significant events, and to use the construction he puts upon them to meet life and make sense of it by a process of anticipation and checking, presumably such anticipation being based on either a kind of statistical estimate or some process of analogy. Thus each individual builds a unique system of constructs, which may be relatively harmonious or be lacking in integration in various ways, and which is constantly undergoing development and modification. In so far as various constraints operate to make for considerable overlap between unique systems it is possible for experience to be communicated and shared. It would seem that a student of language acquisition, which is essentially the contruction by the child of the very system by which most sensible communication is possible, would be wise to take notice of this view of persons and their behaviours. Personal construct theory as applied to clinical experience, however, depends on the formation of verbal constructs, and the relationship of these to unverbalised aspects of behaviour is not clear. In this the notion of a construct has much in common with a verbal schema as conceived in the traditions of Bartlett (1932) and Piaget (1951), though Piaget has more to say than others about the structure of non-verbal systems of knowledge of the world.

If one is concerned with problems of the ways in which children make sense of experience, whether linguistic or not, then the second kind of approach that might be helpful is that of theories of cognitive development. The theories of Vygotsky (1962), Bruner (1964) and Piaget (1966) are all concerned with the identification of changes in children's ways of thinking and are therefore addressed to a similar problem as that of trying to account for children's systematic use of language and for changes in their systems. Indeed a constant theme of cognitive psychology is the interdependence of language and thought, and the problem of their relationship in acquisition is one which will keep recurring in the course of this book. But further points of interest are to be found in the study of thinking. Miller, Galanter and Pribram (1960) showed how over a wide range of skills the essential structure of planning is hierarchical. An overall plan is executed by the separate elaboration of its parts. Further, work on problem solving shows how a systematic alteration or transformation of the perceived structure of the problem often leads to the solution, and that such transformations often have a wide application to a set of problems. Even the very young child experiences systematic transformations of situations which open up new sets of known experiences. Thus, according to Bower and Patterson (1972), the infant behaves at one stage as though he has a structure of knowledge which could be verbalised as 'When I see something moving behind a screen and it doesn't emerge along the same track I can expect to see it when the screen is removed'. Yet the same infant is not aware of the set of discovery experiences open to him by transforming the structure from a visual expectation dependent on events outside his control to one dependent on his own action. Thus he does not appear to expect to be able to retrieve an object which he has seen placed under a cover within his reach. When he experiences such a transformation he soon becomes alert to the possibilities and delights in simple 'hide and seek' games.

Cognitive psychology now includes an outline description of behavioural processes derived from analyses of performance in various aspects of skilled behaviour, from listening to messages to driving cars. Such work had its roots in the need to improve communication systems and signal detection procedures for the armed forces in wartime and good accounts of the kind of studies now derived from it are to be found in Annett (1969). The concept of *skill* is more useful than that of *habit* which underlies learning theory, for, while *habits* are supposedly based on frequency of associations of stimuli and responses as elements of experience, *skills* are complex ways of behaving involving the use of both stimulus and feedback information in the planning and execution of acts. In learning, not only does the probability of a correct response increase, but the 'pay-off' value is important; and the whole act gains in organisational complexity and in speed and fluidity of performance. The main features of skilled behaviour are indicated in Figure 1.2. Incoming sensory data are attended to and selected according to the orientation of the person and to the information he has just processed. Thus much is anticipated rather than awaited and the anticipation is checked against incoming data. This is processed as information by virtue of its context value in both immediate and long term memory activity. Immediate memory processes impose some restriction on amount,

Figure 1.2

A Model of Processes Involved in Skilled Behaviour

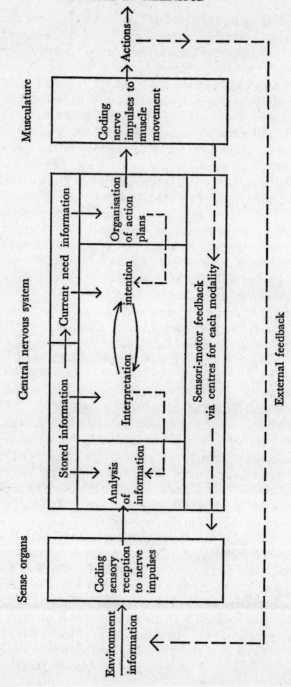

in that while some terms are attended to others might be forgotten. Learning, i.e. storing information in long term memory, depends on the relationship of the information to what is already stored and on the amount of time the information can be attended to and rehearsed before some other data are processed. Earlier learning may facilitate processing by enabling some data to be coded and dealt with in chunks. The production of skilled actions by an individual depends on an overall intention to behave in a way in tune with his orientation and the sense he makes of the situation. The execution of skilled action involves the initiation of action components which have been related in earlier learning and are interdependent according to the musculature and parts of the nervous system involved. These components are smoothed by the activation of delicate counter-mechanisms in the part of the brain (the cerebellum) that has increasingly been involved in earlier learning, and are constantly monitored by attending to relevant sensory data, thus allowing the person to check that his intended actions are being executed as planned (a feedback system). Understanding of the comprehension and production of language must rest in this general framework of analysis of human planning and skilled behaviour, wherein the structuring of utterance perception and production looks like much other human ability. Whether there is any special feature which makes language acquisition different from other learning and so necessitates positing a special innate competence remains an open question. With this preamble it is now possible to try to state formally some of the evident propositions required for an account of language acquisition.

1   The term *language* is an abstract concept, denoting recognition by the user of a complex system of signs and symbols used to encode aspects of the constructions individuals put on experience, and to communicate them. The term itself is a symbol that has been coined by men and therefore rests in the system of use.

2   Language ability is the ability to take part in the activities of using such a system, and to share in the construction and change that it undergoes and has been undergoing for longer than we are ever likely to know. This ability is a form of skill which may be mastered at various levels, and the exercise of which will reveal different degrees of competence.

3   Language acquisition is to be regarded as the development of this complex form of skilled behaviour.

4   Language skill is a system of inter-related subsidiary skills which are developed concurrently, although at any particular time in a child's history one may seem to be developing more rapidly than others.

5   Among these skills the perception and comprehension of speech constitute one major group, while the formation and production of intended utterances form another. These are related in that, once intentional production occurs, utterances must be comprehended by the speaker as appropriate for conveying his intentions, whether they prove adequate or not. Perceived inadequacy may prove a challenge to re-interpret and reconstruct the utterance.

6   The child is an active constructor of both his understanding and his uttering. He is not a passive learner. To be effective in communication he must construct some sense out of his experience within which other people's utterances become meaningful and which can form a basis for his intended productions. His construct systems therefore must treat the language he hears and speaks as an integral part of his general experience, and yet allow utterances to be recognised as part of a specially constructed communication system.

7   The level of structural complexity in an act of comprehension or production is dependent on the power of the nervous system and musculature to sustain it. This depends on the level of control, the degree of differentiation of structure and function, and the capacity to hold some items of information in memory while others are being attended to. Thus some potentialities and limitations in skill at different ages are biological in origin; but others are dependent on previous construction and memorising, leading to more efficient coding.

8   Children produce utterances which show the kind of structuring found in other of their action systems, and which also underlies adult language although this is much more fully developed. Essentially this kind of structuring is the use of hierarchical groupings, and transformations of these, to design finite sets of forms of which innumerable examples may be developed.

9 A full account of the acquisition of language must depend on explanations of processes at different levels of each sub-skill involved and of their inter-relations; but an overall theory must be based on the recognition of the total process as the development of a kind of behaviour that is unique to man, though at various levels of sub-skills it is shared with other species.

These propositions form a framework within which the struggle to develop methods of investigation and formulate appropriate theories of language acquisition might take place. The approach presented in this book is therefore essentially behaviouristic—not in the strictly limited sense of the American Behaviourism of the first part of this century, which still holds sway in some quarters, but in the sense that it is through systematic interpretation and analysis of the observable behaviour of children and their dialogue partners in various situations that inferences about their acquisition of language can be made. It is therefore important to consider what is happening when an investigator observes a child in some kind of situation in which language is used.

STUDYING CHILDREN'S SPEECH

It is obvious that questions about acquisition can be focused on different levels of skill and can be asked by people with different theoretical frames of reference. Inevitably the investigator is an observer with his own interests and with ideas about children's behaviour or about language which influence the description or explanation he attempts, the kind of data he selects, and his methods of observation and experiment. That the scientist is involved in his work in this manner is now being widely accepted. Heisenberg (1958) gives a fascinating account of the differences in this respect between nineteenth- and twentieth-century physics. However it is most important to make the involvement explicit, and nowhere more so than when the field of study is an aspect of human behaviour, and the object of the inquiry is to comprehend the very process which underlies both the interactions between the experimenter and his subject and between him and his science, the acquisition of natural language. Perhaps a comparable recent problem arises when a physicist depends on his understanding of material evidence, his visual perception, and methods of investigation employing light energy, to investigate the nature of hypothetical constructs relating to matter and light. An analysis of what is going on in the research process is vital to understanding what is going on in the physical field. A similar analysis in the field of language acquisition requires a close look at the roles of observer and child.

There are many research tasks in which the person of the investigator is deemed significant only in so far as he is competent in the methods of his discipline and productive of ideas and techniques leading to interesting findings. This principally happens when earlier scientists have thrashed out their disagreements about the object and nature of inquiry and a consensus is established about the aims, the terms, and the methods of research, which will last as long as no one sees reason to change it. But it also happens when the object of the experiment concerns inanimate, or at least non-human, subjects so that personal interaction is ruled out. In the study of child language, however, neither of these conditions obtains and the person of the invesigator is extremely important. Firstly, there is no consensus as to the nature of the phenomenon of language acquisition; rather there are various frames of reference such that any worker has to exercise a considerable amount of individual thought and judgement in defining and intepreting what it is he wishes to study. For example, it is not clear how far the linguist's experience in describing the structures of adult languages is of value in defining the nature of acquisition. McNeill's assumption that the child shares the linguist's experience of having some idea of a sentence colours his whole view of child language. It is not clear to the psychologist, either, what kind of behaviour is involved, nor to the educationist what kind of experience lies behind it or is influenced by it. It is therefore important to recognise that the adult, whether as theorist or observer, is putting a construction on what he observes, and that this is an essential activity in the process of thrashing out some sort of consensus about the nature of children's acquiring language. Secondly, the observer is involved in interaction with the child. Here it is important to distinguish between that absence of objectivity due to interfering human emotions and interests, and that due to human interaction as a prerequisite of the phenomenon. Work on child language by parents has been criticised on the grounds that it is impossible for a parent to be rid of interfering emotions and interests, but brief reference to various studies shows not only that it is possible for parents to control and lay aside interfering interactions but also that a communicative interaction is an essential component of methods of study, and efforts to minimise or eradicate it might be quite mis-directed.

The modern study of child language began in the last century with diary records by parents. These were similar to doctors' case studies or naturalists' field studies. Indeed many of the observing parents were physicians like Sigismund (1856) or biologists like Darwin (1877), and because they brought to their task the attitudes of trained observers in their own disciplines their studies were both reliable and valid. They were interested in the origins and development of features, both within and between species, and thus tended to focus their records on the first year of life, on early cries and babbling, and on phonetic development towards intelligible utterances. The studies show an underlying consensus of agreement as to both the biological phenomena under investigation and the identification of the features and variables to be studied.

A similar consensus is found in the work of philsosophers, educationists and psychologists like Stern (1914), Sully (1896) and, later, Lewis (1936), who also studied their own children, but with an interest in intellectual and emotional development which led them to define functional remarks and developmental stages both within and beyond the first year of life. Yet another consensus is seen in the work of linguists who were able to approach the phonemic and syntactic analysis of forms of utterances in an objective manner. Early work like that of Deville (1891) and Jesperson (1922) was succeeded by more modern approaches by Velten (1943) and Leopold (1953).

As the number of individual studies by parents increased, so each writer was able to make comparisons and contrasts across a range of those within his own frame of reference. This process has led to the growth of important sub-sets of organised knowledge of child language which are still being constructed. Reports from participants at a recent conference on language acquisition* suggest that parental studies continue to play an important role and that parents trained in some discipline are well able to use their training and lay aside interfering interactions in their work.

Underlying all their work, however, is a mute testimony to the

* Forthcoming report of the proceedings at the First international Symposium on First Language Acquisition held in Florence, 1972.

importance of interpretation in the process of observation. Sometimes this is made explicit. Lewis, for example, discussed the observer's interpretations of the child's use of *mama,* and similarly described interpretations of the child's forms for *flower* and *apple,* and how they were derived. At the level of two or three word utterances Bloom (1970) (though as neighbour, not parent) described how interpretations determined the formal descriptions allotted to the remarks. Not only have parents sometimes made explicit their role in comprehension of children's utterances, they have been equally clear about their interpretation of the child's behavioural responses to the speech of others, showing how estimates of comprehension also require interpretative procedures.

When the observer is not a parent the nature of his role as an interpreter becomes even clearer. For example, in their separate attempts to describe the language development of large numbers of children and to establish developmental norms, McCarthy (1930) and Templin (1957) were not able to obtain data for children much below the age of three years, because only by that age were the children in general producing sufficiently well formed remarks to be understood by a strange adult. Brown and Fraser (1963) found that they could not record the speech of two-year-olds without 'training' from the mother's interpretations of remarks. In some cases such training increased intelligibility from 0% to 75% of remarks. In studying comprehension, Herriot (1969) found problems of interpreting the children's responses to the tasks set. Only by varying the relationship of the toys he used, together with the questions about them, could he make decisions as to how children were responding to the indications of tense in the questions, for the task of relating a linguistic form to a referent required the appropriate direction of attention. Herriot's criticism of Fraser, Bellugi and Brown's (1963) work on comprehension by young children lay in observing that the experimenter assumed that the children were able to contrast two grammatical features in relation to two referent pictures, whereas it seemed highly probable from the children's actions that they focused on only one sentence and picture at a time.

As matters stand today the observer's role in studying language acquisition involves therefore two interpretative processes, one of which—the interpretation of the phenomenon itself—is common to early or renewed stages of research in any discipline; while the other—interpretation of the behavioural data—is an essential part of the study of intentional behaviour, and in particular of the use of language. The two levels are undoubtedly related in that decisions or assumptions at the level of analysis of the phenomenon of acquisition affect interpretation in observation and experimental manipulation.

Having shown that there must essentially be a strong interpretative element in research procedure, due to interaction in communication between investigator and subject, what, one may ask, is the role of the child? He is far from being an inanimate object of measurement and manipulation, or even a producer of habitual actions. He is at least required to demonstrate his skills. In so far as naturalistic observations are required he must be available to the observer for adequate periods of time in a setting in which he can be himself. No wonder then that the children studied, particularly at the youngest ages, are so often sons and daughters of the observers, while older children are frequently seen in established nursery or primary school groups, talking with each other as they play and work—children like those studied by Piaget and his colleagues in Geneva (1926) and by Susan Isaacs in Cambridge (1930). At the present time there tends to be a dearth of reports of studies of children of three years or more in home settings. This change in the observer–child relationship is probably due not only to problems of availability of subjects but also to mis-placed notions of the desirability of employing an 'objective' observer and to the direction of work away from single-child studies, from which it is feared that inappropriate generalisations might be made. It is important to take seriously the question of the place of single-child studies in the investigation of language learning. Undoubtedly valid generalisations and knowledge of their limits, based on large scale studies, are useful achievements in a behavioural science; but there is a danger of relying totally on statistical methods, in that so often only fragments of normal communication can be studied with the necessary abstraction, and even then the relationship of the fragment to the processes of interaction and learning may not be clear. For example we know that a very high proportion of children babble at about six months of age, use one-word utterances at one year, two at two years and so on. Yet we cannot say what the significance of such knowledge is for explanations of acquisition, in part because we cannot relate the fragmented acts to behavioural events, and in part because we are not even certain what we are doing when we describe an utterance as 'one-word', i.e. when we make the abstraction of a feature to be studied. Again one is reminded of work in physics. Oppenheimer (1956) claims that no atomic event is, in its essentials, reproducible, for every event is unique. So is each event of change in human learning or interaction. And if this is so, how much more must we regard each child's experience, a complex sequence of many changes, to be a unique story of language acquisition? Thus single-child studies may reveal important patterns which are seen to recur in the life experience of the same child or of different children. Comparison then allows prediction by analogy, which is at least as important as statistical prediction. Some of the most fruitful and interesting work of recent years, work not only directed towards the identification of important developments in children's skills but also to the relationship of these to parental speech models and conversational interaction, has stemmed from the set of three single-child studies made by Brown and his colleagues of 'Adam', 'Eve' and 'Sarah' at Harvard. While such work considerably enlarges our appreciation of what actually happens when children use language, an accumulation of such studies would supply ample material for the worker with a predilection for the statistical approach, and might even be a basis for making sense of statistical findings.

The investigation of language acquisition does not however rest with naturalistic studies. It becomes clear on reading such work that children do not simply show what they are able to understand or produce of a language, but that their performance varies considerably with the nature of the encompassing event, and further, that as their mastery of language improves so their ability to demonstrate their skill becomes more varied. Thus possible methods of investigation multiply. Templin, recognising that context was an important determiner of production, standardised the setting in which she obtained samples of child speech. She used an interview technique in which children were encouraged to talk about toys such as a picture book and a toy car, until enough remarks were produced to satisfy her criterion for a sample. In any study in which comparisons between children or between the same child at different ages are made, some procedure for controlling the setting should be used. Weir (1962) collected samples of her own son's speech in bedtime monologues—an example of the selection of a naturally recurring setting. Berko (1958) compared children's production of English plural, tense and possessive case markers by using a particular experimental task. She designed pictures of nonsense creatures and named them with nonsense words which nevertheless conformed to acceptable sound patterns in English, and, with standardised prompts encouraged the children to complete short sentences about the pictures, thus requiring the use of appropriate markers. Given these basic procedures it is possible to enlarge the scope of investigation by requiring children to demonstrate various language skills at different ages and in different tasks. Much experimental work in the last ten years has been directed to this end, and more clues are available to estimate what sort of skill children possess, but the central problem of how they come to behave as they do, either in the experimental situation or in learning, has not really been faced. Yet it is possible to take the investigation a step further. Linguists, in attempting a description of a strange language, do not only observe the use of the language but also ask native speakers to evaluate their judgements. They ask about the appropriate use of various terms and about the 'grammaticality' of forms they think might be acceptable. As Chomsky (1964) pointed out, this procedure is not available in trying to write a grammar of child language. Brown and Bellugi (1964) have a nice example of a two year old child responding with 'Pop goes the weasel' to a question about correct plural expression. But if the object of investigation is not to write a grammar, but to describe the child's behaviour in using language, it would be a mistake to conclude that no useful questioning is possible or permissible. As the child becomes more knowledgeable about himself and the world and more skilled in his use of language, he may be able to indicate in response to appropriate direct probing just what lies behind the interpretations and constructions he imposes on his language. The older child may also be able to make judgements about his use of language and indicate why he makes them. The author has found such an approach both practicable and interesting for young schoolchildren, as a later section of this book will show. But the first part is devoted to an account of younger children learning to talk, focusing on a study of the speech of her own son, Jonathan.

The main aims of the study were to explore the structure of Jonathan's remarks and the relationship between structure and context of use in order to reach a fuller understanding of modes of performance and acquisition. Ideally one would have liked to know what the child said and understood, together with the structure of the event in which utterance occurred; but this would have involved extensive recording and complicated analysis of the child's utterances and actions, the material setting and the speech and actions of conversation partners. In practice only part of this could be achieved. In the event one major consideration influenced the sampling and the recording; this was the conviction that samples of the child's usual experience were likely to be more valid as a basis for investigation than samples from unusual situations. This severely limited recording capacity, for it necessitated the deliberate exclusion of audio and video recording aids and of assistant observers. Whether situations which incorporate such aids may in some cases be regarded as usual or whether they result in a pattern of behaviour that is significantly different for the child is not known, but most workers have discovered that forms of utterances vary with the situation. The decision to depend solely on the observer as recorder happened to be more sensible than it might otherwise have been, in that she was able to capitalise on certain aspects of family life so that the child was completely unaware of both the recording and the observer's consequent detachment from his activities. It had so happened that the daily life of the mother and two youngest children had included periods in which the mother had sat reading or writing for half an hour or so while the children were playing, and that they had grown accustomed to this and made very few demands on her attention or conversation at those times. Thus it was very easy to make a written record of what was happening without the children being aware of it and without interrupting their activity.

Jonathan was two and a half years old when the sampling was first considered, and two years seven months when observations were formally begun. He and his four year old sister, Hilary, spent their days at home, while three older siblings, a boy and two girls attended school on weekdays. Sampling was based on observations made prior to the actual study. At times when recording was feasible, Johnathan seemed to spend long periods of activity without making many utterances but sometimes he would produce a spate. It was these latter that were to be 'captured', the mother being in a state of readiness to sit down and 'read and write'. Certain situations were highly likely to produce more utterances than others and often these could be anticipated. Examples were mid-morning coffee and biscuits, and obvious settling down with toys which allowed varied and inventive games. These ranged from plasticine, and paint and paper to car layouts and board games, played of course to the children's own rules! Looking at pictures or looking out of the window quite often evoked sustained monologue. It was found that ten-minute sampling at such times sufficed to capture most of a spate of utterances, although as Jonathan grew older the arbitrary ten-minute rule cut off further remarks from the recording. The formal sampling eventually emerged therefore as daily ten-minute observations of his speech in varied play situations. Unfortunately the method of recording precluded observations of Hilary's speech when the children were together, so sampling of conversational exchange was out of the question, but it was possible nevertheless to approach the problem of the significance of dialogue for learning by comparing samples of Jonathan's speech when he was playing alone with those when he was actively engaged in conversation with his sister and, further, by comparing both with samples of social monologues—talking which went on when both children were present but which did not amount to dialogue. Care was therefore taken in obtaining daily samples to provide a fair distribution of these three kinds of social settings. After a period of about three months, however, these settings became difficult to sample. Monologue was tending to disappear, and, as the child become more and more talkative, dialogue predominated. It also became more difficult for the mother to maintain the uninterrupted observer role. This, and an episode of minor illness together with the recording problems mentioned below, effectively brought the study to an end when Jonathan was 2 yrs 10 mths old.

The recording method imposed considerable limitations on the study. Not only was it necessary to limit samples to Jonathan's speech, but after a period of about three months even this became impossible in the 'spate' periods for the child began to say too much too quickly for reliable recording. In making observations the mother wrote a representation of each utterance as it was heard, thus producing a list of written forms. There was no difficulty in deciding what constituted an utterance since pauses and intonation cues made it clear. Other observers have likewise found no problem of this nature. Where utterances were heard as questions or imperatives suitable markers were added to indicate the fact. Margin notes added information to

c

clarify the use or interpretation of forms, and a final note described the social situation and the general nature of the activities of the children. Given the limitations of the recording method, the most important problem, and one which would have existed even if tape recordings had been used, was how to represent the heard utterance on paper. This was a problem at three levels. At the phonetic level the author lacked formal training and she was therefore only able to indicate the child's phonetic performance by using the ordinary alphabet. This meant that very little could be said about vowel production, though more was noted about consonants especially where systematic differences from adult forms were observed. The reliability of recording could not be checked, however, in the absence of tapes, although the author gave much attention to the problem of achieving maximum accuracy within limited aims. Recording at the word level was undertaken with more confidence since the vast majority of Jonathan's remarks seemed comprehensible, and he usually accepted the interpretations put on his speech by his mother in the normal course of events. When he felt that misunderstanding occurred he did not hesitate to show puzzlement, impatience or frustration!

Some remarks however contained items not recognisable as ordinary words. These fell into two categories. A first type was the baby word inherited from an earlier stage, used consistently by Jonathan and comprehensible to anyone familiar with him or instructed in the idiosyncracies of his speech. Thus *lulu* had been used for any roughly circular or spherical object, and understandably extended to a few other objects such as bananas. *Lulu* occurred in this study in reference to modelled plasticine balls, but since the correct words were used for other balls, marbles, a plate, a clock, the sun and the moon, all of which had once been *lulus,* this term was treated as a noun but not used in the vocabulary count. The second type was composed of items of single syllable form which were pronounced as a rather open and lax vowel and were positioned in places where either prepositions such as *to* and *in* or the conjunction *and* were required in adult equivalents. These were found in particular in the earlier weeks of the study, and later similar remarks did in fact contain full forms of the supposedly intended items. The child was therefore credited with the full word. Brown and Fraser (1963) seem to have adopted a similar procedure in their study.

It was considered absolutely necessary, however, that in observation and recording no further assumptions should be made as to the mode of structuring of remarks, yet additional information about their intepretation was required. This was achieved in two ways. When remarks appeared to be of the form an adult might use in the same situation, i.e. complete grammatical and appropriate utterances by adult standards, then it was noted that they were regarded as adult equivalent forms; though it was not assumed that the child possessed the same knowledge of language structure as the adult. When remarks were incomplete or deviant by adult standards they were recorded as they were heard; but when they expressed an identifiable function or relation, the simplest adult form that would express this function or relation was also recorded as the adult equivalent remark. This sometimes necessitated indicating in the adult form what kind of omission or deviancy was thought to be involved. Sometimes additional margin notes were required to register inferred meanings. Sometimes, but rarely, this information was lacking. Obviously there was always a danger that the observer was attributing more to the child than he might in fact have been expressing, but it was hoped that careful interpretation and familiarity with the child would help to minimise this tendency. Examples of the problem will help the reader to grasp what was involved. When tense marking was not adequate it was necessary to indicate whether the child was referring to a previous, an expected or an ongoing event. In some cases one was left in doubt because the immediate past blended so finely into the present, which in turn shaded into the future. A different kind of interpretation was required when Jonathan's remark appeared to break form class rules. For example, it was noted that he was looking at an aeroplane's vapour trail when he said, 'There's a big long'. 'Christmas tree got snow on in the lounge' was said when he was reporting that, in looking through the lounge window, he saw the Christmas tree outside in the snow.

At the end of the recording period three kinds of data had been collected—the child's remarks as heard by the mother, details of the setting in which they occurred and the nearest adult forms judged *at the time* by the mother to be those the child might have used with a fuller command of English. What such a command might imply was an entirely open question. The relationships between the various kinds of information are indicated in

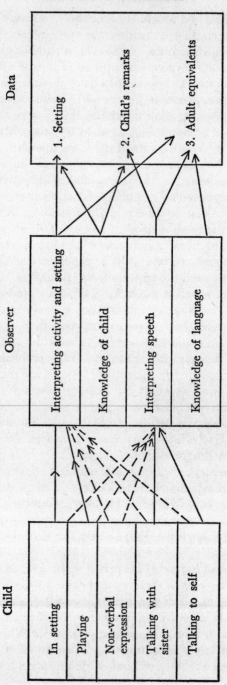

Figure 1.3
Analysis of recording processes

Figure 1.3. The recorded information about the setting was simple and formed a basis for classification of utterances according to the kind of associated play activity, whether it was solitary or shared and whether remarks were part of a dialogue or not. The diagram reminds one, however, that unrecorded information about the setting was part of the basis for the observer's judgements about adult equivalent utterances.

In analysing the recorded data care was needed not to confuse the categories of adult and child speech. Jonathan's speech could be directly analysed in terms of words, markers (bound morphemes marking such features as tense or plurality) and remarks. Indirectly it could be analysed by comparing items in these categories with their counterparts in the adult equivalent forms, which could, of course, be described in terms of the grammar of English. If, therefore, a word of Jonathan's is referred to as a *subject noun phrase,* this is no more than a way of saying that it held that status in the relevant adult equivalent form. As the author has indicated elsewhere (Francis, 1969), the basis of analysis was interpretation founded in effective communication, and descriptions in terms of grammar were no more than an arbitrary and useful research technique.

Some samples of Jonathan's speech are given in Appendix A. The sort of judgement involved in forming adult equivalents is easily perceived. Although levels of confidence were high there was more doubt in some cases than others, especially over such items as tense of verbs. It can also be seen that the nearest adult equivalent was not always quite the form an adult might have adopted, though this was to be expected, given the child's limited vocabulary resources. It was possible to analyse remarks either within the framework which found its fullest exposition in Templin's study (Templin, 1957), or within the phrase and transformational structural systems used more recently. It therefore seemed sensible to make a first analysis to compare findings with Templin's, and then to use the structural descriptions of transformational grammar to explore development in more detail and to test their descriptive adequacy. Since the study rested on speech interpretation which was informed by the author's prior knowledge of the child and by evidence from the situation in which he was speaking, an account of the analysis of remark structuring is preceded by a chapter devoted to the consideration of very early speech and to contexts of learning.

2 Early Speech

UNDERSTANDING WHAT CHILDREN SAY

The foundation of language learning, the establishment of an agreed basis of verbal communication, is laid down long before children begin to produce remarks of two or more words, and so attract the attention of grammar hunters. It has its roots in the purposeful imitation of fragmentary speech patterns as the child learns to control his babbling, and achieves not only the pay-off of communicative interaction but also of communicated meaning. The second nine to twelve months of a child's life is a lengthy and fascinating period of beginning to be aware that vocalisations can achieve effects independently of other forms of bodily expression, and of beginning to make sense of the sound patterning of speech. It is during this time that the basic categorisations of speech are adopted, as sound patterns are understood to function effectively. To put this into linguistic terminology semantic aspects of language are associated directly with phonological.

At about nine months to a year not only does the child begin to comprehend something of adult speech but adults also begin to understand what he is saying. Early studies of child speech made this very clear and there are fascinating anecdotal accounts of the growth of understanding. Taine (1877) described in some detail his daughter's transition from the ability to imitate sound patterns without meaning to her awareness that adult vocalisations were connected reliably with events. Adults inferred this step from her reliable and appropriate responses to their productions of utterances like *Where's grandfather?* He also described how meaning is imposed on the utterance so that the child may not understand it in the same way as the adult. Thus his daughter appeared to associate *bébé* with a framed picture of the infant Jesus, the adults intending that the utterance related to the picture of the infant; but later the child showed, by indicating any framed picture in response to the word, that she understood it differently. She certainly did not connect it with herself as an infant, though the adults had expected her to do so. In tracing the child's ability to use a word purposefully Taine noticed the impossibility of unravelling the transition from attempted imitations of *Papa* to reliable use in appropriate contexts. He also noted the basis of early categorisation, the child using specific names, and names of items of general classes such as animate and inanimate objects. One early word *tem* suggested another category. Since the adults were disposed to expect a naming function, it was not readily discerned that the child was using the term in a demonstrative way to evoke actions of giving, taking and looking. An English speaking child might use an imitation of *that* in a similar way; although Taine was not even sure that his daughter had adopted a distorted version of an adult form, such as *tiens,* or whether she had invented her own.

Lewis (1936) traced the way adults came to understand some of his son's early words. One of the child's early articulations was a repetition of a relaxed open vowel which we can represent by *a.* He used this reliably in several contexts so that sometimes he was understood to be indicating a flower, sometimes a cat, sometimes an apple and sometimes an eiderdown. He later elaborated his pattern to produce forms more like the adult words. Thus he produced *fa-fa* for flower; *tee* for Timmy, the cat; *apa* for apple; and *aidi* (his mother's version) for eiderdown.

In the case of *flower* and *apple* and *aidi* he retained the double syllable with an open vowel which characterised the adult words, but for *Timmy* he closed and lengthened the vowel also into one elongated syllable. When the adults felt they had grasped the association the child was making they approved his usage and guided it by using their version in similar contexts. This inevitably meant that they introduced a strong naming aspect into their use of speech.

Taine and Lewis were not alone in their adoption of the game *Where's X?* as a means of ascertaining that their children showed some of the meaning of the word by looking for the referent. Parents commonly do it. These word games depend for their success on the child's ability to identify the referent, and it is nearly always the case that identification is functional. The strongest experience the child has of a person, animal or object is his ability to manipulate it or respond to it, to know what he can do with it. The child, interestingly enough does not reproduce the *Where's* part of the utterance until he is much older. Indeed, if he wishes to play the game he does not want to check his parents' knowledge of the name; he wants to draw attention to the object and can set his parents looking at it or seeking it simply by using an accepted version of a name with suitable intonation and gesture. If he wants to extend his manipulatory powers he needs new 'names', but then his technique is partly demonstrative. He points to an object and 'agitates' for information, or if he's a little older he says *That?* and later still, *What's that?* It is through the various kinds of functional use of elementary words that the child comes to use appropriately his versions of words that we would label as personal names, and as animate and inanimate nouns. For him they are part of different kinds of experience. These elementary words are therefore learned in ways that would serve to categorise them in the child's mind. Lewis described how his son first used *pay pay* on seeing an aeroplane and then adopted it for a kite. He used *tee* for Timmy, the cat, and then, before acquiring distinctive words, extended its use to a cow, a horse, and a dog, but not to an object or a person. Lewis remarked on the functional basis of this categorisation, seeing the child as responding in similar ways to various animals but in different ways to animals, people and things. He particularly avoided the assumption that the child was naming a concept rather than an area of experience. In this he was very much in agreement with Piaget (1951) who described the intelligence of children under about two years of age as sensori-motor in its nature rather than symbolic or conceptual.

Piaget described the child's organisation of mental activity as schematic. A schema was the mental representation of related perceptual and motor activities. The child who was able to produce his first words was also able to behave in ways which showed that he recognised people, places and things, that he expected them to disappear and reappear as essentially the same in his experience. One can extend this notion of mental organisation to include the ability to recognise and treat sound patterns similarly. This, together with the ability to co-ordinate visual, tactile and auditory information relating to particular experiences, would ensure that, from the earliest reliable usage at about a year, speech for the normal child would be an integral part of his living. Either alone or with others his activities could evoke speech where it was available and functional, while heard or remembered speech might evoke appropriate responses. Sometimes a mental schema might develop without a spoken aspect, sometimes a word would be acquired without a meaning, except that it was interesting or funny in its own right, but for the most part new thought and new words would grow inextricably linked. Such development of mental organisation would imply that the categories and relations of early speech and the categories and relations of early thought are rooted in the same experiences, and that while adults provide the model speech, exercising considerable influence over the selection and shaping of early words, and drawing attention to modes of categorisation, their influence over the organisation of early speech and thought is not strong. The child's basic experience of contact with people, objects, animals, movements and actions is similar the world over, however much environmental and cultural variation there is within these groupings. Adults share this basic knowledge and make it the ground of their communication with their children.

Even so it is shaky ground. Misunderstandings abound at first because the common ground has to be explored together. This is what early communication is about, and categories of knowledge and speech are fluid. As Piaget has pointed out, word classes are not imposed on children as 'reality out there', but words inevitably force some aspects of classification on the child. Cultural differences, in the ways language is used in relation to some perceptible features of life but not others, make for difficulty for adults in establishing agreed meaning. As between young children and adults the fluidity is marked. Adults may have drawn their own boundaries of meanings fairly satisfactorily for themselves, but for young children the possibilities are open. They could be born into any community and learn to adopt the local ways and speech. Moreover, they have their own personal ways of construing experience and may easily make some sense for which there is no accepted linguistic expression, or invent words where they have not yet met one they need. Indeed we can all do this, for while language and thought are inextricably linked, no language suffices to express all our experience. But children's experience, while rooted in the same grounds as our own, is incomparably limited and only partially construed. The mental worlds of adults and children are a long way apart. Thus Stern (1928) reported his bewilderment and fascination when his child at one year used *mama* for mother, father, and nursemaid, then learned *papa,* but also used it for all three, and even called her father *pama.* The boundaries of comprehension and production were fluid and broad.

Our understanding of child speech is not only based on our common experience and our inference from the child's behaviour. Waterson (1970) has produced work that shows a strong relationship between adult and child forms of the same words, such that children do not only attempt to imitate each word but gain systematic knowledge of the sound patterning of the language. In so far as adult and child share this system there are additional cues for adult interpretations of children's utterances. The description of Lewis's child's early words suggested some systematic development, but Waterson has clearer examples. She found several instances of near homonyms in her son's early speech. For example, he used a reduplicated syllable *na-na* with varying degrees of vowel openness for the few words *window, Randall, thunder* and *finger.* He used a similar pattern *bae-bae,* again with varying vowel shape for *butter, Bobby, bucket, birdie, biscuit* and *button.* In each case Waterson was able to show that the child was reproducing the double syllable, something of the shape of the vowel and something of the consonant that carried the greatest sound intensity in the adult form. As he grew older he incorporated more information from the adult models, but new pattern modifications tended to appear not only in one word but in similar contexts in others. Thus while *Bobby* retained the reduplicated *b, birdie, bucket* and *butter* together developed an alveolar feature in the second syllable consonant, yielding *d* and *t* appropriately. The voiced/unvoiced contrast was appearing at the same time. This argued for systematic learning of features in already acquired syllabic contexts rather than the acquisition of perceived or articulated discrete units. Something of the progress from an early to a later form of the same word was illustrated in descriptions of the child's versions of *pudding.* The changes from *pu-pu* to *bubun* to *bupun* to *budun* to *pudun* to *puding* where *u* and *i* represented various forms of the vowels, and *n* a nasal feature, showed something of the complexity of learning involved. The reversal of the voiced/unvoiced contrast in *bupun,* occurred when this contrast was also being achieved in other forms, and for a time some overgeneralisation was noted. Thus during the month when the acquisition was established the child's form for *paper* which contained a correctly reduplicated *p* suddenly acquired a contrast which introduced a *b* to the first consonant, but this was soon corrected.

In spite of these variations in the child's forms of words the adults comprehended them as essentially the same. Waterson's account suggests that anyone familiar with the child's system of word production could to some extent predict the form any new acquisition might take. Such knowledge would undoubtedly assist the adult to interpret the child's utterances, and would help explain why it is that mothers feel what seems to the outsider an unjustifiable confidence in their interpretations of child speech.

By the time children can be understood to be producing more than one word in a remark they are already able to command a small collection of words, most of which are used in connection with what are perceived by both adults and children as discrete objects with some permanence. These are implicitly classified in the child's experience according to the way he can use them, and the classification roughly corresponds with adults' ideas of animate, inanimate and personal names. The child does not clamour for the attention of an apple or a ball in the way he shouts for mother or father, nor does he put his arms around a stool and caress it, or order it about, as he does the family cat or dog; though he may oscillate in his treatment of his Teddy, sometimes handling it like another toy and sometimes hugging it like a pet or person. Sometimes his play suggests that he is testing the boundaries of his constructs, but in general he behaves in accordance with a rough three-way classification. Other words, however are not thought to be like nouns, but they seem to be associated with actions. Taine's child's *tem* was quoted earlier. Scanning the records one can find such items as *no, gone, there, down* and *more.* Sometimes forms like *allgone,* and *getdown* appear to be functioning and sounding like single units. These items do not correspond to any one form class in adult grammar but suggest that the child is adopting some very useful expressions which help him to achieve desired situational changes. They therefore have incorporated in them the semantic aspects of verbs and adverbs. One curious feature of early speech, not remarked upon to the author's knowledge, is that it is quite common to find children using the double-syllable pattern for nouns but not for other words. Thus single-syllable words like *dog* and *cake* have an extra *y* syllable, while words like *car* are reduplicated. Even at two and a half years Jonathan retained this tendency in words like *horsey, car-car, plane-plane,* though for some time in all new words he had adopted the adult syllabic form. It is impossible to know from present evidence whether syllabic form may be used in any way as a primitive category marking system. Knowledge of different adult strategies in relation to this form of 'baby-talk' would be useful.

Analyses of the early two-word utterances of children have suggested evidence of speech categories. Miller and Ervin (1964) found that a few words were used very frequently by the children they studied and were associated with a variety of other words, principally nouns. They called the class of frequent items *operators* and compared them with function words in adult speech. Braine (1963a) carried out a similar analysis and called the operators *pivot* words. These two approaches essentially derived two principal categories, pivot and open classes, and considered that children have some basic grammatical rules which allow them to form such remarks. The productive process is seen as follows. When the child has experienced enough remarks to yield knowledge of *that* as a pivot for an open class including *car* and *dog,* and *there* as a pivot for another open class including *car* but not *dog,* the child knows that *there dog* is a permissible though as yet unencountered utterance. Braine described the process as contextual generalisation and regarded it as something the child learns to do, while McNeill (1970) regarded it as based on an innately determined ability to know the major categories of language and to know how to set about finding regularities of grammar. Neither, however, seems to have entertained the idea that children do not talk for the delight of grammarians or pattern analysers but to achieve something by their use of words. When children put together words that they have learned or used in other contexts they do so because their intentions in the situation make it reasonable to adopt and combine what separate previous experiences have rendered valid.

That this is the case is implicit in Bloom's (1970) descriptions of her analysis of two-word utterances. Basing her work on her interpretations of remarks, she noticed, for example, that the utterance *Mommy sock* occurred in different contexts. In one it was interpreted as *Mommy's sock* and in the other as *Mommy is putting my sock on* (me). To speak of the similarity of syntactic form of two-word remarks is meaningless in the face of such observations, but a classification of similar usages of *Mommy* to indicate a possessor and *Mommy* as an agent yields much more interesting results. It would appear that in comprehending child speech adults use situational information to allocate functions to the words and to infer the intended relation between them. It would be truer to say that they regard spoken words as actions rather than symbols, expressions that are embedded in the child's total activity. The notion that the child is expressing something of a sentence structure seems very far-fetched indeed until his remarks are much fuller and more abstracted from his ongoing activity. This is said in spite of the idea of holophrastic words sometimes found in the literature. True, some words can readily be interpreted as standing for whole sentences. *Jam* may mean *I want some jam,* but only if one neglects how it is that one infers such a meaning rather than *There's some jam.* The word rests as action within action; it does not function as a shorthand form of an abstracted sentence.

Given the many contexts in which a near two year old might combine words from growing vocabulary one might ask what constraints operate to limit his choice of items both as to length of remark and arrangement and combination within it; for although a functional analysis is more useful than a simple pattern recognition procedure it, too, yields a limited number of frequently adopted functional integrations together with relatively few other forms. Brown and Fraser (1963) thought that adult speech was systematically reduced by the child and that the forms of two- or three-word utterances were induced from this limited information. They saw the most powerful constraint as being the limited immediate memory span of the young child, which would not allow him to imitate more than two or three words and would restrict his organising capacity in production. But while children undoubtedly do operate under a severe constraint in this respect, it is not necessary to assume that they learn by reducing adult forms. It is more nearly true to say that they produce their own and that they gain clues as to ordering their selections by recognising ordered elements in adult remarks which function similarly. Much of an adult sentence is 'noise' to the child until such time as he can grasp the functions of different items. His perception of sentences is like his grasp of words. He recognises those parts that are already familiar, especially the heavily stressed, but is alert to new information, especially when it is perceived as distinctively useful.

The perception of adult speech will be one factor in controlling the child's ordering of words, but this will interact with the functional value of remarks. Brown and Fraser observed how a child used *Dad* and *Mum* similarly, although in only 38% of instances was this in an otherwise identical remark. These two words were characterised by initial or final positions, irrespective of length of remark, and functioned as the addressee in adult forms. If the child had any notion of addressing someone by name, and he would be an unusual child who did not respond to his own name at that stage, he would readily recognise familiar names at the beginning or end of adult utterances. Similarly, the same child used *here* and *there* in initial positions in remarks like *Here brick* and *There more block,* where, as introducers, the words had an indicating function and where they performed exactly the same role in adult usage. Moreover both words also occurred in final positions with a locative function, just as they frequently do in adult speech. Other evidence of constraint related to adult speech is provided by McNeill (1966a), summarising the data from the Harvard children, and by Bloom (1970) with her own small sample. Essentially they found subject-verbs, verb-object and subject-object relations expressed in the same order by children as by adults, but, whether acknowledged or not, the description in grammatical terms rested on interpretations as to how the words functioned.

If, in fact, early speech is systematic (although idiosyncratic) in that the sound patterns of words are categorised and used similarly by young childen in ways that are related to adult speech, then parental understanding would be greatly facilitated. Just as the mother might predict something of the phonological form of a new word, so she might also predict something of the structuring of remarks. It is perhaps this sort of implicit knowledge that allows her to reduce her own speech to more simple forms than she would otherwise use, and pitch the model for the child at a level just a little beyond his actual performance but not too far beyond his comprehension. Most mothers appear to achieve something of this kind of reduction.

While many early utterances seem to the outside observer to honour the word order of analogous simple sentences in the language, there are also others that do not and these pose problems for grammatical analysis. Should they be regarded as deviant forms and, if so, deviant from adult grammar or from some supposed child system? To one unfamiliar with the child and the context of use some of these remarks seem ambiguous or even incomprehensible. Miller and Ervin discussed Lisa's *all-gone puzzle* which they felt ought to have been *puzzle all-gone* to match the adult analogue *The puzzle is all gone*. But they did recognise that it was possible the child had heard some form such as *It's all gone, the puzzle is*. What they did not seem to consider was the possibility of the child sampling items which might occur in separate adult remarks, one of which might even have been incomplete but functionally appropriate. Thus the exclamation *All gone* could easily be followed by *The puzzle's gone*. A further possibility is that the interpretation of *all-gone* was at fault. If its function was to express a general experience of vanishing then it might equally suffice to express making an object disappear as the fact of its disappearance, and *hide puzzle* or *put away puzzle* would not have been thought amiss.

Other remarks, however, suggest another possibility, namely that the observer was in error in thinking that the child was constructing a remark in accordance with some abstract rule. In spite of the frequent preservation of sentence order the child's constructions were likely to be guided by her shifting attention and she might well have produced forms better expressed by adults in terms of two sentences. Another example provided by the same authors illustrates the point. The investigator interpreted Susan's *Book read* as a request to read from her book, and asked her whether she wanted him to read the book, thus reversing her word order to that of the usual verb-object in a simple sentence. The child then confirmed the request by saying *Read book*. The authors understood the transformation to be an instance of correction and imitation in the direction of telegraphic speech. But suppose the child's first remark had been intended more like the adult form *Here's a book. Please read it!* It was quite natural and situationally appropriate for the child to adopt her ordering.

It is to be supposed therefore that in comprehending the speech of toddlers, adults implicitly act upon certain kinds of information. On the one hand experience of the child's early attempts to reproduce and use words, and their own attempts to guide them, leads to a readiness to interpret the sound patterning of novel remarks in a way that is likely to be in accord with the child's intentions. In addition to this, knowledge of the ways the child has used words, intonation and word order forms a basis for interpreting the functional categories and relations in new utterances. Word order is not very helpful at first, however, for the child is likely to express category relations in his total activity rather than in the restricted activity of word ordering. Moreover it is readily seen that for the nouns, verbs, particles, adverbs and adjectives of adult speech a suitable grammatical frame can be found for the relationship between any two in any order. This, of course, requires that analogues be sought outside the scope of the single sentence. In a percentage of remarks, the child, influenced by the regularity of his shifting attention during the action in which the remark is embedded, will produce reliable word ordering. He may also acquire some of the adult ordering in the course of frequent experience of its usefulness and in the course of discriminating the sound patterns. But, in the face of the large amount of uncertainty in any prediction based only on the form of the utterance, the adult relies very much on the context of use to check his assumptions of category identity and category relations.

As children gain experience of the use of speech and become able both to glean more information from adult sentences and to produce longer utterances, their remarks become more like those of adults and are more confidently comprehended. The essential feature is that categories and relations become clearly marked in some way and that new categories are introduced into speech. The process may be illustrated by consideration of one remark of Jonathan's. As he sat at tea in a room adjacent to the drive he heard his father's car come to a halt there, and remarked *Daddy car coming*. All three words had existed in his vocabulary for some time, and he had previously referred to *Daddy car*, *Car coming* and *Daddy coming* in similar contexts. The longer remark contained more information so that the adult was less dependent on contextual interpretation, but it still left much uncertainty. Without the situational information the listener might have thought the remark was addressed to Daddy, or that Daddy had said a car was coming. Later ability to add the genitive marker and say *Daddy's car coming* cut out these possible interpretations. But even so, were the listener unable to hear the car, the remark still left open the possibility that the car was expected but was not yet arriving. Only a new category of temporal information in the full sentence *Daddy's car is coming* (*now*) or *Daddy's car will be coming* (*soon*) would remove doubt. Note that the addition of tense markers to the verb did not entirely resolve the problem—additional adverbial temporal identification was helpful.

Word order in English is a form of category relation marking, so that although flexible ordering of two categories in a context of use works well for the young child, the more it becomes necessary for him to combine words unambiguously, either because of communication need or complexity of category relations in remarks of three or more words, the more likely he is to attend to conventional usage. Some of this necessity is rooted in the general conditions of his life. The child who uses two- or three-word remarks is the active toddler who can walk and climb reasonably well but not without some personal risk. He explores a great deal, sometimes most inconveniently, and his parent's felt need to watch over him is reciprocated by his inclination not to wander too far away. But in his third year the child is more frequently to be found in a different room from mother, or in the garden while she is in the house. When he comes to her and talks of activities that she has not observed he is likely to be frustrated by her relative lack of comprehension unless he adopts fuller and more conventional remarks. He is also likely to find a similar pressure in his conversation with other adults and other children. But whatever the reasons for the extension of his skill he comes to mark the functional category relations he has implicitly adopted from the first, and to be ready to mark new ones as he discerns them in construing his experience. At this stage it is much easier for adults to comprehend the child's speech, for it is so much like their own. At three years about 50% of children's remarks are grammatical (Templin, 1957) and the percentage rises so rapidly that it is generally claimed that by four years the child has mastered the basic syntax of his language.

It is because a percentage of remarks match grammatical adult sentences that it is so easily assumed that children of three years implicitly operate in terms of grammatical categories, including sentences. Thus one talks of incomplete and deviant remarks. Yet it would appear that if we comprehend children's speech in terms of adult grammatical structure we may have made a leap from a former basis of comprehension, that of the close speech partner, which cannot be matched by the child. We should be cautious lest we attribute to the child a kind of competence he does not possess simply because we can relate our understanding to our own knowledge of grammar. There are features of child speech that remind one that grammatical competence might not be an appropriate way of describing production.

One point of doubt arises from the obvious fact that the child's mastery of the sound patterning of language is still incomplete. Several particularly interesting aspects emerged in Jonathan's speech. The first was that some utterances which marked simple but full adult remarks were produced as standard one-word expressions. *Whassat?* could be treated as three words, interrogative, verb and demonstrative, but this was stretching a point beyond reasonable limits. Similarly *can't* could not at first be reasonably treated as two words. Another aspect was that although the child at first often made some open vowel sound in positions where adults would expect articles, prepositions, etc., to interpret these as such grammatical forms was anticipatory rather than rooted entirely in present evidence. The written record of speech, where adult equivalent forms are used for words, does not reveal the relative immaturity of the child's speech. Some illustrations may help to do this, and since they are based on consonant sounds they support the notion of consonant harmony developed by Smith (1971). This essentially recognises that children's consonant sounds develop systematically in such a way that the same consonant might appear quite differently but regularly in different contexts. It is not the consonant that is mastered, but consonant features in syllabic context. In Jonathan's case the voiced consonant *th* was articulated as *d* in first positions in syllables as in *dat* (that), *dis* (this), and *dere* (there), but as *v* in mid-positions as in *bover* (bother), *anuver* (another) and *agever* (together). New acquisitions, however, were beginning to show use of *th* as in *then*. The transition from *v* to *th* was started first, the change from *d* to *th* not appearing until a week or so later. Once change began, it spread across all forms, although there was some oscillation. The unvoiced *th* was once or twice represented by *f* as in *mouf* (mouth), but, while this was consistent with the *v* form for the voiced version, there were not sufficient examples to establish a general use. Another example of context-sensitive articulation lay in the use of *l* for *r* as the second consonant after a *b,* and only after a *b,* onset (e.g. *blick* (brick), *bling* (bring), *blush* (brush), *blidge* (bridge) and *bloken* (broken)). When a new word, *brown,* was acquired the change from *l* to *r* occured across the board, but again with some oscillation. All other cases of *r* after such consonants as *t, d* and *c* were pronounced correctly, except that there was residual evidence of a *w* for *r* after *c* as in *cwying* (crying). The *r* was also pronounced correctly as a single consonant in words like *round, road* and *very*, though in *lowwy* (lorry) and *Hilawy* (Hilary) a residual *w* was heard.

Jonathan's pronunciation of his sister's name provided a good illustration of the development of phonology at the two to three year stage. It moved from *Wilwy* via *Wilawy, Ilawy* and *Hilawy* to *Hilary*. The chief features were extension of the syllabic pattern, differentiation of the onset of the first and last syllables, introduction of the aspirated onset, and differentiation to produce the *r* onset of the third syllable, distinguishing the continuants *w* and *r*. By the time the *h* was introduced it was already being used in several older established words like *horsey* and *hurt* and in new acquisitions like *hers* and *hall*, while *lowwy* during this period changed to *lorry*. It was still true that, as in the early stages of one-word utterances, the child's and adult's comprehension of each other's speech required the recognition of correspondence in features of sound patterning related to experience of their use, rather than a dependence on grammatical correspondence.

A second point of doubt arises from consideration of deviant remarks. Because it was possible to describe the child's speech in terms of grammatical categories such as noun, verb, etc., the child using words in much the same way as adults, a remark like *There's a big long* was regarded as deviant, even in terms of Jonathan's own remark structure. Yet it occasioned no feeling of surprise when it was uttered. The child was looking through the window at an aeroplane trail stretching some distance across the sky, and he made the most appropriate word he knew function as a name, although in adult speech it must be an adjective unless there is poetic licence. Jonathan was not using words according to grammatical form in adult speech but according to the way he could make them work. Interestingly enough he went on to demonstrate his search for a name by asking *What's that?* On receiving the answer *aeroplane trail* he repeated it, appeared to be digesting it and then proceeded to demonstrate his skill in making words work for him by saying *Got brown sugar on it*. Sure enough, the vapour trail was breaking up into fragments not unlike demerara sugar in apparent form and colour. It is doubtful whether Jonathan's usage was poetic, for it sounded very pragmatic, as though it was his best estimate as to the nature of the peculiar phenomenon.

Other deviant remarks called in question the assumption that children's utterances are equivalent in some way to sentences in the language. Just as the apparently deviant order of *Book read* raised this question in considering the comprehension of phrase structure, so apparent deviations in marking systems raised similar problems. Jonathan used the sentence *Mine shooting gone* on one occasion. Whichever way one considered the form of the sentence it was deviant. If *Mine* were a noun phrase, why two verbs, especially with different kinds of marker? If *Mine shooting* were a noun phrase, *mine* should have been *my*. But in any case what did it mean? It was, in fact, produced in a sequence of remarks about biscuits he and his sister were eating. Jonathan and Hilary both had a biscuit with the raised outline of a boat on it, and then Jonathan found one with a bow and arrow. His remarks ran as follows:

There's a boat	(his sister's)
Where's my boat?	(searching biscuit tin)
I got a boat	(finding one)
I got a boaty one	(assertion to sister)
Yes, mine's boaty	(comparison with sister's)
Mine's shooting	(a new biscuit)
Gone	(eaten)
Mine shooting gone	

Before coming to any conclusion about the final remark, it is worth noting that Jonathan chose to invent the word *boaty,* using it as he might have used *big* or *broken* or any other appropriate qualifying word in his vocabulary. He then used *shooting* in the same way. Furthermore he used *mine* quite appropriately in two remarks and *my* in a third. These instances were quite consistent with his use of *mine* and *my* in the rest of his speech, which matched adult convention. Given all this information about his speech and its context, the best way of interpreting the last remark seemed to be as follows:

Mine:	expect correct use and consistent reference, therefore
	mine = my biscuit
Shooting:	expect treatment as qualifier of *biscuit*
Gone:	expect *gone = eaten*

The only adult equivalent which would allow this interpretation would be *Mine, which was a shooting one, has gone*. This would make Jonathan's remark 'telegraphic' but not deviant, and would require the recognition that its form was not to be compared with the structure of a simple sentence.

This discussion of the comprehension of 'deviant' speech raises the whole question of the relationship between performance and competence. Chomsky spoke of the distinction he made between the two in terms of the occurrence of errors and limitations in performance which caused utterances to deviate from the forms ideally produced if the speaker's knowledge of the language were unconstrained. It is possible to talk in this way of adult performance and competence, though Broadbent (1970) effectively disputed whether it was meaningful for anyone but linguists! (He found 'native speakers' failing to agree about the grammaticality of sentences). But if in the case of the child it is not possible to know what constitutes deviation, what then becomes of the distinction in explanations of language acquisition?

That children's remarks can only be described via a process of interpretation, resting on the structure of events in which speech is used, has not been made explicit in recent literature, nor have its implications for theories of acquisition been followed through. Interpretation in the course of natural conversation may be said to be the imposition of meaning on an identified speech sound patterning. In the course of reading, the meaning is imposed on the printed words. Note that the meaning is not inherent in the form or pattern, for you may read my writing quite clearly and yet impose a different meaning from that intended by me. And the 'fault' may lie with neither of us, for if our meanings are explained we might agree that both were possible. It is for this reason that the notion of deep structure has been felt to be so important. Chomsky showed how sentences like *Racing cars can be exciting* can be interpreted as meaning that either the activity of racing cars or a particular kind of car can be exciting. The two interpretations would require different syntactic analyses and therefore, in Chomsky's descriptions, different deep structures. Similarly the two sentences *Mary ate the cake* and *The cake was eaten by Mary* would require very similar deep structures, the difference being the additional passive marker and its consequent transformation rules. Note that, although one might claim that the two sentences are based on the same meaning, their grammatical structure is not identical at any level. One must be careful not to confuse 'deep structure' with meaning. How far you and I need to know the possible grammatical structures of a spoken or written sentence in order to agree that two meanings are possible is not easily resolved. Introspectively we seem to be more aware of possible differences because we have experienced those or similar alternatives in the past. Yet linguists, of whom Katz (1971) is perhaps the most outspoken in this matter, claim that communication presupposes the mastery by each speaker of a common system of rules within which each acceptable utterance is given a fixed interpretation. They regard such rules as being those of generative grammar. Such claims see in communication a rigidity and certainty that may be approached with written forms where each sentence is embedded in a text, but is far from being achieved with spoken forms of the language. When a mother and child are conversing they are both engaged in interpretation and quite often when the child is small their measure of agreement is obscure. Children try to understand remarks that, in spite of mother's reductions, are too full of verbally encoded information to be grasped by them completely, and they rely a good deal on situational cues; while mothers, lacking sufficient information in the children's utterances, gain meaning by using their knowledge of whatever else seems relevant in the context. Language learning is constructing meaning for articulated sound patterns, and such learning must rest in the context of the use of speech.

CONTEXTS OF LEARNING

It was a pity that concentration on grammar writing in the 1960s meant that little interest was shown in the situations in which children formed remarks. This was very different from earlier approaches, but fortunately the deficiency is now being remedied. The principal considerations in discussing the relationship between language and context are that actual production might be sensitive to environmental features and further that the manner of acquisition might also be variable. Chomsky (1965) had it that the manner of development was not subject to alteration, but that the effects of environment were to be discerned in triggering, facilitating or retarding an otherwise innately determined procedure. Before describing the study of Jonathan's speech in relation to its context of use it will be helpful to consider what is known of the effects of social and situational factors on the production and development of early child speech.

Several investigations have in the past indicated some sensitivity to environmental effects. Rheingold *et al.* (1959) regarded the vocalisations of three-month-old babies as an index of what they termed social responsiveness. By increasing the amount of smiling at infants, making *tsk* sounds and lightly touching them, as parents might do, they were able to evoke more vocalisations from the babies, and the increase was entirely contingent on the adult stimulations. The authors were inclined to regard the infant response as a form of conditioning, though they admitted that it was possible to regard it as a general form of imitation of the kind called pseudo-imitation by Lewis (1936) when he found that, although vocalising was imitated, the form of articulation bore little or no resemblance to that of the adult. Perhaps Lewis was looking for too close a resemblance. After all, mastery, rather than accidental production, of a discrete voiced sound is quite an achievement for a three-month-old baby. One might ask, however, why the infant should bother to imitate when the form of articulation carries no information. Guillaume (1926) explored this question some time ago and concluded that the infant at that age was not intentionally imitating, but that his behaviour was in a sense purposeful, certain infantile skills being reliably associated with their environmental effects. This was particularly noticeable in the areas of feeding and smiling behaviour, where there was a pay-off value in terms of the satisfaction of basic needs for sustenance and social responsiveness. Rheingold's findings of contingent infant vocalisation suggest that some basic need for mutual communicative responsiveness was being met. Such behaviour is hardly unique to the human species, however, and although it may be a basis for language acquisition it scarcely merits being described as a part of either innate or learned language skill. Yet several studies combine to suggest that in speech production early communicative interaction plays an important part. Irwin (1948) and Brodbeck and Irwin (1946), in studies of the frequencies and forms of the articulations of infants from the first few weeks to the middle of the second year, showed that higher frequencies accompanied more extensive and earlier learning and were found more in middle class than in working class homes, and more within the family than in institutions. This was thought to be related to the quality of care, in particular to the amount of communication of all forms between infants and adults. It cannot be held from these studies, however, that frequency of interaction does more than step up the frequency of children's utterances. The connection with acquisition is obscure. Obviously some interaction is required, but when is enough enough? Possibly, beyond a point, it is not frequency that matters but the associated variation in the model.

The infant also vocalises without adult interaction, uttering as it were to himself, and progressing from the utterance of random sounds. The form of these is determined by chance positions and movements of the tongue, throat and lips, varying with the position, maturity and activity of the child. From six months the baby moves towards an increasingly controlled babbling, when he is able to repeat discrete syllabic articulations and presumably begins to relate his perception of speech sounds to his production. The deaf child, by contrast, begins to babble but his skill rapidly fades. Babbling, which may be increased by social stimulation, is representative of many kinds of repetitive activity indulged in by the child who is playing alone. There seems to be a basic orientation towards improved control of body functions and of operations on the environment. The form of such control is, however, in part a response to the forms encountered in the environment. The babbling child apparently learns to produce something of the articulatory features and the intonation patterns of adult speech, for as he approaches nine months his babbling is recognisably 'in tune' with his natural language, while sound patterns more appropriate to other tongues progressively disappear.

It is not until the child is nine months old or thereabouts that he begins deliberately to imitate something of the adult sound patterns, both in relation to ongoing events and as a form of imitative play. Deliberate imitation is by then a feature of all his behaviour—it has become an acquired strategy of learning, so there is nothing language specific about it, but in the context of communication imitation is accompanied by other strategies which allow vocalisations to be used meaningfully. One of these is calling the attention of the desired listener. No longer is it an affair of crying or chancy babbling—it becomes a deliberate calling or addressing, especially of *Mama, Papa* and any other highly important person in the child's life. The second strategy is that of calling attention to an interesting or desired object. This is often achieved by non-vocal behaviour, but the child soon

appears to learn that vocal accompaniment increases the likelihood of the desired response and patterns his vocalising on adult
forms. At first his achievements are few and very imperfect for
he has only a very limited control of articulation, as has been
shown by observers who have catalogued in detail the early
word productions of their children (Guillaume, 1926; Lewis,
1936; and Waterson, 1970). During the second year, however,
children rapidly develop their naming strategy and show by their
use of words that they recognise not only the naming of specific
objects and people but also something of the naming of classes.
For a time *Daddy* turns out to be any man, and *doggie* might
be any dog or even a horse ! It is also soon discovered that vocalisations can be used in other ways. In games of hide and seek *gone*
and *there* emerge, while a request to be lifted can be conveyed
more fully with *up* than with raised arms alone, and *down* can
add to the value of squirming to be put back on one's feet. *No* is
an early acquisition ! Thus something of the differentiation of
function that seemed to be the basis of the two year old's command of remark structure has its roots in earlier meaningful
vocalising. Environmental factors may facilitate these general
strategies, as when the child has varied and frequent enough
communication with an adult, whether in the form of accompanying everyday behaviour or in deliberate play. But the situation
has more subtle effects. Waterson (1971) has pointed out that,
within general strategies of the learning of the articulatory patterns
of words, each child develops his own personal selection of words,
systematically developing his own imitative skill from his own pool
of information; and as a consequence each child's pattern of
acquisition is unique.

So far only studies of the beginnings of speech have been
mentioned, but sensitivity to the situation in speech production
has also been recognised in studies of the remark structure of
older children. When McCarthy (1930) and Templin (1957)
tried to establish norms and measures of deviation for sentence
length and complexity in children of three years to those of eight
years or thereabouts, they were careful to standardise the sampling
situation, for they knew that the children might well produce
different samples if they were talking to each other or another
adult rather than being observed and possibly prompted. They
also knew that the testing situation—the child being asked to
talk about a particular selection of toys—might evoke a range of

vocabulary and form of remark different from that evoked by another situation. The implication of this is that variation in children's experience of talking with others and in encounter with the environment might not only affect their ongoing production of speech but possibly also the pool of information from which they can learn.

Some more recent explorations of environmental effects have been summarised by Cazden (1972). Discussing work in which she had been engaged with Roger Brown and Ursula Bellugi on the speech of the three Harvard children, she identified features of parental speech that might have influenced child forms, and reported findings about them. Thus the frequencies of use of possessive forms like *Daddy's chair* were seen to match, in that the rank ordering for parents was the same as that for their offspring. Further, the rank ordering of frequency of use of certain prepositions in one of the parents' speech matched that of the order of acquisition of the child. But acquisition was not mimicry—parental speech patterns were taken up because parent and child were sharing the same experiences and talking about the same objects and relations. For some mothers and children some aspects of life are more important or interesting than they are for others. Again we have unique learning patterns, but as always any explanation for acquisition must lie in the functional use the child can make of a novel form. Does he see it working and can he make it work! That this is probably a fruitful line of inquiry is suggested by following through another of Cazden's findings. She and her colleagues reported no evidence of parental reinforcement of children's learning by approving grammatical utterances and witholding approval from others. The only indications of parental correction were not of grammaticality but of usage, so that remarks were required not to be rude or silly, not to be socially unacceptable as responses to greetings, presents etc., and not to be too inappropriate in that a better content word was obviously called for. But Brown and Hanlon (1970) pressed the inquiry as to grammatical acceptibility a stage further, asking whether parents implicitly approved more grammatical forms by responding more appropriately and frequently to them. They inspected the differences in the three child-parent sets of data and came to the conclusion that there was no evidence to support the notion of reinforcement by communication effectiveness. Two aspects of communication were ignored, however. The Harvard parents seemed to understand their children well, and since a parent, with the knowledge of past experience, is highly likely to comprehend both immature and mature forms it is unlikely that he or she will respond inappropriately or ignore the less mature remarks. It *is* possible, however, that differences in the knowledge of parents may lead them to respond differently to their offspring. Thus communication effectiveness could conceivably operate to maintain a high and varied level of interaction between an understanding parent and a child, thus facilitating learning; but it would militate against production by the child of the less understanding parent. Confusion due to inappropriateness of parental responses might also result in deviancy or retardation in learning.

In addition to the question of adequacy of parental response there is also the possibility that communication pressure varies with the context. If the child and parent are talking about events in the here and now, where little elaboration of content words is needed because so much is evident in the situation, then pressure to fill in with markers is minimal. But if the child has to approach the parent in another room with a complaint about a sibling's behaviour, or a report of an event that is not evident to the parent, then infilling might be much more necessary to achieve correct understanding. Grammatical markers do, after all, have some truth value. It would appear that existing studies of child–parent interaction do not incorporate the possibility of evaluating the effects of situational differences.

Brown, Cazden and Bellugi (1969) also explored the possibility that parents exerted an active guiding influence in their child's acquisition of syntax. It was noticed that all three children produced remarks that were followed by parental expansions. Thus *Throw Daddy* was followed by *Throw it to Daddy* and *Eve lunch* by *Eve is having lunch*. Unlike correction, when an adult might preface the proposed correct form with an anaphoric *No,* thus rejecting the child's version, expansions were receptive of the child's remark, taking it up and offering more. Analysis of child and parental speech showed that proportions and frequencies of expansions were not related to acquisition, though overall frequency of occurrence in parental speech was related to the order of emergence in child speech. This was particularly so for the child whose mother spoke least. In addition it was found that this child had acquired more inflections for a given mean length of utterance than had the other two children, yet she received fewest expansions. It was concluded that expansion did not aid acquisition. Slobin (1965) had pressed this kind of investigation further, however, and showed that sometimes children imitated parental expansions. This was thought to be a possible indication of a mode of acquisition, although no analysis of the contexts in which the child did or did not elect to imitate an expansion was forthcoming.

Cazden, while interested in the possible effects of expansion, carried out a small experiment with language-deprived children in a day-care centre in Boston. While some children were treated to expansions of their incomplete remarks, others were treated to extensions, i.e. contingent adult utterances that accepted the child's version but extended the reference. Cazden illustrated the difference by saying that *Yes, the dog is barking* would be an expansion of *Dog bark*, while *Yes, but he won't bite* would be an extension. Some children in her experiment were treated to neither form in their equivalent talking with an adult. Children were randomly assigned to groups of four for the treatments, and tutors were trained to provide them. The treatment was given for 40 minutes daily for three months. The findings were that transcriptions of the children's speech revealed no evidence of expansions aiding the acquisition of grammar, but some evidence that extensions were helpful. Cazden suggested that expansions did not introduce a varied enough element into the child's experience whereas extensions enriched it. She also pointed to McNeill's (1970) comment that expansions might be incorrect versions of children's intended remarks and thus be confusing, and she considered the possibility that they might also be boring, especially in the experimental situation. In their 1969 paper Brown, Cazden and Bellugi came to the conclusion that perhaps the most important aid to acquisition was experience of varied rather than frequent or specially patterned discourse.

That the content of conversation might be important is also indicated by studies relating children's speech to their activities. Although he was primarily considering the development of personality and thought, Lewis's (1963) descriptions of differently structured remarks in different contexts were illuminating. The acquisition of expressions of ownership in dialogue in play, feeding and dressing situations was outlined. Susan Isaacs (1930), again primarily interested in children's thinking, described in detail the learning of relational and logical expressions by children of four years upwards at the Malting House School in Cambridge, learning that took place while they were involved in sorting and comparing play materials, and observing the effects of actions. More recent work is that of Cowe (1967) who showed that kindergarten children used more, and more advanced, speech in housekeeping play and group discussion than in more independent activities like dancing and carpentry. Strandberg (1969) showed that four and five year olds talked more about actual toys and moving pictures than they did about still pictures of the same items, while Berlyne and Frommer (1966) emphasised the novelty effect of fresh experience as a stimulator of questioning.

In exploring children's comprehension of tense, Herriot (1969) came upon some interesting features of the relationship between speech and activity. The nature of the task was that children were required to make a choice between two toys, selecting the one that reflected by its state the temporal relationship expressed in questions. The toys were identical wooden birds able to move in a jerky, tapping way down a pole. The children were introduced to the toy and to a novel verb *gling* to express the type of movement as the experimenter showed them how a third identical toy worked. In the experiment the questions *Which one has glinged? Which one is going to gling?* and *Which one is glinging?* were paired and asked for each appropriate event in which the two birds were involved. A curious result emerged, namely that the three year old children comprehended all three tenses but that they did not do very well with past and future forms when these were presented paired with the present. Herriot suspected that the attention of the children was then riveted on the moving bird so that they did not attend equally to the other bird and to the question relating to it. In order to explore this possibility further he gave the future/present contrast in the same task to children from three to six years of age. He also used additional tasks with two birds to one pole so that singular/plural contrast cues could be added. He found that for the younger children additional verbal and situational cues did not facilitate comprehension; attention still seemed to be directed to the ongoing movement. But for the older children additional cues helped and it became increasingly possible to attend to both toys and to answer both questions correctly. Thus the young children were able to comprehend past and present tenses if no present action was absorbing their attention, but verbal ones failed to 'get through' if the latter was the case. Older children, however, were able to attend to more than one action and to respond appropriately to verbal cues. This finding suggests that much model speech bypasses the three year old's comprehension unless it relates to whatever activity is currently holding his attention.

Soviet psychologists have perhaps been most interested in studying speech and behaviour. They have viewed speech as a second signalling system which has to be learned, and which at first is conditioned to the environmental stimuli which evoke children's non-language activity. With adequate learning and with maturation the child becomes able to use speech independently, and also to use it to control his own actions. Slobin (1966) presented abstracts in English of some publications, in one of which Sokhin (1959) found that children of nearly two years were able to comprehend the prepositions *on* and *under* in everyday instructions where the situation constrained the activity, i.e. where the required action was the most likely or even the only one possible. (If told to put the cup on the table it would be a strange toddler who tried to lift the table on to the cup!) Yet when the directions related to toy bricks the children often placed the wrong one on top, and, in particular, found it difficult to put one under another. They were more likely to hold a brick under the table surface on which the other brick lay than to slip it directly beneath it. Sokhin concluded that the children were able to comprehend the spatial relations in a range of specific instances but that few had a more general grasp that would allow them to comprehend correctly in any situation. They were not only tied to activity, but to specific experiences.

Other Russian work tends to point the same way. Luria and Yudovich (1959), by studying a pair of five-year-old twins who had suffered severe language deprivation so that their speech was more like that of two year olds, were able to compare the twins with normal five year olds. They noted that at first their speech was very much tied to their activity and that they were not able to organise their remarks or take part in games requiring planning, as were the older children, but after a combination of nursery play experience with others, together with every encouragement to talk with teachers and children, both their activities and their speech grew more like those of normal five year olds. Certain supplementary tests of their abilities were revealing. When they were able to show that they understood the names of objects by pointing to them when asked, their understanding of the inflections used to mark functional relations between objects was tested. One twin, who had received special speech training to improve his perception of sound patterning, was able to respond to the inflection marking the instrumental relation *with*. When asked to indicate the pencil with the comb he used one to point to the other, but did not reliably discriminate correctly between the comb and pencil as instrument and object. Yet when given the additional cue of an inflection meaning *at* attached to the pencil he was able to perform correctly. The other twin, however, could not grasp the instrumental relation and simply pointed to both objects. Even the easier marker *at* was not comprehended at first but was readily grasped after training. The second twin was thus only able to comprehend speech embedded in its context of use and where there was no situational ambiguity. The first twin was learning, through his training, to comprehend speech out of its situational context. One of the principal conclusions from the study was that in early speech the understanding of the context is the glue that holds words together in a meaningful relationship.

It is not clear from some of the findings discussed above whether production or acquisition is affected by the experience concerned, but it is entirely logical to expect that, in so far as the structure of language expresses observed or constructed relationships between people and objects in the environment, then variations in experience will present different modes of learning and different pools of information for the acquisition of syntax. Although variations in frequency of interaction may differentially affect the timing and rate of acquisition, others, notably in the kind of interaction, may affect the actual course of learning. There is a subtle and complex relationship between the language content and functions made available to the child and his acting upon them. It concerns the whole quality of his living; his person is implicated as much as his environment. If Chomsky argues, as it seems he does, that, in spite of the adoption by each child of a unique pattern of routes to the full elaboration of his competence, there still remains the evidence of overall abilities to categorise and order language, one is inclined to say that such overall strategies as children may adopt seem to be no different in nature from those they use to order and make sense of the rest of their environment; and in fact to be able to use language they have to treat it as an integral part of their total experience. To claim that some special language competence must be required because no theory of learning which must depend on the forming of associations can in principle account for such structural features of language as category relations and transformations and the systematic embedding of phrases and clauses within sentences, is to ignore the fact that language acquisition is not a matter of learning word associations but of learning new sound patterns in their contexts of use. Research into how children come to do this has been neglected while interest in syntactic structures has predominated, but it would seem essential to probe this aspect of language learning in order to understand how spoken forms are constructed and comprehended.

The recording of situational information in conjunction with Jonathan's speech made it possible to explore how his speech was related to his activity and to the conversational context. It was hoped that not only would aspects of speech structuring be clearer but that developments in learning would be explored. The approach to exploring the forms of Jonathan's speech in its social and situational context was not made by investigating the speech of those around him, but by considering the actual differences in his behaviour in different settings. Three kinds of speech interaction with his sister were a natural feature of his life. He could be observed engaged in dialogue with her, playing in her company but indulging in what can best be described as social monologue, and playing without her, alone and talking pure monologue.

The remarks used in these settings were examined for evidence of structural differences. A simple first approach was to compare the distributions of words as allocated to different grammatical categories in the adult equivalent forms. The results are shown in Table 2.1

Two points of difference seemed worth following up. The ratio of adjectives to nouns suggested that social speech might facilitate the use of more elaborate noun phrases, but since a large number of adjectives occurred in play with paints which Jonathan did not undertake without his sister, and a fair proportion occurred as predicate adjectives following the actual or implied use of the verb *be,* it was not possible to support or reject this hypothesis. The difference between frequency distributions of the use of nouns and pronouns was, however, large and statistically significant. The difference was such that monologue carried a much

TABLE 2.1

Percentage distribution of all words used according to speech setting

Type of speech	Grammatical class									
	Noun	Verb	Adjective	Adverb	Pronoun	Preposition	Conjunction	Name	Misc.	Total
Monologue	25	24·8	18·1	10·2	11·6	6·6	1·2	1·2	1·2	100
Social monologue	18·3	26·6	14·8	9·7	17·7	5·6	·9	3·5	2·9	100
Dialogue	17·1	26·1	14·0	8·8	19·0	5·7	1·0	5·5	2·9	100

E

smaller proportion of pronouns to nouns than did the social types of speech, and dialogue carried the greatest proportion. Since children's speech samples tend to yield a higher proportion of pronouns to nouns as age increases from 18 to 54 months (McCarthy, 1930; Templin, 1957), dialogue may be regarded as the more mature form. It seemed that, for Jonathan, social monologue carried whatever value his monologue held into situations wherein there was first an awareness of the presence and activity of the other child, and then a growing ability to hear and respond to each other's remarks that developed at its best into true dialogue. It was in the context of such dialogue that the use of pronouns was extended, especially in the subject phrases of remarks.

There was an overall tendency for omission of such phrases which was a consequence both of omission in declarative and interrogative remarks and of the use of imperatives and isolated noun phrases. A steady increase in the total proportion in monologue reflected an increase in the tendency to produce 'complete' remarks, while a relatively slow increase in dialogue reflected a higher proportion of imperatives and brief interjections. The distribution of personal pronouns, *I, you, he, she, we,* showed a marked imbalance in favour of the social situations, though there was evidence of their use creeping into monologue. *I* and *you* were particularly found in social speech, *you* and *they* (personal reference) appeared first in social monologue and dialogue, while *she* was used only in dialogue. But, except for *I* and *you,* instances were rare, and the sampling had to be treated with caution, yet the overall trend of expansion from dialogue to monologue suggested that the child was acquiring the use of these pronouns in the context of dialogue, and that his acquired 'knowledge' was being demonstrated in his correct use of the terms in novel applications in his monologue.

Speech in the different settings was also examined for differences in the form of remarks. The findings are summarised in Table 2.2. The total variation from the expected distribution for three equivalent samples was statistically significant. One source of variation was that social speech contained a higher proportion of other patterns than the simple active declarative remark; the speech patterns were more varied. Another source was the high frequency of functionally complete non-sentence forms of dialogue, a frequency to be expected in question and answer and in argumentative exchange. In contrast both forms of monologue

TABLE 2.2

Distribution of different remark structures in three social settings

Remark structure	Monologue	Social monologue	Dialogue	Total
Complete simple active	220	292	218	730
Complete more complex	83	191	132	406
Functionally complete non-sentence	28	32	28	88
Ditto as neg., imp., or interrog.	2	7	18	27
Fragmentary simple active	29	48	19	96
Fragmentary neg., imp., or interrog.	6	7	4	17
Total	368	577	419	1364

$\chi^2 = 37 \cdot 1$ d.f. $= 10$ $p < \cdot 01$

contained a higher proportion of fragmentary, functionally incomplete remarks. In such situations Jonathan did not make his utterances as explicit as he might have done, but dialogue brought out a clearer specification of reference.

An analysis of the distribution of the different kinds of sentence patterns indicated that there was no difference between the three kinds of setting in the proportions of complex remarks, or of the *wh* kind of questions, which Jonathan used quite as naturally when addressed to himself as to his sister; but dialogue and social monologue, in that order, contained more direct interrogatives, negatives and imperatives. It is through experience with these forms that the child ultimately comes to be able to command the well-integrated system of use of auxiliary verbs that allows much of his speech to be called fully grammatical in adult terms.

Other aspects of the move to grammatical forms were marking of number and tense. The use of plural forms was frequent enough to yield a reasonable comparison between settings but the indications were that use had spread right across the board and the social situations did not elicit any important differences. Comparison of the use of tense markers, however, yielded a slightly different picture. There was a tendency to use *put* and *got* more frequently in monologue types which gave a spurious appearance of greater grammaticality, but overall the past tense frequencies were not significantly different. But there was significantly more use of future reference in the social forms, there being a higher proportion of references to the future in dialogue and social monologue, in that order, than in monologue. Presumably the dialogue called forth more avowal of intentions, for this was what the actual references seemed for the most part to express. A curious feature was that whereas the more mature forms of marking with use of auxiliaries were found equally in all settings there was a marked tendency for the less mature forms, the 'infinitive' only, to appear in the social situations, and especially in dialogue. This appeared to be possibly due to a shift from the use of *going to,* as the more common auxiliary, to include the beginnings of *shall* or *will. I going to take* seemed to parallel *I take,* which developed later to *I'll take.* A further point is that dialogue presented the child with some curious problems. For example, Jonathan probably heard forms like *I take this, you take that,* and *When I take it off you'll see a picture,* in both of which *take* has a future reference.

Summarizing, then, the principal differences in Jonathan's speech in the three situations were that he employed more, and more varied, pronouns in the social forms and that he produced more varied remark patterns in those settings—dialogue being the richest source of experience. There was evidence that he was able to listen to and experiment with the various negative, interrogative and imperative patterns in dialogue, and this contributed to his acquiring the complex uses of auxiliary verbs. But this relatively meagre yield of information about how he learned only served to emphasise that this important question required probes of a more specific nature. Some suggestions could be made from Jonathan's experience by considering how he used speech in the different settings.

First, in the social situations he was able to acquire vocabulary. In dialogue he could and did use direct questions. *What's that?* was followed on several occasions by his sister's supply of a word and then by a consequent remark of Jonathan's affirming the naming. Thus in the sequence of his remarks we find *What's that? It's a kettle;* and *What's that? Oh, airplane trail,* when new items were actively sought. In contrast the use of *What's this/that?* in monologue only elicited known words. The function of the question was different. On more than one occasion, for instance, it was clearly used on turning a page, or coming across a new display and was best interpreted as meaning something like *Do I know what this/that is?* In both forms of social speech he was able to hear his sister use a range of words, some of which would be novel to him. When involved in dialogue, in particular, he would at least gain some partial comprehension of their use. On one occasion he produced the two words *tractor* and *rocket,* which were new for him, after they had been used by his sister in talking about some cardboard models their older brother had made and left for them to find. He simply adopted the words, using his own phonological representation which happened to sound more like *tracker* and *crocket,* and interestingly enough savoured them and made them his own in several differently structured remarks.

Also in the social situations Jonathan was able to extend his grasp of remark structure. He did not, however, ask for specific instances or direct examples. There were no questions like *What should I say?* Rather there were samples of dialogue which seemed to offer some means of establishing the use of specific forms. Thus on one occasion the use of possessive forms predominated, so that the remarks *That's mine, That's your baby, This, This mine, That your box, It's yours, It's your box,* followed each other, being interspersed with similar remarks from his sister. The whole set provided a kind of definition of use of possessive pronouns and adjectives. A similar example of the extension of patterning came from play with a doll. Successive remarks *Ooh, falling down, Let's make it fall, I make it fall Hilary, Fall down,* were interspersed with other remarks about the doll falling as Hilary either shared in the operations on the doll or commented on Jonathan's activities. These illustrations of dialogue activity are used to make the point that there seems to be much to be said for the view of Brown and his colleagues (1969) that the child learns best from a varied model, rather than from simple expansion or extension. But they are also used to point out how the learning is set in ongoing activity, with spontaneous shifts of attention and the 'picking up' of the other's interest in phrasing. There is not so much a groping for linguistic regularity as for functional appropriateness as represented in the language modeller's activities. Formal regularity is a consequence of systematic functional usage.

It seems quite natural to suppose that, given the opportunity, a child will engage in dialogue, and will learn from it, but the functions of social monologue and monologue are less clear. Social monologue may, however, have two important functions not, as far as the author knows, really treated in the literature. Piaget, who has had most to say about it, viewed it as a form of play, but two features of Jonathan's use suggest additional values. At first while the two children were playing and talking there were instances of isolated remarks of Hilary's being picked up by Jonathan, indicating that some attention was being paid to her speech although no true dialogue developed. Moreover his own speech included a high proportion of remarks beginning with *Look at* or *See what* which seemed to invite comment. There was a strong impression from the children that social monologue was used as a form of invitation or scanning for dialogue by fishing for the other's response. Moreover, like dialogue, it sometimes contained sets of remark patterns when the children were involved in similar activities, so that Jonathan had the opportunity of listening to a more varied sample than his own. That social monologue reflected something of a dialogue structuring was therefore not surprising, especially since the scanning became more and more successful until at the end of the study social monologue was not easy to find.

In monologue, however, there was no model present. Whatever Jonathan said was not part of a social interaction; it was dependent on others only via his memory. Monologue again has often been treated as play, but the point has already been made that, at a much earlier stage, babbling, which is a form of monologue has an important function when the infant is learning to control articulation. It is possible that the monologue of the two or three year old child might have some particular significance for learning. Jonathan's monologues tended to occur when he was faced with novelty in his play. He might be playing quite quietly until suddenly he saw something fresh and interesting through the window. Or perhaps he came across something novel amongst his toys, as for example new pictures in a book or comic, or perhaps he had some new toy. He then used his available repertoire to comment on his new perceptions and his reactions to them, but as the days passed monologue tended to decline in amount and frequency if the same play situation recurred, although the play itself appeared interesting enough. Yet if new materials were provided, monologue blossomed again. Early in the study Jonathan used to talk to himself when playing with cars, but this talking declined until he happened to include some hardboard pieces of roadway into his play, and then he chatted more enthusiastically. If one asks why the child talked to himself as he played it is important to remember that to some extent we all do this at some time or other. Children, however, seem to indulge in monologue more often, and their use of it is worth considering for it might be functionally important in language learning. Observation of Jonathan's monologue led to the consideration of three possibilities. First it was possible he was using his speech to plan and direct his play, as Luria (1961) has intimated that children do. Sometimes, indeed, he actually expressed his intentions before he carried out an action. It was possible, too, that he was learning to think in verbal terms. Certainly his fuller monologue, used in the face of novelty, contained remarks as complex as any used in dialogue, and included elaborated phrases making distinctions between objects and their properties. Moreover, with familiarity the remarks tended to become more fragmentary and much less frequent. Vygotsky (1962) has seen such a process as the internalisation of speech to become verbal thought. But possibly, too, Jonathan was using his perceptions of objects and relations to enlarge the use of his language. When he was playing he often phrased and rephrased his remarks in accordance with his actions, the speech following the action, not preceding it as in planning. Ruth Weir (1962) has reported a child engaged in similar rephrasing as he lay in his cot and possibly related his remarks to his imagining. Thus monologue may play a contributory part in language development, allowing the exploratory formulation of new remarks in so far as these form meaningful rearrangements of previously learned elements. In particular, since there are no interspersed comments from another, it allows the development of linked or complex remarks and the beginnings of thematic accounts. *There's a lorry going round a corner* occurred in monologue as an almost direct conjunction of *There's a lorry,* and *Going round a corner.*

This discussion of a child's speech in different social contexts has underlined the importance of considering the actual use of different forms in exploring how a systematic structuring is acquired, but it has also stressed the importance of probes into specific learning events. While descriptive analyses of remark structures yield such questions as 'How did he acquire the X patterning?', only analysis of the structure of events in which the patterning is encountered can yield an approach to the answer. Even then one is impressed not so much by the environmental features of the event as by the child's activity in making something of them.

When analysing the events in which children encounter and use speech it is just as important to consider what they are doing and talking about as it is to trace the social aspects of communication. It has often been remarked that young children talk about the here and now, but as they approach school age they gradually free themselves from this restriction until they are able to refer readily to events at other times and in other places. The basic learning of language is achieved, however, in the process of communicating about ongoing events.

It was apparent from Jonathan's speech in the recorded samples that almost all his remarks were tied to ongoing events. His noun phrases identified people, animals, toys, household and garden objects, parts of the body, dress and food all of which he could see at the time in the room, through the window or in a picture. Had he been observed in different but familiar situations the vocabulary would have reflected the fact. The food nouns would have been more plentiful at mealtimes, and more body and dress nouns would have been elicited at bath and bedtimes. A visit to the shops or to the park would have further extended the sampling, for wherever he went Jonathan's speech reflected his immediate situation. On the few occasions when he referred to objects or events outside his immediate sphere of attention the links with his activity were apparent. For instance, once when he was playing with cars he talked of going to London. Only the previous day his father had driven there and Jonathan had waved to him as he set out. On another occasion he recited the name 'Winston Churchill', again while playing with cars. This occurred on the day after he had seen Churchill's funeral procession on television. In both cases a moving car triggered the memory. When he followed a remark about finishing his morning coffee with another expressing the idea of going to the shops he was reflecting a fairly regular sequence of events. These minimal extensions from the here and now represented some of Jonathan's first spontaneous use of remarks that referred to other places and to events more distant than immediately past or anticipated actions, although he seemed able to respond to adults' references with some comprehension. He was still, however, at that level of learning at which he could only confidently extend his vocabulary through his experiencing someone's use of a word while the reference was evident to him.

With each sampling of speech the author recorded the kind of activity that predominated in the setting, with particular notes of detail when these seemed to be of interest. It was soon noticed that there was a relationship between the social and activity aspects of the context. Just as there were three distinct types of social setting, so there were three major features of activity patterns. The child using monologue was necessarily playing alone; but that social monologue should be closely identified with parallel play rather than joint activity and dialogue with joint play rather than parallel, while reasonable, could not have been predicted with certainty. Yet it was so. Any kind of play that necessitated the sharing of activity elicited dialogue. Thus sharing the contents of the toy box involved statements and arguments about ownership. Coffee snacks involved the exchange of information about chosen biscuits, since these had pictures stamped on them. Board games like snakes and ladders, although played in ways most mysterious to the uninitiated, involved taking turns to throw dice and make moves; while play with transport layouts involved agreement and joint planning. Make-believe games like 'going to bed' were also occasions for taking turns, for giving instructions, for rebelling against the other and for joint agreement about the use of actions and objects. On the other hand, play like painting and modelling did not yield dialogue unless the children began to comment on each other's activities, joining together in the use of colours or in talking about the way things were drawn or made. Undoubtedly dialogue would not have emerged unless the children were capable of sustaining it, but knowing the children's predilection for initiating and responding to joint activity of certain kinds it was possible to provide the play settings which would facilitate it and so widen Jonathan's experience of the dialogue forms of speech.

It will be recalled that the samples of Jonathan's speech were obtained at times when experience had taught the author that there was a strong possibility he would say enough to make sampling worth while. At other times the odd remark or two would be made, but no continued effort maintained. What then were the activities during which these bursts of speech were noticed? They could be conveniently grouped. The shared activities included snack times, toy sorting, make believe games, and play with toys which involved shared objects. The parallel activities included painting and modelling and play with small toys requiring considerable manipulation but when both children were independently producing their own outcomes. Solitary play evoked speech when the child was observing novel pictures or scenes, and when he was making novel constructions with toys that required some manipulation. Speech therefore seemed to be evoked not only by those activities that led to sharing but also by those that involved novelty of observation or construction.

A further aspect of the speech and activity relation was that *fine* manipulative or creative play tended to evoke longer remarks and more remarks per sample than other forms of play. This seemed to be predominantly due to the use of more phrases in a remark giving longer predicates with more direct object, particle, adverb and locative phrases. It was also due to the elaboration of noun phrases with more adjectives of number, colour, size and shape. Such remarks required greater cognitive grasp than the shorter forms and it was interesting in this connection that there was no social setting effect. It has already been observed that there was no difference between speech in the different social situations in respect of those remarks comparable with two conjoined simple sentence structures and those containing adjectives in noun phrases. Children's basic structuring capacity, in the sense of amount of message information handled, may be more sensitive to individual differences than to social effects. Cazden (1972) pointed out that in the three Harvard children there was no correlation between the rate of acquisition of negative and interrogative and the mean length of utterance.

The activity settings of Jonathan's speaking could be regarded as pointers to those contexts in which the possibility of acquisition was maximised, in particular to the kinds of play that might be a setting for dialogue or might provide the basis for the thoughtful elaboration of remarks. It cannot of course be argued that production itself constitutes acquisition, but it can be maintained that in order to learn a child at least needs the opportunity to comprehend the use of language in its social and situational context.

A further relationship between speech and activity was noticed when Jonathan's attention was absorbed so that in forms of monologue he produced sequences of remarks relating to a fairly well organised sequence of activity. The cross reference between remarks indicated the beginnings of expression of a story or a theme. Two particular features of more mature expression, the use of complex sentence forms and of pronouns for anaphoric reference were not much in evidence, however. Such forms require the recognition of similar functional categories in separate clauses or sentences so that appropriate qualifying, embedding or cross reference can be made. Thus Jonathan's two remarks *I see that bus* and *Bus stopped* would have been combined in a more mature form to something like *I can see a bus that's stopped,* or, alternatively, anaphoric reference would have been adopted as in *I can see that bus. It's stopped.* Since the child did not lack the necessary vocabulary items one was inclined to suspect that he lacked sufficient command of the organisation rules beyond the one remark level.

It is possible that, in order to relate sentences adequately, classification of the functional categories of two remarks at a time must be well organised. The child's relative immaturity might be a reflection of his general classificatory powers rather than solely a language deficit. Vygotsky (1962) described observations showing that three year olds adopted immature classification strategies when sorting bricks of different shapes, sizes and colours. A common ploy was to select two or three bricks on the basis of one attribute and then to shift attention to another attribute so the collection grew in an 'edge-to-edge' way rather than as an organised whole. (The descriptive terminology here adopted was suggested by Olver and Hornsby in 1966, reporting on the classifying skills of rather older children.) The young child's sequence of remarks sometimes has something of this quality, the last phrase of one remark constituting the feature that focuses attention on to the same phrase as the first feature of selection for the next remark. The remarks about the bus are a typical example.

Another kind of children's collection was shown by Vygotsky to be formed when one feature was chosen to link all the bricks selected, but all other features could be different. Thus a child might collect all blue bricks but they would be an otherwise unorganised collection of all shapes and sizes. This 'key-ring' patterning also seemed to be typical of Jonathan's remark sequences, though the common feature might be in any position in the remark. Examples are: *There's a horsey. I been on a horsey. I going on a horsey,* where *horse* is the common feature; *That your box; It's yours. It's your box,* where *your* in central position is common, and *Put it in the water. Put it on the cotton-wool* where *put it* in first position is shared.

Other collections might be made on a mixed basis, and these were termed 'multiple groupings' by Olver and Hornsby. Some examples of the possible organisation of remark sequences in this way could be found in Jonathan's speech. *Broke. A broke (rough edge where broken) on a car. Car-car on a train* showed 'edge-to-edge' linking, but the next remarks *Pull my train. Who done this to my train?* showed 'key-ring' linking with *train.* A possibility of a more integrating link in the series was seen in that prior to *Broke* Jonathan said *Who's done this to car?* The whole sequence of six remarks contained related information which was expressed in this fragmentary fashion, but underlying it was a smoothness of activity in examining and playing with the toys that lent cohesion to the situation. When remarks were organised with more than one key-ring design, they tended to seem rather repetitious. *There's a bus place. There a car place* were linked at both ends, as were *See baby coming up. See horsey coming up* which were said when making first a pawn and then a knight move up the inclined lid of a box of chessmen. In these examples the

activity seemed to be the basis of expression, aiding the organisation of functional categories of speech in themes of more than one
utterance. This is entirely in line with the notion that the remark
itself was organised in accordance with perceived functional
relations between objects, attributes and movement in which the
child was interested. Although Jonathan was able to comprehend
and use some remarks separately from their situational reference,
as in declaring intended behaviour for instance, many of his
utterances were embedded in activity. This was possibly still a
powerful glueing agent in his speech, holding words in meaningful
and reliable orderings so that marking systems denoting category
relations could be learned. Such systems include the use of phrase
order, word order within phrases, and suffixes denoting number,
person and tense. In other words they are the regularities we
describe as a grammar. What kinds of system children adopt, and
how they become speakers of a 'grammatical' tongue will be our
next concern.

3 The Language of the Pre-school Child

THE STRUCTURE OF REMARKS

Studies of the form of children's remarks have looked either for measures of length and complexity or for evidence of systematic structuring and changes in system. The former are useful to identify a rough level of development, while the latter are more revealing of the nature of speech skill and learning. Jonathan's speech was studied from both angles, comparing it with Templin's (1957) findings and also with the forms described in recent studies of 'child grammar'. An attempt to analyse the structure of Jonathan's remarks based on direct interpretation allowed a test of fit between the derived descriptions and those of the adult equivalents analysed according to phrase structure and transformational grammar. It was hoped that such a comparison would be a test of the adequacy of the theory of acquisition attributing to the child the kind of linguistic competence described by Chomsky and McNeill.

Sixty six samples of Jonathan's speech were obtained during the three months of observation, yielding a total of 1364 remarks and 5250 words. The results of word counts like Templin's are shown in Table 3.1. Comparison with Templin's results for three year olds (the youngest age group she tested) showed that the distribution of all words used compared very closely, though that of different words contained a much higher proportion of nouns to other parts of speech. This was to be expected in comparing a variety of samples from one child with one kind of sample from many children. Calculation of the average length of remark week by week showed a steady rise for Jonathan from a mean of 3·5 words at 2 years 7 months to 4·3 words at 2 years 10 months. Templin found three year olds produced remarks averaging 4·1 words in length. Since Jonathan's speech lay at the immature end of the Templin range a comparable analysis of the complexity of utterances was most easily achieved by using three

TABLE 3.1

	Name	Pron.	Noun	Verb	Adj.	Adv.	Conj.	Prep.	Misc.	Total
Distribution of all words used in samples of J's speech										
Number	185	866	1033	1364	806	504	54	309	129	5280
Percentage	3·5	16·5	19·6	25·9	15·3	9·6	1·3	5·9	1·4	100
Percentage for Templin's 3 year olds	—	19·4	17·7	22·6	13·1	10	1·5	6·5	9·2	100
Distribution of different words										
Number	14	22	206	98	71	34	2	16	12	475
Percentage	2·9	4·6	43·3	20·7	14·8	7·2	·5	3·4	2·5	99·9
Percentage for Templin's 3 year olds	—	12·1	25·5	22·4	11	11·5	1·1	5·8	9·6	99·0

major categories. With adult equivalents as a guide all complex remarks of whatever type were grouped together, all remarks comprising one clause only were allocated to a simple remark category, and those not even having that structure, but being communicatively useful, were assigned to a functional fragmentary category. All three classes were subdivided into complete and incomplete remarks. Comparison with Templin's results showed that Jonathan's speech rapidly approached the three year level during the three months of observation. But while the percentage of correct complete remarks as judged by adult equivalents rose from 34% to 48%, thus reaching the Templin three year level, nevertheless the overall frequency of errors was considerably more than expected. The difference was found principally in errors in attempting to widen the range of verb forms used. At three years, given the rapidity with which his speech was developing, he might well have produced fewer such errors. It was concluded from this analysis that the samples collected were representative of well developed speech of children of about Jonathan's age.

Moving on to consider the form of the child's remarks as compared with the grammatical descriptions of adult equivalents requires a preliminary word or two about the latter. It is important to recognise that such descriptions require the identification of a remark as a sentence or a non-sentence, where *sentence* is an explicitly theoretical term. Chomsky (1957, 1965) seemed to regard a sentence as a string of spoken or written elements that is recognised by native speakers as having a grammatical form and integrity appropriate to the language. This integrity reflects awareness of a semantic completeness such that a sentential meaning may be attributed to the remark even when it is taken out of a context of use. Thus meaning is judged to be mapped in part into the sense of each word item, so that dictionary definitions could be used to identify it, and in part into the grammatical relations between the words. Surface structure cues to these relations are conveyed by word order, additional words, and suffixes or affixes which mark the grammatical function of each dictionary word. Thus while *The youthful mechanic is servicing the car thoroughly* would be regarded as both semantically and grammatically acceptable, *The gebful yag is doobing the moz nakily* would be recognised as nonsense but as having the form of an English sentence. A native speaker would suspect that a particular object or person with a specified quality is operating on another object in a specified manner.

In order to identify grammatical relations in a sentence there is a minimum requirement that it can be parsed into a noun phrase and associated verb phrase, i.e. into forms functioning as the traditional subject and predicate. Utterances which do not have this minimal structure may be perfectly adequate functionally, for example as brief answers to questions, but they are not regarded as useful data for sentence descriptions. Remarks which contain essentially only one subject–predicate relation are regarded as simple sentences; and their phrase structure analyses yield tree patterns like that in Figure 1.1 where, working from top to bottom, each node may be subdivided into lower level categories according to rules relating only to each nodal structure. Such a phrase structuring is not adequate, however, for fully specifying a grammatical sentence. For example, expansion of the verb node to express number, tense and mood requires that complex selection and re-arrangement rules be applied to the ordered elements *auxiliary* and *main verb*. Thus transformation rules are necessary in relating deep to surface structure.

But a description of the syntax of English also requires specification for complex sentences wherein more than one subject–predicate relation obtains. In his more recent work (1965), Chomsky has described these as generalised structures, composed of at least one simple sentence embedded in another which functions as a matrix sentence. Analysis of the deep structure requires that the phrase marker, i.e. deep structure description, of the embedded sentence take the place of some formal category in the deep structure of the matrix sentence; and in 'translating' the deep to the surface form not only are the usual simple sentence transformation rules required to operate first on the embedded and then on the matrix with embedded structure, but further rules of marking, ordering and deleting are required, according to the kind of combination specified by the deep structural description. This treatment of complex sentences will be more readily understood a little further on when Jonathan's complex remarks are discussed.

In comparison with their adult equivalents, 9% of Jonathan's remarks matched functionally adequate non-sentences, 73% were matched with simple phrase structures and 10% with generalised, while 8% were not well enough formed for sentence comparison to be made with any confidence. Of the remarks which could be matched with simple sentences, 78% were declarative while 22% involved negative, interrogative or imperative transformations. There was no true passive form—a point which will be taken up again later.

Three kinds of simple active declarative patterns predominated. All began with a noun phrase and were followed by an intransitive verb, or a transitive verb with direct object, or the verb *be* with an adjective or noun phrase. A few contained prepositional noun phrases or adverbs in the predicate phrase. Although about half of the remarks were recognisable as complete and grammatically acceptable, and therefore matched the adult surface forms, many contained errors and omissions when compared with the adult equivalents. In the following account reference to omissions is always to absence in comparison with adult forms.

In some instances, when the subject noun phrase was judged to be represented by a name or personal pronoun in the adult form, it was omitted, especially in monologue when the child seemed to find it unnecessary to specify what he was talking about. This was mostly the case when he was referring to himself. When recording it was necessary to distinguish carefully between declaratives such as *Put my lulu on there,* a running commentary on his own action, and imperatives like *Play modelling-play* when the child was clearly telling himself what to do next. When present in the child's utterance the subject noun phrase consisted of a proper name, a pronoun, a noun (with or without an article or similar modifier) or an introducer such as *there*. Early examples included *Daddy gone work, I going on a horsie, Bus stopped, There's a polish*. Compared with pronouns and the introducer *there* proper names and nouns were rare. The most frequent pronouns were *I, you* and *it,* the demonstratives *this* and *that* and the possessives *mine* and *yours*. Essentially the noun phrase was represented by a single word and although more modifiers were found in later examples, and subject phrases such as *my lorry* and *Hilary's tower* occurred, the qualification of the subject noun lagged behind that of predicate nouns. The simplicity and lack of variety in the subject noun phrase gave a curiously formula-like quality to the remarks, especially when the predicate was short.

Different predicate patterns, however, gave variety to the remarks. Frequently the verb *be* was followed by an adjective or noun phrase as in *Daddy be cross, It's hot, That's mine,*

That's my flower, I'm on a rocking horse, but often in this kind of remark the *be* was omitted as in *This warm, This mine, That your box, That Andrew's, There another one* and *Car on a train.* The omission was inferred from the way the remark was used and from the structure of other remarks in the particular sample. Quite often the child seemed to oscillate between producing the full pattern and that with *be* omitted. The omissions became fewer, however, as the study progressed. Other predicate patterns were based on intransitive verbs. Most of these yielded very short remarks, especially since auxiliary verbs were frequently omitted, but some included prepositional noun phrases such as *I going on a horsie.* Yet other patterns were based on transitive verbs and included direct object noun phrases. All predicate noun phrases tended to be more fully represented than the subject noun phrase, but no more than two post-verb phrases occurred in any one utterance in the first month of the study, and this was achieved in patterns like *I put them on a draining-board, Put my brick on there,* and *I make a polish on a table.* Figure 3.1 summarises the phrase structure relations of the adult equivalents of simple active declarative remark structures produced in the first month. The omissions of modifiers and auxiliary verbs are comparable with

Figure 3.1

Omissions in remarks matched with simple active declarative sentences at age 2 years 7 months

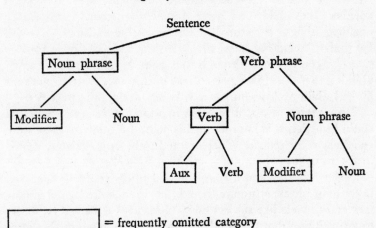

those noted in studies of other children. Brown and Fraser (1963) called the incomplete sentences of small children telegraphic speech. Jonathan's simple remark patterns were therefore not excessively idiosyncratic; they were in many ways characteristic of other children at a similar stage of development. Inspection of Figure 3.1 indicates that omitted elements were all from first positions of phrases and this suggests strongly an intimate relationship between the organising and processing capacity of the brain and the structure of language. It is as though, having decided to say something, the child can only afford to encode the subject and verb very simply lest he fail to organise all his utterance, or forget how to complete it. A strategy of simple subject but fuller predicate coding may also be reinforced if the child can successfully act upon the assumption that his listener easily recognises what he is referring to but doesn't know what he wants to say about it. The author knows of no studies which would indicate whether this particular distribution of omissions is characteristic of English speaking children of Jonathan's stage of development, although reported examples of other children's speech do not yet appear to contradict the possibility, and Bloom (1970), in a study of three American English speaking children, has observed a strong tendency for sentence elaboration to develop first in the predicate. Not only would more information about English speaking children be valuable, but more light might be thrown on the question of systematic omission in production if we could also know how children learn to speak languages with very different grammars. At this stage of the argument we are faced with an open question whether the child has some innately endowed competence enabling him to structure his incomplete remarks in line with his native language, or whether the language has been so consistently constructed (through the ages in relation to human abilities) that the child's perceptions of it in use, together with his limited abilities, lead him to adopt his productive strategies.

Some comment about remarks to which no sentence structure could be assigned is in order at this point, for many of these were complete noun phrases which seemed to be appropriately nested in the context of the child's activities. This observation, together with the fact that more complete utterances could be analysed in terms of phrase structure though they frequently lacked important constituents like subject noun phrases or verbs, led naturally to a conclusion that the child was operating with words that were nuclei of linked phrases in adult forms, but not with what we might confidently term sentences. That some combinations of phrases allowed a match with simple adult sentences indicated partial, but not complete, mastery. The transition from an incomplete to a complete phrase structuring of sentences seemed to rest on an integration of two major patterns. One was based on the subject noun phrase which appeared to act as a pivot for a subsequent open class of constituents. In the other major pattern the subject noun phrase was absent and the verb acted as a pivot for a subsequent open class comprising noun phrase, particle, adverb and prepositional phrase. Except that phrases could be more elaborate the structures were reminiscent of the pivot-open patterning noted by Braine (1963a) in samples of two-word utterances of younger children. What one is really saying is that the analysis shown in Figure 3.1 in terms of deep structure is derived from remarks whose forms might be represented as shown below :

Pattern 1
Subject noun phrase + selection of one or two of :
                verb
                adverb
                adjective
                noun phrase
                prepositional noun phrase

Pattern 2
Verb + selection of one or two of :
                noun phrase
                particle
                prepositional noun phrase
                adverb

Pattern 3 (integration of 1 and 2)
Subject noun phrase + (aux +) verb + selection as for 1 or 2

The integration appeared to involve transitive verbs and the verb *be* in both its main verb and auxiliary roles. Once established it linked the patterns by effectively being an additional phoneme to the subject noun or pronoun, as in *I'm, it's, you're* and *the car's.*

A special kind of patterning was seen in verb and particle constructions. Twenty remarks in all were like *I lift it up,* a structure where the object noun phrase lies between the verb and its particle. When this phrase occurs as a pronoun in English such separation is compulsory. We never say *I lift up it.* But when the phrase contains a noun, separation is optional. We can say *I lift the book up* or *I lift up the book.* Now Chomsky regards the particle separation as a transformation such that sentences containing it would have a more complex transformation from deep structure than those without separation. Yet Jonathan produced no sentences without separation. He used both pronouns and nouns, but appeared to know only the separated form. That he was depending on surface structure seemed to be further indicated by the fact that the actual verbs and particles used were almost always identical with the verbs and prepositions such as *take off, put in, put on,* used in sentences like *I put this in a coke-bucket.* It seemed likely that the child had only one construction pattern for three different kinds of sentence structure and that the common feature was a similarity of meaning in the functions of the patterns.

If one turns from a formal to a functional categorisation and translates the remark patterns above from the terminology of grammar, the following patterns are obtained, where *object* might be animate or inanimate :

Pattern 1

Subject noun phrase	+ *other phrase*	*Example*
Agent	+ action	I finished
Object	+ movement	Car going
Object	+ location	Car on a train
Object	+ attribute	Baby cold
Indicator	+ object	There steps
Indicator	+ attribute	This warm
Indicator	+ possessor	This mine

Pattern 2 (subject noun phrase not present)

Verb	+ *other phrase*	*Example*
Action	+ manner	Sit up
Action	+ location	Gone in my mouth
Action	+ time	Falling now
Movement	+ direction	Gone up there
Operation	+ object	Open a gate

Pattern 3
Subject noun phrase + verb   + other phrase

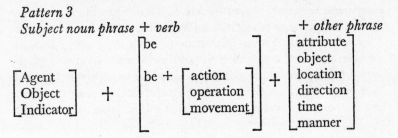

This type of analysis is like that suggested by Schlesinger (1971a). Integrated patterning to develop full sentences is shown in pattern 3, where the bracketed constituents indicate that the child made a selection of items according to the appropriate functional relations in his utterance. Such patterning involved fuller expression of relations indicated in pattern 1 or the organisation of relations from both patterns. In pattern 1 development of the verb *be* as a link, whether as auxiliary or main verb yielded acceptable sentences. To use patterns 1 and 2 together the child had to come to combine two foci of attention, an agent or object which could be represented as in pattern 1 together with an action, operation or movement which could be represented in left hand categories in pattern 2, and would carry with it further necessary and optional selections from the right hand categories of the same pattern. Further categories were included later, thus *I make a big bang with my chair* appeared to be composed of functional phrases: I (agent) + make (operation) + a big (attribute) bang (object of operation) + with my chair (instrument).

It will be seen that this pattern analysis of simple active declarative remarks suggests the hypothesis that Jonathan was adopting certain strategies in his structuring of such utterances. First, he was using words which he had learned to be closely associated with his perceptions of people, objects, movements, actions and qualities of the same; though an observer would be inclined to assign these words to the form class categories of noun, verb, adjective and adverbs because an understanding of Jonathan's usage allowed a comparison with corresponding adult performance. Second, he used most of these words in a way which led to a comparison with phrases in adult equivalent remarks. They seemed to be the nuclei of phrases. Third, as his speech developed he learned to combine more such phrase nuclei in appropriate remarks and to 'mark' their function in some way. Thus, when he used it, he regularly placed the subject noun phrase first, as though it were his principle focus of attention. Whether he used a subject phrase or not, the verb took next position in ordering, and whether the verb was used or not, other predicate phrase elements followed in a fixed order. Although extended predicates were relatively few the order of items selected never varied from direct object (noun, pronoun or proper name), verb particle, prepositional phrase indicating manner, direction or location of action or operation, and phrase indicating time of action. The name of the addressee might precede or follow the remark, but never occurred within a simple form. Given that remarks interpreted as simple active declarative forms were being described, it was fair to say that Jonathan always used correct English phrase order, that given the selections he made he could not rearrange many phrases without producing incorrect forms, but nevertheless he did not use all the options open to him in English. For example, as already mentioned, he did not use the predicate form verb + particle + noun phrase, but neither did he place adverbial phrases before the subject noun phrase. For instance he said *There's a big ball in the garden* but not *In the garden there's a big ball*. The only instance of variation was that once he put the adverb *now* at the beginning of a remark in *Now I lift it up*.

Inspection of other simple forms, of negatives, interrogatives and imperatives showed the same patterning, modified by some of the relevant marking systems and transformation rules. There was no instance of a full passive form with the agent phrase following the verb, but neither was there a full shortened passive without the agent. The nearest approaches were in *That's tangled, It's broken* and *Tree knocked down,* but the absence of a full passive form of *be* made one extremely doubtful whether the child was treating the subject noun phrase as though it functioned as the object of some action upon it. On the other hand the form closely resembled structures described as *subject noun phrase* + *be* + *qualifying adjective*.

Since 73% of Jonathan's utterances were matched with simple sentence structures, and approximately a further 8% with simple phrases, it can be concluded that since the patterning of remarks was relatively restricted much of the variety rested with the choice of vocabulary that formed the nuclei of phrases. A hypothesis that his linguistic competence was based on the deep structure grammar of simple sentences, while superficially attractive, would not be adequate to account for the systematic limitations within his competence.

It must be emphasised that the phrase structuring of Jonathan's speech may have been idiosyncratic, but from what one can gather of other studies there seem to be remarkable similarities between his speech patterns and those of other English speaking children, such that it might be the case that children at a comparable stage of development have adopted similar ordering strategies. Slobin has been interested for some time in cross-cultural studies of language learning, and he reported (1966) that there seemed to be a widespread tendency for young children to adopt a rigid ordering in sentence construction. Almost universally the equivalent of the English subject phrase was uttered first, and then this was followed by a predicate in which each child adopted a fixed order strategy although no particular order was universal. This obtained no matter how the adult language treated phrase order as a way of marking differences. In making this generalisation one is aware of the still relatively limited number of available studies and of the problem of ascertaining what exactly is happening when a child constructs a remark in a certain order. Miller and Ervin (1964) point out that although the short utterances of the two year old sometimes seem to be violating order rules it is almost always possible to conceive of alternative adult analogue sentences. Thus *all-gone puzzle* could conceivably be *The puzzle is all gone* or *It's all-gone, the puzzle is* and we do not know what 'model' sentences the child has heard. Similar remarks have been reported in the speech of other children. Braine (1970) uses the examples *See it baby* and *Baby see it*, both taken as meaning *See the baby*. There are interesting problems in intepreting these remarks and also in making sense of early child speech in languages relying on inflection rather than word order. Finnish supplies a case in point, and Bowerman (1969) reported studies of two children, one of whom adopted a fixed ordering while the other retained flexible but unmarked order. In the latter case one infers that category relations inherent in simple utterances were understood but unmarked by the child. That such an inference might be justified is indicated, not only by the fact that the child was understood, but also by an interesting finding by Schlesinger (1971b) that unmarked category relations are a feature of the Israeli sign language used by the deaf. If one assumes some prior comprehension of such relations then children's early word order-ing might be regarded as a first stage in category marking.

Since the model language undoubtedly finds some part in the context of learning it is worth noting that Greenberg (1963), after studying a varied sample of thirty languages, concluded that in declarative sentences with nominal subject and object the dominant order is almost always one in which the subject pre-cedes the object. It is tempting to think that this pronounced tendency to begin a declarative remark by specifying the main topic or focus of attention and to proceed by elaborating or commenting on it is a universal psychological orientation. One thinks of the procedures of mime, and of the actions accompany-ing, say, the showing and describing of a valued object. It is not surprising then that young children are likely to adopt the pre-dominant adult ordering. But in learning words which we recog-nise as nouns and verbs, and which are phrase nuclei, children relate them to familiar objects and actions; and in comment or predicate they are likely to construct their own ordering which may or may not be aided by imitation of adult forms. Not until the child grasps the locally agreed means of marking phrases will he become more flexible in his ordering and perhaps even shift from a 'deviant' mode to the adult ordering of his native tongue. A restricted ordering is thus seen as a step towards the ability to elaborate and relate phrases in the manner required by the adult community.

So far only the structure of simple remarks has been considered, yet about 10% of Jonathan's utterances were attempts to form remarks that were interpreted in such a way that their structure had to be matched against the generalised phrase-markers of complex sentences. As with simple remarks it was possible to consider whether such descriptions were helpful in accounting for his skills. Essentially a generalised phrase structure involves the embedding of one simple sentence phrase marker within another, which is regarded as the matrix sentence. Some examples will illustrate what is meant by this.

Conjunction may be effected when two sentences differing only in one phrase and sharing the same deep structure occur together and are combined. Thus *John ran well* and *Mary ran well* could be conjoined to form *John and Mary ran well,* and the generalised phrase-marker would look like that shown in Figure 3.2.

Figure 3.2

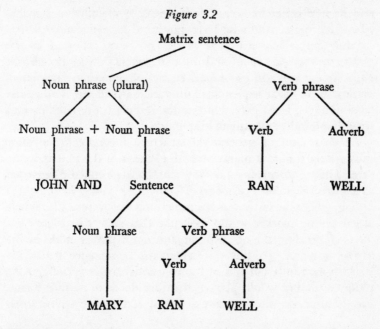

This phrase marker would thus account for a string *John and (Mary ran well) ran well*. Transformation rules to delete the duplicated identical verb phrase would be required to achieve the correct form *John and Mary ran well*. Since all phrases can be singular or plural there is a possibility of conjunction at any phrase head in the matrix structure.

Jonathan apparently attempted nine conjoined patterns. Not once did he set the embedded form in the subject noun phrase of the matrix sentence, but he did attempt combinations in predicate phrases. Thus he tried *Lorry go up and down* and *Come and see my car*. Other forms were less complete. In *It's raining, pouring* he omitted the *and* and in *Puffing and raining* he omitted the introductory *It's*. Some forms were unusual. *I look and see boat* implied a searching and finding which would not be expressed so concisely in adult forms, whereas *Put a wheels on and put a wheels on* would be likely to be expressed more concisely or with some variation. A surprisingly long remark involved several conjunctions. In *I go in lounge and in breakfast room and go in front room and go in hall,* he attempted first to join predicate prepositional phrases and then to join complete predicates. The result was much more cumbersome than an adult equivalent, and in fact could be seen as the simple conjoining of remarks which he might otherwise have produced as a linear sequence, the full simple sentence *I go in lounge,* being followed by the phrase *in breakfast room* and the two sentences without subjects *go in front-room* and *go in hall.* In fact all Jonathan's conjoined remarks were linear sequences of utterances which might otherwise have occurred separately. Phrases and sentences preceded by *and* were found independently in his remarks.

Another kind of generalised structure theoretically involves substituting a phrase marker for an element in the matrix structure. Thus *I discovered the boy was hiding* could be regarded as compounded of *I discovered something* and *The boy was hiding,* where the latter was the something discovered. The generalised phrase marker would look like that shown in Figure 3.3 Such embedding might occur at any noun phrase node in the matrix sentence, yielding different complex sentence structures. In each case different sets of transformation rules applied to the phrase structure would also yield rather different surface forms. For example, *I wanted the boy to hide* would involve a generalised

Figure 3.3

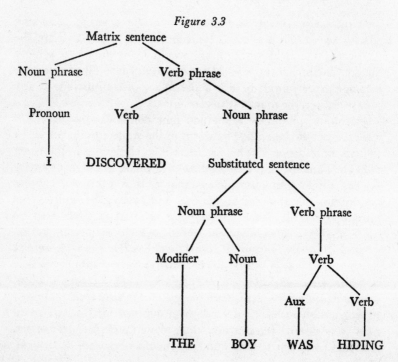

structure like that of *I discovered the boy was hiding,* but different
rules would have to be applied to achieve the correct verb form
in the embedded sentence. Most of Jonathan's complex remarks
seemed to involve substitution, but although he attempted between
thirty and forty such remarks the patterning was very restricted,
being limited to sentences like :

(i) Look + (what + noun phrase + verb phrase) } e.g. *Look what a horse's doing.*

(ii) Noun phrase + (see) + (noun phrase + verb phrase) } e.g. *I see you got it.*
(say)
(know)

(iii) Noun phrase + (want) + (to + verb phrase) } e.g. *I want to see television*
(like)

(iv) Noun phrase + make + (noun phrase + verb phrase) } e.g. *I make it fall*

Although he varied the words chosen to fill the noun and verb
phrase categories, this was his sole source of variation, and as in
the case of simple sentences and conjunctions his limited set of
patterns seemed to be based on predicate elaboration through
linear sequencing of phrases. Except for the first pattern it seemed
more likely that he was running two remarks together but dropping redundant repetition. *I see you got it* might have been a
combination of *I see you* and *You got it,* and *I want to see
television* a joining of *I want to see* and *See television.* The first
pattern was possibly the latest to develop and was almost certainly
related to question forms. *I know where's a car* seemed to combine
I know and *Where's a car* in a way that suggested the message
'I know the answer to the question *Where's a car*'. All in all,
generalised phrase markers and associated transformation rules
did not provide a satisfactory description of Jonathan's sub-
stitution-type complex remarks. His production strategies were
less complicated and more fragmentary.

The third kind of generalised phrase marker to be used to
consider complex remarks involved the use of one sentence structure to qualify a noun in another. For example *The boy found a
purse* and *The boy explored the attic* might be combined to form
The boy who explored the attic found a purse; or *The boy exploring the attic found a purse;* or even *The boy in the attic found a
purse.* The generalised phrase marker would look like that shown
in Figure 3.4. Similar constructions would allow the qualifying

Figure 3.4

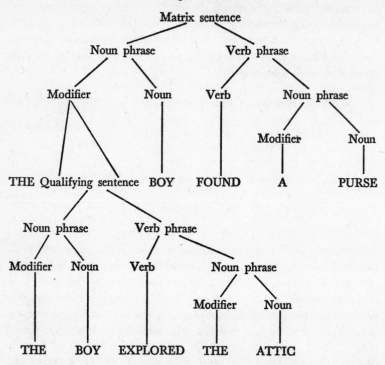

of any noun in the matrix sentence. Transformation rules would be required to yield the appropriate surface form from the structure *The (the boy explored the attic) boy found a purse,* and such rules would require at least some deletion of deep structure elements.

Jonathan attempted a few remarks that could be compared with such constructions, but again only a limited range of patterns, and using predicate elaboration. Thus he tried *Look at cars in there, there's a lorry going round a corner.* There was no use of relative pronouns. If he were constructing complex forms in anything like the way they are described in generalised phrase markers he had adopted those which required the more complex transformation rules including considerable deletion. This seems a highly unlikely state of affairs and it is much simpler to suppose that, as in the case of conjunction and substitution his attention moved in such a way that he slipped in a sequential or linear way from one surface structure to another. It is easy to see the surface combination of *Look at cars, Cars in there,* and *There's a lorry. Lorry going round a corner,* when the child's attention was on the same cars and the same lorry.

STRUCTURE WITHIN THE PHRASE

While very short remarks composed of two or three words can often be recognised as meaningful utterances and can be matched with full adult sentences, the construction of a fully grammatical remark requires not only the ordering of an adequate sequence of nouns, verbs or adjectives functioning as phrase nuclei but also whatever elaboration of these is necessary for fully conveying the speaker's intent. According to the customs of the language community noun phrases may require qualification to convey such features as number, gender and descriptive attributes, while the verb phrase requires marking of such features as number, tense and mood.

Studies of child speech show that with some of their earliest two word remarks children begin to expand the noun phrase, particularly by using words we recognise as articles and various kinds of adjectives. Jonathan produced isolated phrases like *big load, poor Christmas tree,* and *pinky one* while he was still not making more than half his remarks complete by adult standards. Fuller remarks like *Got brown sugar on it, There's a funny big load, Where's Andrew's brown car?* and *There's another little one* suggested a varied use of noun qualifiers, although, as in all remarks, predicate phrases were the ones that tended to be expanded.

McNeill (1966a) gave an account of the development of the noun phrase in which he regarded the child as first using a very general class of any qualifying word preceding a noun and later differentiating this class into categories of demonstrative adjectives, articles and other qualifiers. These sub-classes were regarded as optional but, if used, they preceded the noun in the order given above. Subsequently possessive adjectives would be differentiated. He suggested that children have command of categorising and ordering rules derived from the same kind of linguistic competence as that which he supposed allows them to recognise and order phrases within sentences, namely, a knowledge of basic grammatical relations within the sentence.

But in the process of drawing this conclusion McNeill only

looked at a limited range of evidence. He did not seem to have considered that words that act as qualifiers in noun phrases may also be used in other positions in a sentence. Nor did he compare the use of demonstrative and possessive adjectives with corresponding pronouns. How is one to classify a child's *that* in *That a car* and *That car going?* When observing Jonathan the author could only analyse the basis of her interpretation, and what transpired was that inference from his total behaviour led her to consider that in the first case Jonathan was indicating an object and naming it as a car, while in the second he was identifying one particular car about which he had something more to say. Thus the adult equivalent forms were *That's a car* and *That car is going*. What would appear to be a knowledge of two grammatical classes with different relationships to the other categories in the sentences might be a knowledge of two discriminating ways of using the sign *that* to mark different kinds of communication intent, namely indication and identification. Systematic usage would mean that remarks like *That a car* were never unitary noun phrases, and this was indeed the case with Jonathan's speech. In a noun phrase he used either demonstratives or articles but never both. Brown and Bellugi also noted that, in their observations of child speech, constructions like *That a blue flower* never appeared intact as a noun phrase preceding or following a verb. Jonathan's use of possessive names was similar to his use of demonstratives. For example preceding a noun, *Hilary's* served to identify a particular object as in *Hilary's van there,* but standing alone it served to indicate one as in *Take Hilary's.* A discriminating categorisation of possessives and demonstratives on this kind of basis would account for their unlikely co-occurrence as adjectives preceding the noun, for in drawing someone's attention to identify an object the use of both would involve redundancy. The differentiation of qualifying words described by McNeill in terms of word classes might be explained therefore, not in terms of grammatical competence but in terms of learning to discriminate different functions. By the time his speech was carefully observed Jonathan had even learned to mark such discriminating use of possessive adjectives and pronouns. Thus he consistently used *my* and *your* before nouns and *mine* and *yours* as pronouns, as in *That's your baby* and *I want to take yours* and *Yours not jumping* and in *Put my lulu on there, That's mine* and *Mine go in there.*

His use of descriptive adjectives also seemed to be discriminating. In English, as we have seen, young children use these adjectives both before and after nouns as in *brown sugar* and *car red,* and adult observers tend to interpret the latter as *car is red.* The child, however, may be discriminating between a use before the noun which increases the specificity of his reference and a use afterwards which simply gives information about, or qualifies, the object named. This would be in line with his tendency to use an identifying word before a noun. But in this case the use of a second adjective before a noun would not be redundant; instead it would increase identifying power. Thus a two stage process of attention focusing might be involved in which it would be natural first to use a more general identifier like *my* or *that* or *Hilary's,* and then to use a more specific clue such as *red, big,* etc., so that noun phrases like *my yellow one* and *Andrew's brown car* would be formed. If the distinction between *red car* and *car red* is between identifying and qualifying, then the insertion of *be* in the latter might be expected to come quite late in development, for it would be more a grammatical luxury than a necessity. A four year old's question illustrates the point : 'Why can't we say "Christmas Happy" as well as "Happy Christmas", because Christmas is happy?' This serves to remind us that while the identifying adjective does not follow the noun in English, qualifying adjectives may precede the noun in a phrase or follow it with an intervening verb like *be.* Some adjectives, like *red,* function both as identifiers and qualifiers and in the latter case in child speech may be found before or after the noun. It is difficult to tell from the literature just how children use phrases with qualifying adjectives especially in the early stages of two- or three-word remarks, but in Jonathan's more mature speech such phrases occurred predominantly in predicate positions with an accompanying indefinite article or modifier. The rather open *a* was increasingly differentiated into words like *a, some* and *more.* There were isolated noun phrases which could not always be interpreted but these often carried an implicit predicate function in that they answered questions or seemed to follow an implied *That's* or *There's.* Only towards the end of the observation period did such phrases function as subjects. This was probably related to Jonathan's strong bias towards using indicators or identifiers at the beginning of remarks, thus effectively first drawing attention where he wanted it most. It seemed, then, that Jonathan elaborated noun phrases according to the way he was using the noun. If he wished to indicate something, he would use a minimal structure consisting of a demonstrative or possessive pronoun or a name. If he wished to identify a particular object about which he was saying something further he would place a general and/or a specific identifier before the noun. If he wanted to refer to one item among several possibilities, or to an amount of some available material, he would place an indefinite modifier and/or a qualifier before the noun. If he was not using the phrase in an implicit or explicit wider relation he retained the option of placing a qualifying adjective after the noun.

It was of interest that Jonathan did not use the definite article readily. While omissions of the indefinite occurred predominantly in the subject position, when a noun was used like a name as an indicator, as in *Birdie chasing it,* there were clear omissions of the definite in all phrase positions, e.g. *There's sun, over there,* and *I want to go in lounge.* Sometimes *a* was clearly used for *the* as in *What's a matter?* and *It's in a way.* Clear expression of the definite article took the form of *de* or *the* and occurred only three times in the first month of the study, four in the second and eight in the third. It was, perhaps, strange that Jonathan could express definite indication with demonstratives, and indefinite with *a, some* etc., but did not use the definite article. The author's impression was that the demonstratives and possessives were easier to learn because they were associated with definite actions of pointing, snatching, allocating, etc., while awareness of choosing one item of several was also easy to associate with a verbal marker, as in *I want a biscuit,* but there seemed to be no way of demonstrating *the.* The task of identifying the word and discriminating it from *a* both in his own and other's speech probably required greater cognitive maturity. A case worth considering in this context is reported by McNeill (1966a) where he discusses Japanese ways of marking subject nouns of sentences. The two markers he refers to, *ga* and *wa,* appear frequently in adult speech but they carry different meanings. If the author's interpretation of McNeill's account is anything like correct it appears that *ga* carries something of the function of the indefinite article in that it marks reference to a specific yet indefinite object, but it also carries something of the identifying function of demonstratives in that it identifies one object from a known set. *Wa,* on the other hand, bears some similarity to *the.* Curiously enough, Izanami, a two year old, only used *ga,* although her mother employed both markers, and used *wa* twice as often as *ga*. Did Izanami experience something of the same cognitive problem as Jonathan?

Although Jonathan made no errors by adult standards in his selection and ordering of items in noun phrases there is evidence in the literature of errors made by younger children. Brown and Bellugi (1964) reported *A your car* and *A my pencil* from a child, Adam, at just two years. It is quite possible that when first learning to use such words children made inappropriate judgments in categorising. Possibly Adam at that stage treated *your* rather as we treat *of yours*, i.e. as a qualifying form, and had to learn to readjust.

Discussion of children's use of the indefinite noun modifiers hinted at the distinction between count and mass nouns. In English the singular and plural forms of count nouns are generally distinguished by marking the plural with the addition of a bound morpheme, as in *bed* v. *beds*, or with a change of vowel, as in *man* v. *men*; though in rare cases there is no plural marker, as in *sheep* v. *sheep*. Mass nouns do not carry a marker, but their pattern of association with modifiers differs from both singular and plural forms. Thus one can say :

I should like (a) pear
or
(the)
I should like (some) pears
or
(the)
and *I should like (some) milk*
or
(the)
but not, *I should like a milk*
nor, *I should like (some) milks*
or
(the)

There is evidence of plural forms of concrete count nouns in the very earliest of children's two-word utterances, and Brown (1957) was able to show that children from three to five years old could distinguish between mass and count nouns. He used nonsense syllables to name items shown in pictures, and found that children used appropriate modifiers and markers when they used these 'new' words in sentences. Jonathan was not able at first to use all the appropriate markers in his speech. He used plurals correctly for count nouns and allied these to the plural demonstrative adjectives *these* and *those* and to other modifiers such as *some* and *more*. A distinction between *coffee* when some was spilled and *coffees* when two cups were poured suggested that he had some grasp of the semantic distinction between mass and count nouns. He was also able to use *some* and *some more* correctly with both plural count nouns such as *bricks* and *cars,* and with mass nouns *milk* and *water,* and did not use them with singular count nouns. He was only just learning, however, to use *a, the* and *some*. It seemed as though all three were differentiated from a basic *a,* because correct usage followed earlier forms like *There's a windows, Bus got a lights, Put a bricks on a lorry* and *Where's a polish?* The use of *some* may have been aided by its prior occurrence as a pronoun and in association with *more,* as in *I got some* and *I got some more*. It was certainly clearly articulated first in such contexts.

It has been noticed by several observers that children between two and four years of age tend first to adopt a limited set of separately acquired correct plural forms and then systematically to apply particular marking rules across all plurals, sometimes extending them inappropriately. Cazden (1972) summarises these over-generalisations by showing how *s* can be added to nouns with no plural form, e.g. *peoples;* vowel-change plurals in both singular and plural forms, e.g. *mans* and *mens;* mass nouns, e.g. *milks;* and pronouns and adjectives, e.g. *twos, somes, pinks*. Miller and Ervin (1964) found that at the stage of systematic application children also soon added the appropriate marker to new words, these being in fact nonsense syllables of English sound patterns. Thus, having been told that a novel object was a *bik* children referred to two such objects as *biks*. The voiced plural, sounding like a *z,* followed voiced consonants, as was appropriate in English. They also found that children used the syllabic plurals of *churches* and *glasses* rather later than the simple *z* or *s* forms, preferring for a while to use the unmarked *church* and *glass* for both singular and plural instances. Ervin (1964) argued that some sort of extension by analogy was being performed—that the errors of over-generalising plurals indicated more than imitative learning. Jonathan's use of plural markers indicated that he was coming towards the end of the stage of over-extension of plural rules. There was ample evidence of appropriate marking in such words as *lots, shops, bricks, cups* and *steps* with the unvoiced *s*, and in *cars, rollies* and *eyes* with the voiced *z*. There was even an instance of the syllabic marking in *houses*. When over-extending his rules, however, he changed from earlier use of *children* and *chessmen* to *childrens* and *chessmens*. Within two months however he was again using the correct forms. The argument of analogic extension requires that the child recognise the quality of plurality that is to be expressed in a marking system. One might therefore expect that other evidence of the child's recognition of number might exist in his speech. Some of Brown's and Bellugi's (1964) samples of early phrases show the use of the numeral two, as in *two sock, two shoes*. Jonathan, being slightly more mature, used a range of numbers from *one* to *six*, but in spite of using plural markers regularly elsewhere, he at first failed to use them with numbers. Thus he said, *two carriage,* and *I got four paper,* (four sweet wrappings); but on the very next day he said *two coffees,* and thereafter no similar plural marker was omitted.

In order to produce a fully grammatical sentence not only must the noun phrase be fully developed but the verb also requires elaboration. The grammatical categories and relations embodied in the expansion are summarised in Chomsky's account of the auxiliary transformation, though care should be exercised not to take this as a description of the mode of acquisition of competence. In Figure 1.1 the predicate phrase is subdivided to yield, amongst others, a verb node. This may itself be further subdivided into auxiliary verb followed by main verb. The auxiliary can then be thought of as composed of past tense and number markers to be applied to the main verb as necessary; modal verbs and the auxiliaries *will* and *do,* which do not entail an alteration to the main verb; and the auxiliaries *have* and *be,* which require past participle (coded as *en*) and present progressive (*ing*) suffixes respectively to the main verb. Thus in order to be able to generate correct forms of verbs from the underlying structure, summarised in Figure 3.5, it is necessary to select and reorder elements of the auxiliary, and place them as suffixes to the main verb. In forms like the pluperfect tense the task of transformation is quite complex, but even in the simpler tenses it requires that some element of the auxiliary be first generated before the verb and then transposed to the suffix position, as shown in Figure 3.5. Examination of children's speech may indicate whether they demonstrate anything

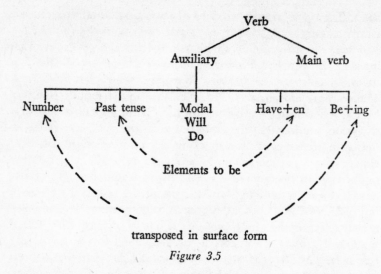

Figure 3.5

like this sort of competence or whether their utterances suggest some other kind of skill.

In early remarks the verb is essentially one word which represents some action, operation, movement or state of some person or object. Sometimes, as when a particle carries the main semantic weight because the verb is weak, as in *take* and *put,* it is the only part of the verb produced. Miller's and Ervin's (1964) subject, Susan, used the particles *on* and *off* without main verbs just before she was two years old. These, with *up* and *down,* seem to occur often in early speech. Otherwise the main verb is the first part of the verb to appear and remains unchanged for several months. It was expansion of the main verb that played a large part in moving Jonathan's speech significantly towards grammatical acceptability during the three months of observation, allowing him to express something of the ideas embodied in tense and mood. That children first adopt the main verbs, unmarked, is perhaps not surprising, for in English these may appear the most intelligible forms. They are used in imperatives, in both second and first person forms, as in *Make a tower* and *Let's make a tower.* They also occur in modal construction like *I can make a tower* and in the future tense *I'll make a tower.* Thus they form the heart of the expression of instructions, demonstrations and intentions which loom large in communication with very young children.

Cazden (1972) concluded from a survey and analysis of studies of child speech that the first elaboration of the verb was the addition of the present progressive marker *ing* and that the marking of the regular past tense and the present indicative followed soon afterwards. Over-generalisation was also observed. There was evidence of all three in Jonathan's speech but they were by no means always used when the observer judged that they were indicated. In English the indicative form is indistinguishable from the imperative except in the third person singular when an *s* is required *(I want, he wants)*, which is thus the only means of ascertaining the child's use of the appropriate marker. Jonathan did use it on occasion e.g. *She stands up,* but he often failed to do so, producing items like *It go, She want,* and *He have.* He also produced an error in the plural form when he was learning to use the singular, saying *They goes.* This suggested that the earlier apparently correct forms may not have been properly discriminated. The present progressive *ing* was often not used when it was judged appropriate, e.g. *I bring mine* for *I am bringing mine,* although it was in fact used intermittently over quite a large range of verbs, and always when needed for *going* and *coming.* For some reason, although *ing* was well learned with *come* and *go* and was increasingly used with other verbs, its use did not extend across the board for the expression of the present progressive tense as completely as did past tense or plural markers. The author suspected that, although the child was able to discriminate fairly clearly between completed, previous actions and present events, he was not able to be clear about a distinction between present progressive and immediate future reference. When, for example, he was modelling a piece of clay into a ball and said *I make a lulu,* one could understand that he was aware both of his concurrent action and the almost immediate end product. Should he have said *I am making a lulu* or *I am going to make a lulu*? Obviously, from the adult point of view the *ing* was missing, but one could not be confident about the position of omission, and this lack of confidence reflected the level of discriminative difficulty faced by the child. The past tense was used much less than the present, and most of the instances were of irregular participles or simple past forms like *lost* and *made.* The regular past marker was used, however, with a range of verbs as in *finished, stopped, crashed, spilled, missed* and *switched,* although it was not always used when needed. It was missed, for example, from

Mummy knock. .... There were instances of over-generalisation in such cases as *drawed, droppened* and *usened*. The latter two seemed odd, but some clang effect of extension from *happened* and *wakened* may have taken place. The total impression gained from the study of Jonathan's marking of the verb was that he showed awareness of the tense differences but was only just beginning to mark them systematically and correctly. His errors of omission and over-generalisation were like other children's but were of his own making. Independent evidence of tense discrimination came from use of phrases like *yesterday, now* and *in a minute.*

It is clear from this account of main verb markers that while young children do not demonstrate the use of auxiliary elements before the verbs, they yet add those markers which figure in the theory of transformational grammar as auxiliary elements generated before the verb and then transposed. This sort of 'jumping the gun' has already been described in relation to deletion transformation in adjectival and relative constructions. Again one must say that it is to make a gross and unjustifiable assumption to think that children generate their remarks in any way that conforms to the generative theory of transformational grammar. Instead they seem to acquire markers which express perceived functional differences and to use these systematically when they recognise their function.

The first evidence of systematic use of an auxiliary element before the verb seemed to be of the use of the modal verbs *can* and *will,* especially in their negative forms *can't* and *won't.* These can, of course, stand alone and yet convey fuller meanings if used in context. If the building of a tower is suggested the child does not have to answer *I can't build it. I can't* is powerful enough. It may be that this allows the modal verbs to set naturally before the main verb when both are used. Jonathan was well able to use these modals with main verbs when the observations were begun and also used the expressions *have to* and *should* during the observations, although forms of expressing conditional or uncertain moods of the verbs were absent. Other studies suggest the latter expressions come later in English speaking children, and Slobin (1972) reports Russian studies showing similar development. It seems to be widely thought that the order reflects aspects of cognitive growth.

The auxiliaries *have* and *be* developed very slowly, as did the use of *do* and *will* as auxiliaries, although the main verb *do*, a general term for action verbs, was used as in *I do another* and *Two did it* quite early. There was perhaps not very strong pressure on the child to develop the auxiliaries in active declarative sentences since he could adequately mark past and present tenses with suffixes, and could use *going to* as a form of future reference. Equally he was not required to develop *have* and *be* as main verbs since *got* substituted for *have* and the omission of *be* passed unremarked. He did, however, begin to fill in both auxiliaries and main verbs, and interestingly did not ever use *got* as an auxiliary *have!* The first steps appeared to be the addition of an *s* to subject pronouns and nouns preceding the verb as in *That's mine, It's your box, It's raining, That's falling down, A car's coming* and *He's going there*, but from the first month *I'm stuck, I'm on a rocking horse, I'm going* and *We're turning* presaged the establishment of a more discriminating and extended use. When forms like *it is, he is, they are, those are, this was,* and *Hilary was* began to appear it was evident that an independent auxiliary was being used rather than a marker on the subject, yet the whole process from marker or elision to independent word guaranteed the maintenance of agreement between subject and auxiliary. A similar development of the auxiliary *have* was noted, where an *s* added to third person singular subjects developed to *has*, and a *ve* added to other subjects developed to *have*. During the three months, however, Jonathan's use of auxiliaries was not reliable at any stage. He might easily still omit them even at the end, but his accurate learning was aided by the selection of elisions as his first imitations from adult speech. Whether children generally adopt this strategy is not known, nor whether there are comparable examples in other languages. When surveying Jonathan's developing use of the elements of the auxiliary verb it was impossible to tell whether he related those which preceded the main verb to the suffixes on the verb. There was a strong impression that he adopted three unrelated systems, main verb marking, adding main verbs to modals, and inserting auxiliaries *have* and *be* only when they were already strongly related to subject noun phrases as elided main verbs in their own right. His strategies ensured that he arrived at a stage when his sentences were fully grammatical and could be described in terms of the auxiliary transformation, but it would be difficult to say that even implicit knowledge of such a procedure was a part of his competence.

An important feature of the development of auxiliaries, however, is that they are involved in the differential development of
declarative, negative and interrogative remarks, and their use
has implications for the notion of knowledge of so called deep
structure as a part of linguistic competence. It will be recalled
that early in the first chapter, when the notion of the deep structure of a sentence was introduced, it was remarked that negative
and interrogative forms could be regarded as having the same underlying structure as corresponding active declarative sentences,
except that each carried a marker denoting its function and
indicating the transformation rules required to generate the correct surface structure. Thus together with *sentence* at the head
of a phrase marker should go at least one of the items *declarative,
negative* and *interrogative*.

The negative transformation essentially provides rules for the
use of *not* or *n't* in sentences so that the negating word follows
the auxiliary verb, or the inserted auxiliary *do* if no other is
present. Thus the essential question to ask of child language is
whether the child appears to adopt this kind of structuring or
whether he arrives at the same end in some other way. Negation
in action is evident in infant behaviour well before it is accompanied by an uttered syllable which may reasonably be interpreted as the forerunner of the *no* that amounts to a verbally
expressed rejection of some proposed form of behaviour. By the
time the child is producing two- or three-word remarks *no* often
figures amongst them. Klima and Bellugi (1966) noted that in the
speech of three children the negative either preceded or followed
the rest of the utterance, but never occurred within it. They
therefore proposed that the child was using a rule of the term
no + sentence or *sentence + no*. Sometimes *not* occurred instead
of *no*. Bloom (1970), however, has argued that in her observations
the child's *no* often referred to a previous utterance which was
being rejected, while the rest of the remark was an alternative
positive assertion. Thus she regards Klima and Bellugi's example
of *No the sun shining* as an illustration of her kind of observation.
Perhaps hers belong to an earlier period when such use of *no* is
all the child adopts, whereas Klima and Bellugi's belong to later
development when it is only one of several kinds of use. Bloom's
criticism seems valid however, and there are examples of anaphoric
use of *no + sentence* in Jonathan's remarks. Such use naturally
continues to occur, whatever the age of the speaker. The next

important development noted by Klima and Bellugi was the use of negative modals and the use of *no* or *not* between subject noun phrase and main verb, with the auxiliary verb omitted. They saw evidence here of transformation rules from the basic *negative + sentence,* and referred to this as the second stage of development. In the third stage they noted use of auxiliary verbs and of *can* and *do* as freely related to either positive or negative forms, and therefore concluded that more complex transformations were available.

Jonathan's negative remarks included examples of all the forms described in Klima and Bellugi's analysis, but certain features raised some interesting questions. An examination of his 24 uses of *no* led to a classification into 15 correct instances when it stood alone, or when it was used anaphorically and followed by a negative supporting statement as in *No, not that one* or an alternative positive assertion as in *No, me take a tray,* and into eight incorrect instances when it functioned as the imperative *don't,* as in *No get out of bed.* The additional instance was a special case to be referred to again, *I can no reach it.* The interesting feature of the incorrect imperative use was that it looked like Klima and Bellugi's early examples of *no + sentence,* yet its surface structure was *no + predicate* and it was not a declarative sentence. If a similar interpretation could legitimately be put on other children's remarks then the whole deep structure argument is called in question. It is tempting, reading the examples in the literature, to think that even those which may not be imperatives or anaphoric references look more like *no + predicate phrase* than *no + sentence.*

Jonathan's use of *not* occurred 47 times, all in the second two months of the study—sampling of negatives was low in any case in the first month—and it was clear that in 15 instances it stood in the place of either the auxiliary or main verb *be + not,* as in *My knee (is) not getting better* and *I (am) not ready yet;* and in 10 further instances there was neither a subject phrase nor a verb *be* as in *(It's) not falling* and *(It's) not yours.* Of the remaining 22 examples 17 were correct forms including *It's not, I'm not, He's not* and *That's not* preceding a main verb or a predicate noun phrase. Only five other forms occurred, *Not go in front room, Hilary, You not get up, You not get those bricks, No, it better not* and *I not drop it* (past tense). These suggested a move towards the use of words like *must, had* and *did* in ways which had not yet been adopted, and they did raise the intriguing question as

to whether a child's active search for expression might be a powerful force in directing his attention towards features of the model
speech. Often children seem to invent and make do when their
command of language does not quite meet their need. But, to
return to the point, the bias towards the use of *not* without the
accompanying *be,* and its occurrence in forms *not + predicate*
led to a second look at the Klima and Bellugi examples. Similar
examples were to be found—thus again it might have been better
to regard this form of early negative as *negative + predicate*
rather than *negative + sentence.*

Jonathan used negative modals *can't, won't* and *don't* as Klima
and Bellugi observed children doing from their second stage
onwards, but he also used auxiliaries with negatives, especially in
the latter part of the study. Examples like *You didn't do it, It
doesn't work, I don't like Pinkies* and *I haven't got a brush*
illustrated his developing skill in the third stage. The remark *I
can no reach it* suggested that he was developing a *can/can't*
contrast which was not previously evident. But how had he
attained this skill? There was no real evidence to show that he had
ever used a negative before a subject noun phrase except in
anaphoric reference. His use of *no, not* and negative modals
all placed it immediately before a main verb, and since his
development of true auxiliaries showed strong elision attachment
of *be* and *have* to the subject phrase, and his development of
negative auxiliaries tended to ally the *n't* familiar from modals
to the auxiliary, he was never inclined to place a negative in a
position from which it had to be transposed. His remarks at all
times reflected surface structure, and this was in keeping with the
other aspects of remark structure already discussed. The basis
of his categorisation of negatives was functional, discriminating between negation of a prior event, statement of what is and is not,
prohibition of another's act, and recognition of inability or refusal
in himself or another. His choice and positioning of markers for
these categories, distinguishing between *no, not* and modals
seemed to reflect the surface structure of adult speech and to
approximate more closely to it with his developing ability to
expand the verb.

Klima and Bellugi also described the development of the use
of questions in child speech and discussed it in terms of transformational grammar. They noted a first stage in which, as all
observers have remarked, children used intonation and facial and

body expression to convey their questioning while otherwise the form of their utterance was like a declarative remark. Klima and Bellugi likened their competence to the possession of a deep structure sentence plus question marker; but, as in the case of negatives, such a procedure implied that the child's competence included some nuclear structuring which might be described as sentence formation. If, however, it is difficult to show that the young child does anything other than acquire a strategy of linear sequencing of phrases when uttering what might be interpreted as declarative remarks, then the same is true of early interrogatives. A second kind of early question was the *wh* form where the child made remarks like *What that?, What cowboy doing? Where kitty?* and *Where milk go?* Klima and Bellugi suggested that only a very limited patterning was shown, such that children merely prefaced a declarative remark with a *wh* word, and such words were tied to a limited number of verbs. At stage two negative questions were introduced as in *Why not he eat?* and *Why not me can't dance?* This stage paralleled the introduction of negative modals in declarative sentences, and since Klima and Bellugi treated these as transformations they incorporated this treatment into negative questions. Otherwise no new transformations were suggested, but by stage three various developments had taken place. The auxiliary was being used in declarative remarks; and while in questions it was first used as in a declarative, intonation conveying the question, before long the subject noun phrase and auxiliary were being inverted and questions like *Can I have a piece of paper?, Are you going to make it with me?* and *Does the kitty stand up?* were being posed. The prior use of declarative auxiliaries followed by question inversion was interpreted by Klima and Bellugi as evidence of possession of a transformation rule. Further transformations were seen in the *wh* questions. First, in sentences like *What we saw?* the initial *what* referred to the direct object noun phrase in the following part of the remark, which by itself did not constitute a complete utterance. Second, although the move came later than in direct questions the *wh* questions began to incorporate auxiliaries and the auxiliary inversion was adopted. Thus in stage three, because utterances became completely grammatical, it was possible to describe them in terms of the linguistic descriptions applicable to adult sentences. But such a possibility might have little to do with the way the children's remarks arrived at such grammatical acceptability.

Jonathan's speech at the time of observation included questions, and, in Klima and Bellugi's terms, was spanning stages two and three. In fact in those questions requiring a direct affirmative or negative response he used all the techniques they described. He depended on intonation alone whether an auxiliary was present or not, as in *You want this?, I have a crane?, You haven't finished?* and *You seen my tyre?* He also used auxiliary and verb inversion as in *Is it yours? Can I go down there?, Wasn't it funny?, Can I have some more paper?* and *Is it an H?* His inversions were few, however, only 11 instances being found, and they were limited to the *Can I . . . ?* and *Is (wasn't) it . . . ?* patterns. There were however, nine instances of questions formed by adding a tag question to a declarative form as in *That's falling down, isn't it?, That wrong, Hilary, isn't it?* and *I draw a brown car, shall I?* Brown and Hanlon (1970), deriving their findings from the speech of the same three Harvard children as were studied by Klima and Bellugi, regarded tag questions as a more mature form of question, coming later than main sentence inversion, but Jonathan's use of *Shall I, Have you?* and *Will you?* as tags before he was able to construct remarks beginning with them suggested a different line of approach. It seems possible that truncated questions such as *Can I?, Have you?, Isn't it?* and so on might be adopted by children either as leads into fuller forms, or as tags. Brown and Hanlon suggest a close relationship between the child's choice of form and the model speech, for they observed differences between the three children's finer strategies of development.

Brown (1968) has already suggested that the child learns *wh* question forms independently of others, and that he gains many cues from question and answer exchange with adults. Klima and Bellugi remarked on the limited patterns of *wh* questions even with later auxiliary inversions. Jonathan's patterns were also limited, except for three examples, to *where's* or *what's* plus a noun phrase or a predicate, as in *Where's the black king?, Where's a plane gone? What's that?* and *What's mine doing?* or to *Who's done this/that . . . ?* The additional three examples were *What are those? What are mine doing?* and *What goes on here?* The use of elision for the main verb *be* suggested learning that was closely associated with the declarative remarks *There's a . . .* and *That's a . . .* though the development of *be* to include the use of *are* after *what* suggested that with the general growth of use of this verb some analogic extension of the use of *what* was becoming possible. The use of a limited range of patterns, even if analogic extension was thereafter adopted, suggested a functional rather than formal basis for children's interrogative skill, usage not some special linguistic competence. *Is it?* and *Can I?* marked two different kinds of questioning, one a search for agreement or confirmation and the other a request for permission. *What, who* and *where* marked questions seeking information about objects, persons, actions and locations.

The safest conclusion to make about children's use of interrogatives seems to be that there is evidence of systematic but not extensive use of various forms, and that children do not appear to learn to invert declarative forms; but they seem to learn question forms independently, first using intonation alone and then learning useful, but limited, separate systems of affirmative and negative truncated questions, tags and *wh* forms which they attach as markers to otherwise declarative remarks. Often this leads to apparent auxiliary inversion, but if *Can I?* and *Have some more paper* are separately learned their juxtaposition necessarily results in what may be described as an interrogative auxiliary transformation. Eventually analogic extension and discrimination in the face of mismatch with adult models will guide children to make the adjustments which lead to a more complete interrogative system, acceptable to their adult community. Indeed it is possible that it is experience with truncated questions used alone and as markers that leads the child to notice those features of auxiliary development in declarative remarks that seem to be more a grammatical gloss than a functional necessity to the three year old.

When analysing children's elaborations of phrases one is impressed by the evidence of system and order, and intrigued by the apparently deviant structures. As with the overall phrase structure of remarks one can sense an important difference between (a) the kind of basic categorisation which sometimes reveals unusual judgements rather than errors, and is remarkably similar from one language to another, and (b) marking systems for these categories and their relations. These latter seem to depend partly on imitation from adult models which vary quite considerably, partly on the ability to recognise markers and partly on analogic extension, the mixture yielding systematic but somewhat idiosyncratic kinds of error. There seem to be important differences between learning how to categorise and how to mark the categories.

To describe a child's competence in terms of patterns of surface forms is to go counter to the trend since Chomsky, which has been to describe it in terms of the hierarchical deep structure of sentences and to assume that the integrating mechanism of sentence production and perception is a special syntactic competence. Yet such descriptions can only be made if the child's functional use of words is such that the adult grasps his meaning, and assigns form class categories and relations to his remarks. The real integrating mechanism may be the construction of relations between perceptions of utterances, people, objects, actions and qualities of these, in ongoing events. Patterns of utterances are then similar when events are construed as similar. The foregoing considerations suggest the possibility that attributing the patterning of child speech to some knowledge of grammar, equivalent to the ability to adopt and relate formal categories, might be misplaced. The child's competence may in fact be far less abstract and may rest in an ability to relate words to broad functional categories in his knowledge of the world. Such an ability would place certain epistemological constraints on the structuring of remarks and, because both knowledge and speech would be partially shaped by the adult community, would progressively lead to the development of more adult-like remarks.

4 Schoolchildren Talking

MORE COMPLEX SPEECH

While pre-school children rapidly learn to talk more skilfully they have some way to go before they attain adult abilities, and certain developments can be traced in speech in the first years at school. One index of change might be the mean length of utterance, which has been found by students of child speech to be a moderately reliable measure, though it is somewhat sensitive to context. A moment's reflection on adult performance however raises problems of its possible greater sensitivity to context. Berger (1967) made recordings of café conversations in which he found a mean length of not quite seven words per remark, with a range from one to twenty or so words, but a skew distribution so that the longer remarks were much less frequent than the shorter. He commented, however, on the limited vocabulary and the use of elision and shortened forms compared with more formal speech. An analysis made by the author of the length of remarks in a video taped discussion between university teachers yielded a mean length of 15 words with a range from one to 55, but a mode of only eight words in a unimodal distribution. A remark was in this case taken to be either a functionally complete non-sentence or a sentence which had no more than one independent or matrix clause, no matter how many dependent clauses might be involved. Curiously enough only 3% of remarks were incomplete and therefore not included in the count, and very few of the remarks were ungrammatical. These two samples of adult speech serve to show that while some quite remarkably long grammatical remarks are possible the most common length is about eight words or so.

When a child's utterances reach this level we may regard them as being more typically adult in respect of length. Templin found a rise in the mean length of children's remarks in interview conversations from 4·1 words at age three to 7·6 at age eight years, though the rate of increase was low from four to five years. Such a finding was probably accounted for by change in the remarks attempted by children. There was a downward trend with age in the proportion of incomplete remarks, no change in the proportion of simple remarks, and an increase in that of complex remarks of various kinds. This suggested that up to four years the children were mostly gaining an improved command of the phrase structure of remarks, and that from four to five years they enjoyed a period of consolidation at this level, but that after five years improving production of complex structures resulted in longer forms. There were, of course, complex structures attempted at all ages from three onwards, but the proportions were low for the younger children. Grammatical deviations were common in the speech of the younger children, and appeared to be at a maximum between four and five years. This would be consistent with a period of consolidation when elaboration of phrase structure with the necessary growing command of regular and irregular forms of markers was one major task, and more accurate development of complex remarks was the other.

Reports of children's use of various kinds of complex remark have appeared from time to time in the literature. Watts (1944) summarised the position by indicating that several writers seemed to have made over-strong claims about the complexity of the speech of children up to five years of age. He welcomed Isaacs' (1930) report, but emphasised the bias towards high intelligence in her sample of children at the Malting House School in Cambridge. She reported the use of dependent temporal, noun and causal clauses at the mental age of six and a half years, and of conditional and qualifying clauses a year later. Other kinds were infrequent. Watts went on to show, with his own work on the construction of tests in English, that correct use of clauses based on connectives, such as *although, because, unless, whether,* and *neither,* was still being attained by some children in adolescence, and only about 50% of responses using these forms were correct at eight years.

More recent work has been based on analysis in terms of phrase markers and generalised transformation. Menyuk (1969) has described the further development of rules of tense agreement as extending into the tasks of the school child, and has also illustrated the developing use of some generalised transformations. She observed about 50% of her sample of children using some of these at three years, and about 70% at seven years. Her samples were small, however, and only selected transformations were illustrated. Carol Chomsky (1971) explored the comprehension of four different transformations by children of five to ten years, using children's actions to test their understanding. She found the younger children experienced considerable difficulty, but it was not clear from her report whether they had trouble understanding the sentence structure or whether the tasks predisposed them to jump to incorrect conclusions more readily than the older children.

Perhaps the most difficult problem of developmental studies is to find an index of complexity of utterance which will be general enough to apply to all remarks and reliable enough to reflect increasing productive competence. Templin's index of grammatical complexity did not discriminate clearly between phrase and clause levels of difficulty and cannot be used in conjunction with estimates based on a transformational grammar. These present problems, however, in that some kinds of transformation seem harder to use than others, and some of the difficulties seem to be related more to the amount or kind of thought required than to the complexity of syntactic description. It was at first thought that perhaps those transformations involving more rules and deletions than others might be more difficult, but this does not seem to be the case. Moreover, only those transformations that are specifically related to sentences more complex than simple forms are likely to be of interest if one is looking for an index of structural complexity. Those that are equally necessary for both simple and complex sentence forms are not really relevant. But even in the case of complex forms it is the basic sentence complexity rather than the kind of transformation rules that would seem to be the more reliable index. The author has explored the possibility that the insights about sentence conjunction and embedding that have been produced in the search for a transformational grammar might provide a more systematic framework of analysis than the traditional clause and phrase approach. The question of difficulty and order of acquisition is open to empirical investigation. The rest of this chapter outlines an attempt to make some headway with the problem in a study of the speech of young schoolchildren.

For the first part of the investigation the author selected a sample of children of five to seven years who might be expected to show a good command of English for their age. The project was discussed with the headmistress of the infants' department of a school in north Leeds. The receiving junior department of the school had sent a high proportion of children to selective secondary schools during its history, and the neighbourhood was a middle-class residential district. The headmistress and the Chief Education Officer readily agreed to the project, and the author first spent one morning per week for most of a school year observing a 'family group' class of children from five to seven years old, undertaking pilot studies, and devising suitable tests and materials for an investigation that ultimately included more than an exploration of productive competence. The subjects for the full investigation were all the children admitted to the school who were born between 1st September 1962 and 3rd April 1963. They had entered school either in September 1967 or April 1968 and were placed in classes formed from their own age group, the organisation of the school having been changed from family to horizontal age grouping at the end of the pilot study year. The children were not tested until they had been in the school for at least a full term and had had time to become familiar with it and with the author's occasional presence in the building. The same group of children was tested at six-monthly intervals, the mean age at the first testing being 5 years 9 months and at the last 7 years 3 months. Of the original 54 children four left the district, and of those who remained throughout the testing 20 were boys and 30 were girls.

From information supplied by the headmistress about fathers' occupation, it was found that in only one case did it seem likely that a child came from a home below social class three in the Registrar General's returns. Roughly half of the children came from social classes one, two and three(a), though the categorisation was not always certain. After a school medical inspection the headmistress reported that none of the children had a diagnosed hearing deficit. Two of the children were of non-English-speaking descent, but their parents had been in England for a considerable time, had learned to speak English well, and the language at home was English. The children's scores on the tests were above average, so there seemed to be no valid reason for excluding them from the sample. The best available index of intelligence for the group was the vocabulary score on the Stanford–Binet scale (Form L–M, Third Revision) at the final testing. The group mean score was 8·88 with a standard deviation of 2·06 and a range of 3–13. The mean score represented a vocabulary age of about 8 years 8 months, while the mean chronological age was 7 years 3 months. This index should not be regarded as anything more than an indication that the mean intelligence of the group was well above the norm for their age.

On a later occasion the author selected a sample of children from two schools in south Leeds and gave them some of the same tests. There were 12 boys and 12 girls at each age level represented in the north Leeds testing. The majority were from one school, but because classes were small it was not possible to make up the full sample and the remainder were selected from the second school so that the required age distribution was sampled. These children lived in an inner-city redevelopment area, some in new corporation-owned flats or houses and some in late nineteenth-century houses due for demolition. Factories and houses were, in places, only yards apart. In several cases there was no father with the family, in others they were unemployed, and in those where they were both at home and in work their occupations were those of social classes four and five. Principally because of re-development these children moved from school to school more frequently than those in the north Leeds school, and it was thought better to sample at each age level than to follow one group for two years. The Standford–Binet vocabulary score for these children at age 7 years 3 months was 8·1, a score which indicated that they lagged behind their north Leeds contemporaries by about six months. It should be pointed out that although their background was in some respects less favourable, their experience in school tended to be of smaller classes. The local authority was concerned to some extent with compensatory education. A further point of interest was that they were not a particularly roving population. Often the children had extended family contacts locally, and their speech had the characteristics of the area. Mention of Richard Hoggart's writing of the stability of Hunslet is not irrelevant here.

Devising procedures to test structure in speech was not easy. Different situations elicit different speech patterns, and the inter-view techniques and recorded conversations often used in investi-gating speech result in patterns that are at least in part a product of the speech partner. If a comparative study had been intended then a method comparable with that of other workers would have been required, but the author wished instead to establish a descriptive analysis of sustained portions of child speech that would allow comparison at different ages, and if possible comparison with adult speech. In the pilot study the children were encouraged to tell stories, but while some were able to do this well, others seemed to be at a loss for ideas. Furthermore the variety was such that there was no good basis for comparison. It was therefore decided to try telling the children a short story and asking them to retell it. This generally worked well when suitable stories were found. Surprisingly they were not like those normally used in school. They did not appeal to the imagination, nor require extended comprehension, for such stories were not at all easily retold. Instead they were short; they contained limited vocabulary; and they were very simple stories modified slightly from a collection of young children's bedtime tales. Four stories (see Appendix B) were selected and altered so that the length and sentence patterning of each were very similar. The children's productions could then be compared both with each other and with the model story. For this task the four stories were presented to the north Leeds children so that each child heard a different story at each testing, the order was randomised and each story was presented to a quarter of the children at each testing. The south Leeds children only heard one story each but all four were used randomly at each age level. In order to maximise production the children were read to individually, for this allowed the reader to ensure maximum attention from the child. (Listening to a tape-recorded story cannot be so readily controlled.) They were first instructed to listen to the story carefully so that they could tell it again afterwards 'in their own way'—not exactly like the reading. After hearing the story they were asked to retell as much as they could remember. Their story was recorded, and if they halted in the telling the children were encouraged by suitable interjections and expressions such as *Yes?, What happened next? Can you remember any more?* Care was taken to avoid prompting in such a way as to elicit a sentence structure intimately related to the prompt. In the few cases when a child seemed unable to respond beyond a few words the recorder was switched off and the child questioned. Rarely was he able to volunteer any further information so the limited recording was accepted. If, however, he indicated that he could tell more with a second try he was recorded again, but when this happened the second recording differed very little from the first. All the children had been introduced to the tape recorder before the story task, and they had been promised that they could hear their stories replayed if they wished. The promise was not always exacted, but it was kept, and the children enjoyed listening to their own voices. In order to establish some measure against which to assess the children's speech when the north Leeds children were tested, the stories were similarly read to 25 undergraduate students, 12 male and 13 female, and their retelling was recorded. They had been told the purpose of the exercise but were not told the criteria to be adopted in analysing the samples. They were sensibly co-operative.

STORY REPRODUCTION

A preliminary comment must be that both children and adults adhered to the semantic content of the stories to a remarkable extent. One was reminded of Bartlett's (1932) experiments on story recall where the first attempt usually resulted in a fairly accurate but reduced version. The amount of reduction varied considerably, especially by the children, but even more variety was evident in the construction of the stories. It was obvious that phonological learning was still going on, and although there was no endeavour in this study to link such learning with grammatical structuring, it should be remembered that attention to the surface structure of sentences is important for discrimination of significant structural units. The following are representative of the longer and more complex examples, and illustrate some of the errors and difficulties in sentence construction. They are presented with the sentence boundaries determined as described later in the text and with repetitions of words or phrases omitted.

1. (Age 5 years 8 months)
One day Kanga saw that Jumbo was looking very sad. She said, 'What's the matter, Jumbo?' 'I have to get one of my toofs tooken out and you don't really like having your teef tooken out.' 'Well if when you go to the dentist when it's night-time you put the toof under your pillow and then you get a bright shiny sixpence in the morning.' So he went to the dentist. And when he waited for bedtime, and when he had his tea, after his tea he went up to bed. And Kanga came in. And she looked under his pillow. Then she went away, back to her house, crept out quietly, as quiet as a mouse. In the morning Jumbo waked up. He didn't see a

sign under his pillow from a toof. But just where he put the toof he saw a bright shiny sixpence.

2.   (Age 5 years 10 months)
Koo loved eating biscuits. He knew perfectly well that his mother didn't allow him to eat the biscuits. One night when he went to bed in his mother's lovely soft pocket he ate and he crunched for nearly an hour. And when he had eaten all the biscuits he couldn't get off to sleep because there was not enough room for him, for the crumbs had gone all in his mother's pocket. He said 'Oh dear.' So he couldn't get them out. So he lay in his mother's pocket with his. . . . He was very cold because his head was hanging out and his toes. And he didn't like sleeping because the crumbs were all rumpled up. In the morning when Kanga found out what he had done she nearly had to stand on her head while the little kangaroo brushed them all out. And he said to his mother he was very sorry and he would never eat biscuits again.

3.   (Age 5 years 11 months)
She was always knitting. One day Busybody went out. And she saw a strange thing. She went to Teddy's house and knocked on the door loudly. Teddy didn't answer because he was in the bath. Busybody just opened the door and walked straight in. But when she always walked in she put her ball of wool in her pocket. And when she went into Teddy's bedroom she saw the boot and went into the bathroom. Teddy got out of the bath and tripped down the stairs. Busybody just walked out without saying sorry.

4.   (Age 5 years 7 months)
And he went anywhere. And Teddy asked him to go to his party. And he thought. And he couldn't. And he worried. And he tied a knot in his tail so. . . . And he worried so much that he couldn't sleep that night. And when he woke up in the morning it was nine o'clock. And he was supposed to start work. So he dashed out like an express train. Then he ran to the milk. . . . Then he ran round the town like a racehorse. Then he went home and tied the knot out of his tail, brushed his face. And he rushed out of the door and locked

it up and then ran to Teddy's. Then he knocked on the door. And then Teddy looked at him. He was so surprised. Then he began to laugh. And he said, 'Oh, you're too early for me. . . . ' 'I've come to the party,' he said. 'You're too early, it's tomorrow is the party.'

5. (Age 7 years 3 months)
One day Kanga met Jumbo looking very sad. She said, 'What is the matter?' And Jumbo said, 'I'm going to the dentist to have a tooth out.' Nobody likes having teeth out. But Kanga said if you have magic teeth is is very exciting. She said that she knew a friend who said he had magic teeth, and when he had teeth out he put them under his pillow and in the morning he had a sixpence there instead. Jumbo's face brightened when he heard this. And he went off to the dentist. And as soon as his tooth was out he asked if he could have it. He took it home in his pocket. And he was waiting all day for bedtime. As soon as he'd finished his tea he went upstairs. And he put the tooth under his pillow. And in the night Kanga came up to see if he had remembered about his tooth. And he was fast asleep. So she crept down quietly and out of the house. The first thing Jumbo did as soon as he got up next morning was to look under his pillow. And there was no sign of his tooth. But there was a brand new sixpence there instead. As soon as he was dressed he went off to tell Kanga all about it.

6. (Age 7 years 3 months)
Koo lived in a soft pocket in Kanga's pinafore. One night Koo took some biscuits to bed. He knew he shouldn't take biscuits to bed. And he munched and crunched the biscuits for nearly an hour. And when he had eaten the last biscuit he found out that the pocket was full of crumbs. He knew he couldn't throw the crumbs out or Kanga would see them. So he tried to curl up like he usually did. But he couldn't because there was not enough room. So he had to sit on the top of the pile of crumbs. And his head and feet popped out. And his toes and head got frozen. In the morning Kanga found out that her pocket was full of crumbs. And she had to stand on her head for about an hour while Koo brushed the crumbs out. Koo felt very sorry for Kanga.

7.   (Age 7 years 1 month)

Busybody knitted in the bath and in the street and in the shop. One day when Busybody was walking along, knitting in the street, she saw a boot hanging out of Teddy's window. She was so anxious to know why the boot was hanging there that she knocked at the door very, very loudly. And Teddy was in the bath. So when he was in the bath he didn't open the door. So she opened the door and walked straight in. And she dropped her knitting on the doorstep. And she had her wool in her pocket when she knits. So when she walked upstairs a trail of wool came behind her. When Busybody went into Teddy's bedroom Teddy came out of the bathroom. And when Teddy came out of the bathroom he tripped over the wool and fell downstairs. And Busybody shouted at Teddy. And she said, 'Why is that boot hanging out of your bedroom?' So he said, 'Well, it fell in the bath, so I left it out to dry, Nosey-parker.' So she went and hurried home. And she didn't even bother to say thank you.

8.   (Age 7 years 5 months)

Wonky was always late. One day Teddy asked him to a party. Wonky was so afraid of being late that he tied a knot in his tail. He was so uncomfortable in bed. So he couldn't go to sleep that night. In the morning when Wonky woke up he looked at the clock. And it was nearly nine o'clock. He started work at six o'clock. He pulled the milkman's cart. And he got out of bed and ran downstairs and outside. He pulled the cart. He went so fast that he broke all the bottles. So they had to go back for another load. When he had finished he went home and brushed his face and went to Teddy's house and knocked on the door. Teddy opened the door. And Wonky said, 'I've come to the party.' Teddy stared at Wonky. And Wonky thought the party was over. Teddy said the party was yesterday.

As a first stage in the investigation of the samples the model stories were analysed into words and sentences. The latter were taken to be any strings of words which functioned as complete grammatical and semantic units and which did not contain more than one independent clause—or, in terms of transformational grammar, more than one matrix sentence. They might therefore be simple or complex. These sentences were then analysed into phrases so that matrix and embedded *sentence units* could be identified from the sentence forms and inferred meanings. The reader will recall that some indication of what might be involved was given in the analysis of adult equivalent remarks in the account of Jonathan's speech. A further description of the procedure for story analysis will be developed a little further on. Suffice it to say for the moment that it was possible to carry out such an analysis, which yielded an indication of sentence complexity in terms of the number of sentence units comprising a single sentence. Such an index was independent of the kind of transformation involved in describing the sentences, and was logical both in terms of syntax and of difficulty in construction, since more information or message content is involved in combinations of sentence units than in any unit separately.

Armed with the analysis of the model stories the author proceeded to attempt a similar analysis of transcripts of the recorded versions. This was not too difficult. Much of the material was grammatical, and where an incomplete remark occurred it was decided to count it as a sentence unit only when its verb root and dominant (subject) noun phrase were represented in the total remark. Repeated words (often associated with hesitation) and altered words were not counted. The reader will have appreciated by now that the model stories were treated like the adult equivalent remarks in the earlier study, but that in this case, since the spoken samples were structurally of the same order as the model, no situational information was required for interpretation and description. Some questions arising from this treatment will be considered when the sentence descriptions are discussed in more detail.

The variation in amount of reproduced story was reflected in the counts of numbers of words. For the children there was a steady increase with age in the average length of a story, though even at the last testing this was well below the adult level, which was itself short of the model. Table 4.1 gives indices of sentence length and complexity and the total number of words per story at different ages. The mean sentence length for the children was greater than that for adults in Berger's café conversations but not as great as the average for the model stories. The students, however, produced sentences that were on average longer than the model. The ratio of sentence units to sentences proved to be a

TABLE 4.1

Speech in the story reproductions

	Average no. words	Words per sentence	Sen. units (clauses) per sentence
Children			
North Leeds (N=50)			
5 years 9 months	65	8·6	1·63
6 years 3 months	78	8·8	1·65
6 years 9 months	103	9·2	1·73
7 years 3 months	119	9·5	1·86
South Leeds (N=24)			
5 years 9 months	66	7·4	1·48
6 years 3 months	84	7·5	1·44
6 years 9 months	101	8·6	1·67
7 years 3 months	116	8·1	1·76
Adults (N=25)	230	12.3	2·37
Model (N=4)	326	11·5	2·34

useful index, showing a reliable increase with age for the children and an adult level exceeding that of the model. Since the north Leeds children were studied longitudinally it was possible to estimate the significance of the score differences and the reliability of the measures. As reported elsewhere (Francis, 1974b), both the differences between testings and the reliability of the scores of amount and complexity were statistically significant. Longer samples from the children would probably have increased the reliability, as would the use of the two more reliable stories (Jumbo and Wonky).

The differences between testings were similar for both groups of children; but the south Leeds group, while maintaining a similar length of story, seemed to be about half a year behind their north Leeds contemporaries in their scores of sentence complexity. They were not less fluent, though they appeared to be less mature; but, when children from both groups were matched for age, sex and Stanford–Binet vocabulary scores (15 matched pairs), the differences in complexity scores almost vanished. Since the story vocabulary was not particularly exacting, and complexity scores correlated with vocabulary scores for both groups of children, it was supposed that the differences in sentence structuring skill were possibly related more to variations in general intelligence than to social differences. (The Stanford–Binet vocabulary scale correlates at the 0·9 level with the scale of general intelligence.) That the ability to integrate information in a more explicit and complex way should relate to intelligence would scarcely be surprising.

The main source of change in the children's speech was a decrease in the proportion of simple sentences and a corresponding increase in that of combinations of three or more sentence units. In order to make a closer comparison of developmental trends, the south Leeds children at the fourth testing were matched as carefully as possible for birthdate and sex with a sub-group of the north Leeds children, care being taken to ensure that this was not a biased sample of the whole group. The student sample was also reduced to 12 males and 12 females by omitting the story of the last female to be tested. In Table 4.2 the percentage distributions of sentences of different levels of complexity are shown. The students produced proportionately more sentences of four or more units than was characteristic of the model, while the children produced fewer. The children, moreover, produced more single unit sentences. The corresponding frequency distributions yielded statistically signicant differences between the model, the students and the two groups of children at the last testing. The differences between the two sets of children were such that the north Leeds children produced more three-unit and longer sentences and fewer one- and two-unit forms than expected if they and the south Leeds children were regarded as a homogeneous group, while the reverse was true for the south Leeds children. In spite of these differences, however, some children occasionally produced some very complex sentences, and a few of their stories were comparable with adult samples; but the children who achieved these also had high scores on the vocabulary test, taking them to the ten or eleven year level.

The children's stories quoted above indicated some of the grammatical errors. An exhaustive analysis of these was not undertaken, but those of the south Leeds children were counted and compared with those of the sub-group from north Leeds. Errors of tense, number, agreement and use of auxiliary verbs were found in both

TABLE 4.2

Percentage distributions of sentences of different degrees of complexity

Sentence units per sentence	North Leeds (N = 24) Testing				South Leeds (N = 24) Testing				Adult (N = 24)	Model (N = 4)
	1	2	3	4	1	2	3	4		
1	34	29	30	22	45	45	34	28	14	11
2	39	39	36	31	28	36	35	39	24	33
3	15	20	20	25	20	16	16	19	26	31
4	7	7	7	12	4	3	8	8	17	15
4+	5	5	7	10	3	0	7	6	19	10
Total	100	100	100	100	100	100	100	100	100	100

simple and complex sentences. Errors made in relating sentence units within complex sentences consisted of the use of the perfect tense when the pluperfect was required, incorrect word order, omission of necessary *and*, failure to achieve correct pronoun agreement, and the use of inappropriate relational words. Difficulty was most noticeable with *lest, otherwise, because, as . . . as, so . . . that, if . . . then, or* and *although*. Piaget (1928) and Watts (1944) have commented fully on such difficulties. Given the equivalence of the total numbers of words used, the south Leeds children made significantly more errors than those from north Leeds, but this was largely because they systematically inverted the use of *were* and *was*, as in *he were* and *they was*. While not standard English this was correctly learned from parental models, and as they produced longer stories so the incidence of the inversion increased. The north Leeds children made more errors with the pluperfect, but this was related to a higher incidence of both correct and attempted use. When both these errors were ignored there was no real difference between the two groups, though the incidence of error was lower for the north Leeds children. In both cases the proportion of errors decreased with age. Perhaps the model stories were not challenging enough to be more revealing, though a more difficult model might have inhibited production altogether!

The language abilities of the two groups appeared to differ quantitatively rather than qualitatively, the south Leeds group being delayed in development compared with the north. Yet one cannot avoid considering the possibility discussed by Bernstein (1972), that although both restricted and elaborated codes might be available, they might not be used similarly by children of different social classes. In his earlier papers he thought that an elaborated code, a fuller, more explicit and accurate form of the language, might be used generally by middle-class children and a restricted code might be the only version available to the less advantaged. In the light of this view Hawkins (1969) explored differences between the ways children described a series of scenes depicted in cartoon-like pictures. The elaborated code would require more explicit noun phrases and internal references from one sentence to another in the story, whereas the restricted code would lead to a widespread use of pronouns, demonstratives and indicators, making reference directly to the pictures (exophoric reference) and not maintaining a clear and coherent account.

Hawkins reported that middle-class children were the more explicit and gave more informative accounts. They used more nouns and adjectives, while lower-class children relied more heavily on pronouns, demonstrative adjectives and location indicators such as *here* and *there*. The middle-class children's stories gave accounts that were comprehensible without the pictures, but those of the lower-class children lacked nouns essential to convey meaning without pictorial support. In the light of Bernstein's later views Hawkins' findings might be taken to show that in a picture description task the middle- and lower-class children chose to use language rather differently. But one still has to ask whether there are circumstances in which the elaborated code is equally available to both classes of children.

The storytelling task used with the Leeds children proved to be a useful means of looking at this question. The stories of 12 boys and 12 girls from each of the age levels tested in each area of Leeds were analysed for the relevant data, to make a comparison with Hawkins' study (Francis, 1974a). Since the total words and total sentences units at each age level were very similar, it was possible to make a direct comparison of the incidence of various features of noun phrases. While both north and south Leeds children made some use of exophoric reference, as described by Hawkins, it was relatively slight and tended to decrease with age. There were no differences between the groups. An analysis of the distribution of pronouns, nouns, descriptive adjectives and other modifiers for both groups again revealed no significant differences. Lastly, to be quite clear about the differences between specific and exophoric reference, a closer comparison was made. Nouns and names were obviously specific, but pronouns, demonstrative adjectives and locatives might be either specific or exophoric, depending on whether they referred to something already made explicit or to something with no clear specification. Thus, in *Wonky was worried. He was invited to a party,* the *He* was clearly related to and dependent on *Wonky*. But, in *He was worried. He was invited to a party,* while the second *He* was dependent, the first was exophoric. It was thought that exophoric reference might well be associated with confusion and pronoun error, so this aspect of the stories was also checked. But it was found that on no score were the groups significantly different. It could only be concluded that the story reproduction task had led the south Leeds children to use the same code as the north

Leeds, and that both found an elaborated code available. Presumably this was because the model stories set an example, and the children did not assume that what they were talking about was otherwise evident to the listener.

Further exploration of children's abilities required more detailed analysis of sentences. The scheme to be outlined here was developed during the pilot study and was designed to explore complexity, not in terms of those transformations of basic sentences that apply within the simple sentence, but in terms of the major construction patterns of complex sentences. The simple sentence as seen by linguists, and as identified in this study, comprises at least a subject noun phrase and a verb phrase, while complex sentences are seen as versions of one or more simple sentences embedded in another simple, but matrix, sentence. In order to specify the embedding it is necessary to have a clear description of the structure of the matrix form and then a further description of the embedded version. Linguists have devised descriptions in terms of transformational grammar but these always specify a known sentence, and the procedure for first defining the structural relations involved in 'raw data' has not been explored. In the analysis of conversation and the speech of young children, the utterance, or remark, has been recognised as a functional unit, but it does not correspond reliably to a syntactic unit such as a sentence; only at the morpheme and phrase levels is there a a close correspondence between functional and formal units. Young children speak in relatively segregated remarks, or very short sequences of such; but once the speaker tends to produce coherent sequences analysis into units requires further explanation. Moreover, since the discourse is not characterised by the 'telegraphic' and fragmented structuring of early speech, it is possible to speak of a sentence unit in the sense that it constitutes what is to any native speaker a recognisably complete expression, regardless of its context of use.

A first requisite is that the discourse should be meaningful to the analyser. This was seen to be the major premise of analysis of Jonathan's speech, and is an indispensable circumstance for a discovery procedure. The problem of how far the meaning imposed by the analyser and that imposed by the speaker are in any sense either similar or identical is obviously of interest to philosophers and psychologists, and is an everyday problem for most of us who engage in discussions with our friends; but if the circumstances are such that the measure of agreement is maximised then it is possible to say the meaning is grasped well enough for the purpose in hand. This claim was made for the analysis of much of Jonathan's speech and is now made again for the analysis of the children's stories. Here it is made with greater confidence in that the common experience of speaker and analyser was more explicit—the model story—so that the semantic relations expressed in the spoken accounts were readily identifiable. This is not to deny a margin of error, but to claim that it was necessarily small.

Given an awareness of the semantic relations, then it was possible to begin to identify from the transcripts the noun and verb phrase relations that constituted the minimal requirements for a sentence unit. The next problem was to determine the sentence boundaries. This was done on a basis of defining the phrases which, together with the nucleus noun and verb phrase, supplied a unitary network of semantic relations such that a whole string of words constituted a recognisably complete expression. Quite obviously this meant including in the sentence phrases which were not necessary for the completion of such an expression but, although optional, added to its fullness rather than to that of an adjacent expression. For example *he carried it home in his pocket* consisted of the necessary *he carried* and the compulsory *it* (given the particular subject–verb relation) together with the optional *home* and *in his pocket*. The next stretch of words in this particular item of discourse was *he waited for bedtime*. To have put the sentence boundary after *it* or *home* would have left the phrases *home* and *in his pocket* meaninglessly isolated or nonsensically attached to the next items *he waited*. In this case the solution was clear, but in some instances the transcript and the shared meaning still left the matter unclear. In particular, a phrase like *next day*, expressing the time of an action, might equally well belong to a sentence unit on either side of it. In these cases the actual recording often resolved the matter, for the intonation, stress and timing patterns of native speakers are not unimportant features of some aspects of sentence structuring.

The outcome of the decisions so far described was the formulation of a simple sentence description which is shown in Figure 4.1. The phrase numbers were for reference only—no fixed order or relationship was implied. The figure was based on three assumptions. One was that noun phrases are essentially case marked; the second was that the subject noun phrase in a sen-

Figure 4.1

The simple sentence

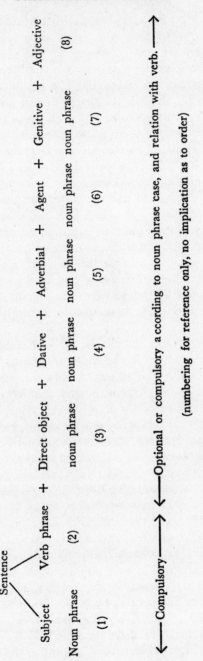

tence might be of any case, but once it was related to a verb the relation would determine what other noun phrases were compulsory or optional for a complete sentence; the third was that the sense of a sentence would enable the listener or reader to recover the phrase case markings. The possibility of other noun phrases being required in the description of other data was not overlooked, but there seemed to be no problem in principle in extending the range of predicate categories. Indeed the fifth category—adverbial noun phrase—covered several kinds and was in fact subdivided when this seemed useful, as will be seen shortly. The reader will have recognised in the figure a parallel between this sentence description and the statements made about simple remark construction by Jonathan. It is also much more a framework for rules relating meaning to surface structure than for the Chomsky type syntactic rules. The reason for this was simple— it was not possible to analyse the children's spoken stories into sentence units without first being sure of the semantic relations expressed. In this the model story was a guide, taking the place of the adult equivalent remarks used in the analysis of Jonathan's speech.

The simple sentence description only sufficed to account for a proportion of sentences in the children's stories. Other sentences included additional verb and noun phrases regarded by linguists as transformations of embedded sentences. When sentences are seen in this way one of the most notable features is that, if the additional forms are compared with their supposed simple sentence bases, the most invariant element common to both is the verb root. Thus the most readily identified element of an embedded sentence unit, whether viewed as a surface or deep-structure embedding, is the verb. Using this rule it was possible to describe many of the children's sentences in terms of combinations of sentence units indexed by their verbs. Thus many sentence units were comparable with the main and dependent clauses of traditional grammar. For example *He ran upstairs and got into bed* was regarded as composed of two sentence units, the two predicates indexed by *ran* and *got* sharing the common subject *he*.

Before a fuller description of complex forms is undertaken, one or two problems remain to be considered. One problem was that in thematic presentation there were not only features of sentence relations that involved structural organisation, there were also features that involved word selection. Thus pronouns might be used when repeated reference was made to an object or person, and sequencing strengtheners such as *and, then* and *so* might appear to relate sentence units which were in fact quite independent structurally. Such word selections were not regarded as indices of sentence complexity. A further problem was that some noun phrases denoted relations that went beyond those of the simple sentence description. Linguists tend to regard these as the surface result of deletions from embedded sentences in the deep structure. Examples were given in the account of Jonathan's speech, but other examples might be useful here. The double nominal *my brother, the mayor* can be regarded as derived from two sentences *my brother* and *my brother is the mayor*. The nearest examples in the data from children's stories were *Wonky, the donkey* and *Jumbo, the elephant* but these could be treated as extended nominals like *John Baker* and it was decided not to credit the children with the more complex description on this evidence alone. Another form, the genitive construction, e.g. *Kanga's pocket,* was also treated as a combination of genitive and object noun phrases within the simple sentence, although again some linguists tend to regard the genitive as indexing an embedded sentence such as *the pocket is of Kanga*. The decision not to credit the children with an embedding was based on the case marking argument already referred to and on the recognition that such genitive constructions are common in early speech and do not seem to require a matrix sentence.

A more difficult problem might have been phrases like *in his hurry* which Watts (1944) regarded as an economical form of *while he was hurrying*. In such a case not only is the embedded sentence re-ordered and reduced, but there is an alteration from verb to noun. The relationship between word classes and relations involved in this kind of expression would be a fascinating topic in itself, but had such expressions occurred in the story data the author would have hesitated to infer embedding without further evidence, using instead the adverbial noun phrase description. A developmental study of the use of such phrases would help to resolve the problem, for, although Chomsky (1965) described some in terms of deletion transformations, he did so on an *ad hoc* basis, and it is not clear whether the child faces a problem of more abstract vocabulary or more complex syntax.

Finally the most difficult problem was posed by the use of adjectives and phrases that functioned like relative clauses. The latter were fewer in number and the problem is illustrated by the following sentences : *He put the car in the garage; He saw the car in the garage; He borrowed the car in the garage.* In the first the phrase *in the garage* is indubitably a reference to where the car was put, i.e. an adverbial noun phrase according to the scheme in Figure 4.1. In the third, to infer an adverbial phrase one would have to have contextual information that made such an unlikely thing possible. To borrow a car implies the act of using it rather than the agreement to do so. The most likely interpretation is that the phrase is equivalent to the relative clause, *which is in the garage.* In the second, the decision is more difficult still. Was he in the garage with the car or not? Only with an answer to that question can a decision be made. Even then, and also in the third case, supposing a qualifying function is indicated is one entitled to infer a complex structure? In the few cases in which the problem was encountered the author decided not to infer a deletion from an embedding, but to rest on the possibility that the children had direct production rules which permitted the expression of the qualifying relation by the use of a phrase following a noun. This decision was also influenced by the awareness that such phrasing occurred in early speech. The question of adjectives presented most difficulty. Chomsky presented a good argument for describing adjectives in noun phrases as the remainder after deletion of embedded sentence units. For example he regarded *The sleeping child,* as being derived from *the child* and *the child is sleeping.* Approaching the analysis of raw data, however, one is aware that the functional relations conveyed by the use of adjectives are not faithfully reflected by this treatment, and that they are related to the whole qualifying function. If we take an undoubted complex form such as *the boy who missed the bus will be late for school,* we see that two separately perceived events are related. One cannot simultaneously report the boy missing the bus and being late for school. Similarly *the cleverest boy came into the room last* also refers to two separate perceptions—one of the boy in skilled activities of some sort, and one of his entry. Thus it is intuitively like the first sentence and one would not be too unhappy about inferring some complexity. But *the red mug is on the table* seems to refer to what can be encompassed in one observation event, and the relations expressed thus belong to a simple sentence structure. Such was the author's disquiet, but having regard to the parsimony exercised in other problems, and to the unresolved problem of the young child's use of qualifying adjectives both before and after nouns, the decision was made to count all adjectives appearing in the context *modifier + adjective + noun* as indices of an embedded form.

What then were the categories of expressions that were treated as subordinate sentence units, and how did they relate to matrix sentences like the simple sentences of Figure 4.1? The non-subordinate category of sentence units comprised simple sentences, either alone or as the matrix units of complex sentences. There were then logically four different ways of embedding a sentence unit in a matrix sentence. It could be conjoined with a set of one or more phrases, it could be substituted for a compulsory noun phrase, it could be inserted to qualify a noun phrase, or it could be added in place of an optional noun phrase. The latter allowed two major possibilities, one that the additional unit elaborated an adverbial function, such as indicating the location in time or space of some happening, or that it expressed a perceived logical relation between the expressions of the matrix and subordinate sentence units such that separation destroyed the relation.

Conjunction was recognised by a plurality of phrases occurring in any position in the matrix sentence frame, and by the use of *and* or *but* to join them, though the latter was used rarely. When the subject noun phrase shared two predicates, as in *so she opened the door and walked straight in,* the form was described as *Conj. pred.* It was used frequently, and sometimes extended to cover more than two predicates, when any *and* except the last might be omitted. Another pattern was the conjunction of subject noun phrases sharing the same predicate, as in *and his head and feet popped out.* This was labelled *Conj. 1.* When two verbs shared the same subject and further predicate as in *and he munched and crunched the biscuits for nearly an hour* the form was labelled *Conj. 2.* Once, two different combinations of subject and verb shared the same further predicate, the pattern being described as *Conj. (1+2).* Two further predicate positions were occupied by conjoined phrases, the direct object noun phrase and the adverbial phrase; these were labelled *Conj. 3* and *Conj. 5,* respectively. Finally when adjectives were combined after *be,* as in *Kanga's pocket was warm and soft,* the form was labelled *Conj. adj.*

Substitution units sometimes took the place of noun phrases in matrix sentences, but in some cases they were related with words like *that, what* and *who,* and in others the verb was modified to take an infinitive or participle form. Direct substitution was seen in *some people said she knitted in the bath,* where *she knitted in the bath* was substituted for the direct object noun phrase in *some people said (some sentence).* This type of substitution was therefore labelled *Sub. (3).* Direct speech was labelled as *Sub. (3) ('–').* When relating words such as *that* were used, they were regarded as additional information about the relation. *That* was an indication of something it was possible to express in a simple sentence. *Why* was an indicator of an answer to a problem expressed in the substituted sentence. Such substitutions were labelled according to both the noun phrase position occupied and the relating word. Thus, the substitution in *she found out why it was there* was labelled as *Sub. (3) (why).* When verb forms were changed these were indicated in the label. For example, in *He wanted to go to the party, to go to the party* was labelled as *Sub. (3) (inf.);* and in *Nobody likes having teeth out, having teeth out* was labelled as *Sub. (3) (ing).* No distinction was made between *He wanted to go to the party* and *Teddy wanted Wonky to go to the party* where the subject phrases of the embedded units were different, though correct comprehension required that an implicit subject identical with the matrix subject be recognised in the former example. A distinction was made, however, between *He wanted to go to the party* and *He was anxious to go.* In the latter there was no NP(3) position in the matrix sentence, and it was decided to describe the embedding as a special, adjective dependent, infinitive form of qualifying the matrix subject phrase. Had a sentence like *The doll is easy to see* occurred, the same procedure would have been adopted, but with the recognition that in comprehension an implied other was doing the seeing.

There were several kinds of qualifying pattern based on the sharing of a common referent by a noun phrase in the matrix sentence and the expressed or implied subject noun phrase in the qualifying unit. Relative pronouns were often used to indicate this relation. In *She saw all the crumbs that were in Koo's bed,* the qualifying unit *that were in Koo's bed* related to the direct object phrase *all the crumbs* in the matrix sentence, and such a qualifying unit was labelled *Qual. (3) (that).* Sometimes the verb was in infinitive or participle form only, as in *She saw a boot hanging out of the window.* This was labelled *Qual. (3) (ing). He went to sleep curled up in a ball* was labelled *Qual. (1) (ed.)*

since it was felt that *curled up in a ball* qualified the subject noun phrase *He*. Where an adjective qualified a noun the form was labelled *Qual. adj.* with the appropriate number of the noun phrase.

Other embedded sentence units took the position of optional adverbial noun phrases in the matrix sentence. Some defined the time or place of a happening and took the position of locative noun phrases. They were labelled *Loc. (5)* and given an additional marking word indicating the temporal or spatial relation involved. Thus in *when he went to bed he put his tooth under his pillow, When he went to bed* was labelled *Loc. (5)(when)*. Other adverbial units conveyed purpose, consequence and other logical relations between the events referred to. A few were informative of the manner of an action, using the conjunction *as*. Given other data this category might have been much enlarged, but with the present data examples were classified with the general category of adverbial units, which were predominantly logical. Each instance was labelled, *Adv. (5)* with its accompanying defining label word such as *because, so . . . that* (consequence of purpose) *or, if, etc.*

Once this kind of analysis was complete it was possible first to explore the construction of complex sentences in terms of the combinations of categories of sentence unit. There were six major categories : simple or matrix sentence (sen.), conjoined unit (conj.), substituted unit (sub.), qualifying unit (qual.) and the optional adverbial units (loc. and adv.). There was clearly no important difference between the relative frequencies of use of these types in the speech of the adults and children, though the model made use of rather fewer conjoined units. Sentences ranged in complexity from simple units to patterns of five or more, though the latter were relatively rare. The number of possible combinations and arrangements of six types of unit was great, but some restriction seemed to operate in practice to avoid ambiguity and awkwardness, and possibly to match relative frequencies in use in English. A wide variety of patterns was used, however, reflecting the flexibility of the language. The general rule for deciding the order of sentence units in a complex sentence was to identify the elements of the matrix, to adopt the order in which other units were embedded in it according to Figure 4.1 and to continue with the order of embedding of further units in each other.

Examples of the treatment will make it clearer. The sentence

He knew perfectly well that his mother didn't allow him to eat the biscuits was broken down into :

S_1 = matrix = *He knew* something *perfectly well*
S_2 = embedding, replacing *something* in S_1 = *that his mother didn't allow* something = Sub. $(3)_1$ (that)
S_3 = embedding, replacing *something* in S_2 = *him to eat the biscuits* = Sub. $(3)_2$ (inf.)

The complete description was $S_1 + S_2$ [Sub. $(3)_1$ (that)] $+ S_3$ [Sub. $(3)_2$ (inf.)]. It can be seen that the index numbers allowed each embedding to be specified fully as to both the matrix unit in which it immediately rested and the phrase position within that unit that it occupied. Joint embedding such as *When he brushed his face and when he tied the knot out of his tail he ran to Teddy's* was specified by indexing both embeddings into the same matrix. The description read S_2 [Loc. $(5)_1$ (then)] $+ S_3$ [Loc. $(5)_1$ then)] $+ S_1$. It will be realised that these descriptions were of so called surface structure, and no assumptions were made about deep structure or the transformation rules required to treat the embedded units as equivalent to simple sentences. The analysis was based on decisions about the relative functions of sections of the complete sentence as it made sense to the listener.

At the two-unit level in the model and in the productions of all three groups, adults, north Leeds children, and south Leeds children, matrix units were combined with examples from all five of other units. There was a strong preference for placing the subordinate unit within or after the elements of the matrix unit, though it was frequently grammatically permissible to place it first. This preference extended to, but was rather less evident in, the more complex forms. While the percentage frequencies for both adults and children for placing a subordinate unit in first position were similar, they were lower than those for the model stories. This possibly reflected differences in style between spoken and written English. Optional locative and adverbial units were the most frequent type of subordinate unit to begin a sentence, but substitution and qualifying units were also found to occupy that position.

With complexity beyond the two-unit level the number of possible arrangements increased rapidly. The model stories, there being only four, contained a limited selection at each level, and in every case this was exceeded in all three groups of reproduced stories. For three-unit sentences all three groups produced about the same number of different arrangements, and all but one of the model patterns were reproduced by all groups. Several patterns were produced more than once. For four-unit sentences differences emerged. There were eight model sentences, all different, only one of which was reproduced by all groups and three of which were not reproduced at all. The adults produced 35 different patterns, 16 of which were shared with the children, but the latter together produced a further 37 different patterns. These figures were derived from all four stories from 24 children in each group. It was a clear case of variety increasing with number of instances, and the north Leeds children were able to produce more different patterns than the south Leeds in part at least, because they produced more four-unit sentences. The same effect was seen in sentences of five or more units. Here none of the model sentence patterns was reproduced, and of 34 different adult patterns only one was shared with the children. Together they produced a further 33 different patterns, only one being common to both, and the north Leeds children contributing the larger share. It was clearly evident that the model stories exercised no constraint on sentence construction at the level of selection and arrangement of different kinds of embedded sentence unit.

Structural variety was not only achieved by using different selections and arrangements of embedded units but by choosing different kinds of patterning within the major categories. But a curious feature emerged at this level. Although each story was told differently, there were few differences overall between the models, the adult stories and the children's versions. Thus in the case of conjunction, 80% of all instances for all groups were of the *conj. pred.* type. For other instances neither group of children nor the adults failed to produce the patterns given in the models, but neither did they produce additional varieties except for the isolated instance of *conj. 1 + 2*. A similar picture obtained for substituted units, though the children and adults together produced a slightly wider range than the model. Almost all the substitutions were in the object noun phrase position (NP3), a contrast with conjunction, which was more widely distributed. The only difference of note between the groups was that the proportion of direct and indirect speech or thought varied. The south Leeds children used a higher proportion of direct speech, both groups of children used more than the models, and the adults used least. They, on the other hand used more indirect forms, and in this respect the south Leeds children used the lowest proportion.

In the use of qualifying units the children again slightly exceeded the range given in the model and matched that of the adults. As with conjunction they referred to a range of matrix noun phrase positions, but there were interesting group differences. The model favoured qualification of NP1, NP3, and NP5 in that order, but both adults and children preferred the order NP3, NP1, NP5. Perhaps, again, this reflected a difference between spoken and written English. The south Leeds children were least inclined to qualify the first noun phrase and most ready to modify the third, while the adults spread their qualifying more evenly over all three positions. The use of additional location and adverbial units also revealed a slightly wider range for both children and adults than for the model stories, but again there was considerable similarity.

It appeared then that there was a fairly close correspondence between the performance of the model story writers and the storytellers in patterning within the sentence unit, though there was wide freedom to combine these units in various ways. This may well have been a consequence of the semantic structure of the stories and it was not possible to say how far the children were stimulated or constrained by the stories. It was evident, however, that there was no real difference between the relatively advantaged and disadvantaged children in ability to construct the various kinds of sentence unit, though there was a marginal difference in ability to express relations between them in complex sentences, and an even more marked vocabulary difference. The implications for education are that perhaps less attention need be paid to basic grammatical skill than has recently been advocated, and more should be paid to exploring situations in which children are encouraged to talk and to listen to thematic speech, and especially to fostering the acquisition of vocabulary.

Evidently the children were able to organise spoken language much more competently than young children of three to four years, who organise phrases into remarks that increasingly match sentence structures. The five to seven year old children were able not only to use full simple sentences but also to employ an increasing proportion and variety of complex forms. The combination of what might essentially be expressed in two or more simple sentences required such embedding procedures as were described in terms of conjunction, qualifying, substituting and adding. These were still being learned, both in the extent to which they were practised, and in the adoption of appropriate intersentence relation markers. Two aspects of the development of complex forms were evident—that their use required both the cognitive skills to relate events in terms of cause, consequence, condition and other logical relations, and the processing skills to hold the relevant amount of information or message content together in verbal form.

Some insight into this skill was anticipated in the use of the second task to investigate language abilities. Since the same basis for analysis of structure was used for both tasks, further comments will be reserved until the recall task has been described.

SENTENCE REPETITION

In order that their skill might be explored further, the children were required to repeat individual spoken sentences immediately after hearing them. It has generally been found that young children's imitations of adult model sentences tend to be structured more like their own everyday speech than like that of the adults. Ervin (1964) checked spontaneous imitations by children of two to three years against their free productions in the same dialogues with adults. She found that their structure was comparable with that of the non-imitated utterances. Here the judgement of imitation was based on the fact that the child's remark was an essentially unchanged, though deleted or 'incorrect' version of an immediately prior adult utterance in ordinary conversation. There was no assessment of intentional reproduction. Fraser, Bellugi and Brown (1963) had previously attempted to elicit imitations from children of a similar age and had found that although these reproductions were often like spontaneous speech the more controlled condition sometimes led to an increase in accuracy in reproduction, though not necessarily with comparable comprehension. Slobin (1965) pointed out that, while children spontaneously imitated adults' remarks in forms like the rest of their speech, nevertheless when adults expanded the children's incomplete utterances, thus drawing attention to the expansion, the children tended to imitate the expansions more carefully. Thus it would seem likely that in directed recall the child would pay more attention to accurate reproduction than he might in the course of conversation. Yet Menyuk (1963, 1969) found that children of four to eight years reproduced some model sentences in forms comparable with their normal speech, and not with the grammatical structure of the model, and that they even tended to 'correct' to their own version model sentences which were deliberately ungrammatical at levels judged to be within their competence. It seems that, provided sentences are long enough or difficult enough to test subjects beyond the 'echoic' level, recalled forms provide a basis for a description of linguistic abilities. The pilot study work with north Leeds children enabled the author to construct sentences which proved to be interesting tests. Length was kept constant while structure was varied. These sentences were not presented to the south Leeds children, and the following account is therefore based on results from the 50 children from the north of the city. Where comparison is made with adults these were 20 undergraduate students.

Both simple and complex model sentences were used at each testing. Each was constructed from 12 different monosyllabic words checked against Burroughs' (1957) word list of common words used by infant school children. Simple active sentences were designed to contain five phrases, a subject noun phrase (NP_1), a verb phrase (V_2), a direct object noun phrase (NP_3) and two optional additional noun phrases. By adjusting the number of words in each phrase, and by substituting an agent noun phrase for the direct object noun phrase, it was possible to design five-phrase negative (N), interrogative (Q), and passive (P) sentences, and sentences combining pairs of these forms, and even all three (NPQ). Complex sentences of two sentence units were designed by constructing a five-phrase simple matrix sentence and using an embedded sentence unit qualifying either NP_1 or NP_3 instead of one of the optional noun phrases. Three-unit sentences were similarly designed except that the second optional noun phrase was replaced by a further qualifying sentence unit embedded within the first embedding. To construct four- and five-unit sentences within the 12-word limit it was necessary to use sentence units that substituted for NP_3 in each matrix. Thus in terms of traditional grammar both relative and noun clauses were used. These were taken to be a fair means of testing for ability to reproduce complex forms, because they are commonly found in the speech of children of five to seven years (Watts, 1944). It would have been possible to have designed different combinations of matrix, qualifying and substitution units, varying the choice of relevant matrix noun phrase, but a fuller exploration would have required a different approach. As it was the variation introduced by qualifying either NP_1 or NP_3 in the matrix sentence allowed those of the latter design to be regarded as sequentially ordered sentence units while those of the former were seen as being nested constructions. Since the testing was only a part of a wider exploration of language abilities, including spoken, literary and analytic skills, a fuller use of recall tasks would have been burdensome for the children. As it was, the nested constructions were not given at the first testing. The results from this limited investigation suggest that a more comprehensive and intensive exploration might be of interest. Examples of the sentences used are given below:

Simple sentences

A	Those clowns will play their tricks on the stage for some time.
N	Our class will not sing these songs to the school this week.
P	A den was made by the boys in that tree last spring.
Q	Did your friend take his pet to their house the next day?
NP	Those sheep were not chased by that dog to the farm then.
NQ	Didn't a bird lay some eggs in that nest this year?
PQ	Can their coats be hung by the girls on those pegs now?
NPQ	Wasn't a hook fixed by the man to that door once?

Complex sentences

Sequential:

2-unit	The child found a shoe then that had come off her doll.
3-unit	We saw a man who caught the thief that stole his purse.
4-unit	She hoped he knew that boy had seen the train go past.
5-unit	We thought you heard me say she knew the door was locked.

Nested:

2-unit	The van that has turned by those shops dropped a box then.
3-unit	My friend who saw the dog that took her bag chased it.
4-unit	The lad who thought he heard me call ran to my house.
5-unit	The girl who heard us say we hoped you won came next.

Being administered as part of a series of language tests the recall task was given to the children in sub-sections of no more than six sentences at a time, these sections being separated by tasks of a quite different nature. Thus practice and inhibition effects were minimised. The order of presentation was that of the list above, for pilot work had indicated that the more complex sentences presented most difficulty, and that the difficulty was such that when randomised presentation was tried the early giving of complex forms did not result in any better performance for those items but did introduce an inhibition of response to those and to other items in the same set. It was therefore decided to present the items in the anticipated order of difficulty, and thus to maintain confidence and possibly maximise performance. This, of course, is the kind of procedure adopted in the Stanford–Binet type of intelligence test.

The simple sentences did not prove to be too difficult for many children to achieve perfect recall of at least some of them, and they were therefore not all included at the fourth testing. Since there appeared to be no discernible change across the age span the results for the second and third testings when the children were between six and seven years are reported here.

Several kinds of error occurred. Omissions tended to be of complete phrases, or of the latter part of a sentence when a child stalled, apparently searching for a particular word at an earlier point. Often, however, the grammatical structure of the sentence was maintained, although errors pointed, not to simple reproduction, but to a process of reconstruction. Thus although words might be incorrectly ordered, as in confusion in word list reproduction, this only happened where it was possible to exchange words of the same form class. Thus articles and other noun modifiers were shifted, as also were nouns when it was semantically feasible. Some of the lost phrases seemed to be consequent on the selection of an incorrect noun earlier in the sentence. Another type of error pointing to reconstruction was the substitution of a semantically appropriate word in place of a model word. The following examples illustrate this point, the bracketed words being the child's version.

Did the train run (set off) from the station. . . .
Our class will not sing these songs to the school (people, children). . . .

Did your friend take his pet (cat, dog). . . .
Hasn't the nurse parked her car by (near) your gate. . . .
That tin was seen (found). . . .

In that errors of number maintained correct number agreement between modifier and noun and between subject and verb, it was again seen that reproduction was a process of construction, and it was held therefore than even at the simple level the children's competence was being tested. There was, however, no evidence that negative and interrogative patterns led to more difficulty in recall than did simple active sentences. There was no difference in the amount recalled, and the distribution of errors according to phrase type showed remarkable similarities. In all cases the subject noun and verb phrases were best recalled, with the compulsory direct object noun phrase next and the optional noun phrases, taking the final positions, containing most errors. As was to be expected the final phrase was rather better recalled than the penultimate. Within phrases the prepositions and the nouns were more accurately recalled than were the modifiers. One cannot help but see in this a reflection of earlier 'telegraphic' speech.

Recall of passive sentences made it even more clear that some language competence was being tested. Comparison of passive and active forms showed that the passives contained more errors in the agent phrase which replaced the direct object noun phrase in the active form, had more omissions and displacements of phrases and were even converted to active forms. Taking the second and third testings, the negative was only converted to an affirmative form 11 times in 400 sentences, the auxiliary inversion to mark an interrogative was omitted only once, but the passive agent phrase was omitted 137 times and the passive was converted to an active form 17 times. Analysis of all active and passive forms showed differences between them in the distribution of omissions in the predicate phrases to be statistically significant. The passive taxed the children in quite a different way from the active, negative and interrogative forms. Several reasons might be suggested. A tendency to treat the grammatical subject as the logical subject might have led to failure to incorporate the actual logical subject into the sentence. There was actually no reversible passive used, and a grasp of semantic relations possibly led to conversion to an active form. The surface passive agent marker *by* might be

K

confused with the preposition *by* meaning *beside* and a tendency to confuse agentive and locative phrases might ensue. Given these possibilities it seems that whereas accurate recall does not necessarily tell us anything about a child's competence, errors indicate a tendency to reconstruct according to cues derived from the surface structure. These do not necessarily lead to a reliable grasp of underlying grammatical relations; but reconstruction indicates an awareness of semantic relations, possible functions of phrases in sentences and a limited set of earlier learned rules realising the relations between semantic content and the way it is conventionally expressed. Some further exploration of response to passive forms will be discussed later, but the outcome of the tests of recall of simple sentences was the finding that even at the youngest age tested, between five and six years, the children showed that except for the passive they were well able to reproduce accurately, and that errors tended to reveal a process of reconstruction that nevertheless achieved a grammatical and semantically acceptable sentence.

Complex sentences taxed their abilities more heavily, but although results showed differences between subjects and between sentences there was no reliable change with age. The complex sentences were also recalled by adults, however, and there were considerable differences between them and the children. A general feature of the reproduced sentences was that few words were omitted in isolation. When omissions occurred they tended to be of complete phrases or sentence units (clauses). Moreover, the finished product tended to be altered where necessary so that even when omission occurred it was both semantically and syntactically acceptable. In other words the children were not only trying to reproduce the sentences, they were producing sentences in English.

Since the test was primarily designed to test competence in structuring sentences of differing numbers of constitutent sentence units, the responses were first scored according to the number of these represented at least to the extent of a verb and relevant noun phrase, irrespective of level of accuracy in reproduction. Since the sentences contained different numbers of units, the best comparative measure was the percentage of sentence units omitted in each case. The figures for the three testings from age 6 years 3 months to 7 years 3 months are given in Table 4.3. At the first testing at 5 years 9 months no nested constructions were tested,

TABLE 4.3

Sentence unit omissions in complex sentence recall

Sentence	Percentage units omitted			
	6 years 3 months	6 years 9 months	7 years 3 months	Average
Sequential				
2-unit	3	4	4	4
3-unit	40	15	21	25
4-unit	20	18	26	21
5-unit	41	38	33	37
Nested				
2-unit	9	4	13	9
3-unit	29	21	22	24
4-unit	—	29	11	20
5-unit	—	34	34	34

though the findings for the sequential were similar to those for the later testings. The two-unit sentences presented little difficulty, but there was a marked increase in the percentage of omissions for sentences of greater complexity. Overall differences between sentences were statistically significant, though there was little change from the three- to four-unit level. This possibly reflected the change from qualifying to substitution units, but further investigation would be required to test the responses to different kinds of sentence unit fully. There was, however, no significant difference between the sequential and nested forms, though in no case was a double subject qualifying nesting used. Such a task might have been more difficult.

Comparison of children's and adults' scores of correct words, number of words and number of sentence units showed that adults achieved almost perfect recall, though some slight loss occurred in the more complex sentences; whereas for the children there was a marked deterioration from the two- and three-unit level. These findings were very much in accord with those for the storytelling task, where the children were beginning to show more competence at the three-unit level but did not match adult performance. As was the case with simple sentences, the errors revealed that the children were not simply attempting passive recall but were actively constructing their replies. Changes of number, person or tense in one word were nearly always accompanied by necessary agreement changes in others; the following are examples, the model being bracketed, *the shoes* (a shoe), *this desk* (these desks), *the cloud brings* (the clouds bring), *you think* (she thinks), *needs* (will need), *went* (had gone) and *fell* (had dropped). Adverbial phrases and adverbs not having a fixed position in English sentence order were produced in different but appropriate positions. When memory was taxed so that clauses were restructured, the response was sometimes a fully grammatical but different complex sentence, and sometimes a partial breakdown into separate sentence units, as in the following examples: *The girl found a shoe off her doll then. The child found a shoe last time and it came off her doll.* (The child found a shoe then that had come off her doll.) *The van that turned by the shops then. Some boxes fell; The van that had turned by those shops then. There was a box dropped; The van dropped a box near those shops then.* (The van that has turned by those shops dropped a box then). *My friend who saw the dog. She took it and chased;*

My friend saw the dog that took her bag and chased it. (My friend who saw the dog that took her bag chased it).

Sometimes, because units were forgotten or altered, children changed the remainder of the sentence to make it grammatical, as in *He hoped he would see the boy on the train that passed.* (She hoped he knew the boy had seen the train go past.) *The lad who thought I called ran to my house.* (The lad who thought he heard me call ran to my house). *We thought you said the door was locked. We thought you heard the door close.* (We thought you heard me say she knew the door was locked). Perhaps the most interesting finding was that not only were embedded units omitted where the remaining construction was acceptable, but a telescoping of units with the omission of the predicate of one and the subject phrase of the next also occurred. An example was given above in *We thought you said the door was locked.* The relevant omission is shown bracketed in the model thus, *We thought you (heard me) say she knew the door was locked.* Such restructuring suggested not only a tapping of grammatical competence, but also a dependence on semantic knowledge, for responses were neither anomalous nor irrelevant to the model sentence. Indeed in omissions crossing unit boundaries they required recognition of possible semantic relations other than those expressed in the form of the given sentence. It was as though the children reconstructed not from a grammatical analysis but from acceptable arrays of semantic relations. Further evidence of change that reflected semantic reorganisation was seen in the word and phrase errors. Examples were, *for some days, every time, sometimes,* (for some time), *shut,* (locked), *who, which,* (that), *second, last,* (next), *robber,* (thief), *leg,* (paw), *near,* (by) and *fallen,* (dropped). Sometimes the error was not so much a synonym as an appropriate alternative in the context, as in *The cat will find more fish* (milk) *in her dish. . . . The child found a shoe then that belonged to* (had come off) *her doll, Those clowns will play their tricks at the circus* (on the stage) *for some time, The lad . . . ran* (came) *to the door* (to my house) and *She hoped . . . the boy had seen the train hurry* (go) *past.* There was strong evidence in these examples and in others like them that sentence recall was based primarily on semantic competence, with grammatical competence taking a subsidiary role.

These explorations into the speech skill of young schoolchildren gave some insight into the way children's language competence develops beyond the early remark stage. Whereas the remarks of two and three year olds were perhaps better described in terms of strings of phrases, those of five to seven year olds were best talked of in terms of sentences. Yet the integration of sentence units was not fully grammatical, and recall showed weakness at those points whose absence in earlier speech had led to its being described as telegraphic. Both in story reproduction and in sentence recall the children seemed to be primarily concerned with the organisation of simple sentence units into a meaningful array. Two strategies predominated. When a matrix remark was extended by developing an embedded unit within it, the arrangement was often sequential, since the embedding came at the end of the matrix predicate phrase. When two remarks were related by some logical connective, again a sequential structuring occurred. Yet these strategies provided an ample basis for the generation of a wide variety of remark patterns, most of which were acceptable in English. One was reminded of the small child dealing similarly with phrase patterns, having at hand not a fully grammatical sentence pattern but a sensible sequencing of phrases partially conforming in their organisation to the rules of the parent tongue. The principal differences between the 'phrase' and 'sentence unit' levels of organisation of remarks lay in message content and rules of marking. The simple sentence unit was a maximally explicit expression of the functions of the related phrases within a simple remark, and the complex sentence was the correspondingly explicit expression of the relations judged to obtain between simple units. The simple remark required rules making phrase relations clear, while the complex remark called for rules making the phrase relations across units unambiguous. (It should be noted in passing that while explicit expression reveals the complexity of thought behind the remark, absence of organisation in expression cannot be taken necessarily to imply paucity of thought. The discussion of language 'codes' made this clear; and much that is thought is only implied, even in mature and profound expression, for powers of comprehension supply the absent information.) While the young children mentioned earlier in this book were occupied in learning to mark the phrases of simple remarks, rarely attempting to go beyond this, the school-children had almost completely learned these rules and were in the throes of finding their way to forming more complex remarks acceptably. In neither case could one confidently ascribe a knowledge of grammatical deep structure to the child, although the concept of a sentence was invaluable for descriptive purposes. For the child one could only safely assume an organising ability based on what was perceived by him to be a sensible combination of meaningful phrase patterns, conforming, as far as he had learned the rules, to the accepted ordering and marking of adult speech. Thus even in children at six or seven years of age it is possibly an error to consider any special linguistic competence in the Chomskyan sense. But before a closer exploration of structuring ability is reported, a different aspect of language must be examined, for schoolchildren do not learn about language from speech alone but also from the experience of learning to read and write.

5 Early Stages in Literacy

BACKGROUND TO READING

Whatever their previous experience, school life introduces all children to an environment in which they are expected to learn to read and write. It should not be forgotten, however, that a continued experience outside school is the background against which this expectation operates. School, moreover, emphasises a subset of the functions of written language—the reading and writing of accounts of events, and the use of the number system. While some concession is made to other experience, the net effect for children may well be to achieve a feeling of separateness from the world outside school, where they are accustomed to seeing written signs on buildings, buses, bottles and boxes, signs that are names of people or places or contents, rather than any other form of language. They see advertisements where the writing does *not* say what the picture is; they observe parents' handling of bills, orders and personal letters; and they see bold headlines contrasted with small print in newspapers and on television and cinema screens. They encounter numerals, and both capital and lower case lettering. They find most of this experience belongs to the world of adults and older children; much of it provokes curiosity but not necessarily any sense of importance for themselves. It is fun sometimes for a child to be able to show that he can identify the correct bus as well as anyone else, but rarely is it really necessary for him to recognise a written symbol. It is not even necessary to be able to recognise pictures, though this is much more a part of his world, and the idea of drawing to represent something is familiar to all except the most deprived pre-school children in Britain. This is where comics have such an appeal. But the best means children have of communicating is to use their own bodies and voices and to 'read' the gestures, movements and voices of others. This they are not aware of doing. Speech is part of living, here momentarily and gone with the actions that accompanied it. Recalled—yes, but deliberately stored—no. Recounted—yes, but reflected upon—no. Children are not aware that they use a language.

But in our culture, while still naïve about speech, they are expected to enter the world of literacy. As parents and teachers, we can see this attempted both by the child who wants to get there and by the one who is coaxed or dragged or shoved into it. There is, of course, no guarantee that the wanting will result in achieving nor that lack of desire will prevent it, but the child who actually protests, whether silently or noisily, is not likely to get very far. What makes children want to read, what makes them willing to be taught, and what makes them resist? These are important questions, and both motivation and experience are relevant factors to be explored in assessing what effect the written language has on children's language competence. Further investigation into how children learn to read and write and what they think of reading and writing is also required. This chapter describes how such exploration was made with the children of the north and south Leeds schools whose speech was described in Chapter 4.

Reading ability was assessed with the Schonell graded vocabulary test, and the rank-ordered scores were compared with those obtained from assessment of progress in the school's reading schemes. Correlations of the order of 0·9 were obtained, so the Schonell test was taken to be a reasonable measure for comparison across all three schools. Norms were of less interest than rank ordering which was used to compare reading skill with other language abilities; but at 7 years 3 months the mean reading age for north Leeds was 7 years 2 months while that for south Leeds was 6 years 10 months.

Experience of reading was explored by questioning the children while they were being given small rests between the various language sub-tests used in the investigation. The questions were answered readily, often with supplementary information; but while the responses seemed valid, how far they could be taken to represent experience reliably, as distinct from being impressions on a particular occasion, was doubtful. In the case of north Leeds, where the same children were questioned on three occasions, the responses showed some changes. Not always did the same children report the same experience and sometimes they volunteered reasons. For example, they said parents didn't read to them any longer, or Mummy was busy with the new baby, or the child himself could read better now. Such responses tended to confirm earlier reports and at the same time to explain change. On average, however, the reports tended to give the same picture of the group on the three separate occasions. Because the responses seemed to be both valid and moderately reliable they were judged worth reporting.

One of the questions was the direct 'Do you like learning to read?', which yielded an affirmative in the vast majority of cases, though there were obvious degrees of enjoyment. One or two, however, frankly said they did not like it and one could feel much sympathy for them. They were by then approaching seven and were well aware that they had made little if any progress; and in one case in particular the boy concerned knew what was difficult for him, and was most frustrated that he could not achieve a better synthesis of elements he could well identify separately. None questioned the desirability of learning to read. All their responses reflected an acceptance of the value of such a skill, although not all, especially at the younger ages, seemed to have any confident knowledge of why they thought it desirable. The question 'Why do you think reading is important?' yielded a fair proportion of 'don't knows' while the majority of children reported that either teacher or parents said so. One or two, however, looked ahead, beginning to realise the fun of gaining their own access to stories and poems and to information related to hobbies. One child was even moved to comment that he would feel silly if he were a father and couldn't read to his son! A related question, asking the children what they would like to read if they could manage it, was more revealing. While a proportion of children from both north and south Leeds had fixed their ambition on the next school reader in their series, and a further proportion mentioned some simple story book at an equivalent level, a significantly greater number of north Leeds children seemed aware of the possibilities offered by poetry, history and children's books at a more advanced level. This seemed to be not so much a consequence of any differences between schools as of differences between home backgrounds. Both groups of children spoke of older brothers and sisters, but it was the siblings of the north Leeds children who had the more advanced books.

Yet, in both groups of children, over 90% reported that they themselves had comics and books at home, though it seemed that those of the south Leeds children were fewer, simpler, and often duplicates of school readers. Nevertheless reading was not entirely alien in the homes of these children. The same high percentage of parents of both sexes, 70% or more, were reported as seeming to enjoy reading and the children were fairly explicit about what they read. Newspapers, magazines and library books figured prominently in the replies of both groups, while the south Leeds children also reported parents as reading comics and crime stories. The difference in background was not a difference between reading and not-reading, or between valuing it and under-valuing it, but rather it seemed that differences must lie in the quantity and quality of what was read, differences that probably reflected the education and lifestyles of parents.

As to the actual practice of reading at home, only 10% of children felt that they were not read to by adults; some others reported that parents used to read to them; yet others were read to sometimes; while about 35% reported listening to a story nearly every night. Bedtime story reading was the most common experience, and there seemed no difference between north and south Leeds children except that in north Leeds fathers were more involved. This possibly reflected the actual availability of fathers rather than any difference in interest. Both groups of children reported some attempts to read aloud to parents, although about 30% of children in each group did not think they ever tried. In this activity fathers were much less involved. When asked about reading to themselves about 15% of children reported never trying, again a roughly equal proportion from each area. This was the only practice in which there was a definite trend with age, the proportion not reading by themselves dropping as skill was gained.

The general relationships between reading ability and children's reports of home experience were summarised after finding the numbers of children with reading ability above and below their age norms who reported frequent or occasional or no experience of being read to, of reading aloud to another, and of reading alone. There was no difference between the figures in the case of being read to, but in reading to another and reading alone the better readers reported significantly more frequent experience. This was most marked for reading alone. Obviously a spiral of success was set up in which those children who made progress found practice increasingly rewarding; but there was no guarantee that parents' reading to children influenced reading ability, though the practice was obviously enjoyable in itself and might have had some other value in relation to language skills.

It was interesting that the overall patterns of experience and their relation to ability seemed similar for the north and south Leeds children, but there were ability differences between them, the mean reading ages for the north Leeds children being from one to three months higher. This was less than might have been expected from a recent national study (Davie *et al.*, 1972) and it was not a statistically significant difference. One suspected however that the differences in background which were only hinted at in this study, namely in number and kind of reading materials available and valued, might later lead to greater advantage accruing to more of the north Leeds children. Differences in schools might help to compensate, however, and it must not go unremarked that the local authority was already assisting the south Leeds schools to the extent of a better staff–pupil ratio, and a boost in the supply of attractive books. The children had more opportunity of practising reading with individual tuition than had their contemporaries in the north of the city.

This difference apart, the approach to reading in the schools was very similar. In their first term at school, children became familiar with their new environment, in particular with their classrooms where items of furniture, equipment and personal lockers were clearly labelled. Pictures and posters and items of the children's work adorned the walls and these often had short accompanying legends. The children were being introduced to the notions that written forms could be directly associated with objects, that they could function as labels or naming devices, and that groups of them could hold fuller information about events or pictorial representations that had something to do with them personally. When the children began to use books they worked their way individually through the school's reading schemes. In all three cases the children first met encouragement to 'Look and say', but a more analytic and phonic approach was soon dovetailed into this as they responded to it both in individual and group learning. Writing was encouraged early so that children learned to read and write at the same time. None of the three schools used the initial teaching alphabet, and none adopted a rigid adherence to any particular approach to reading.

In many ways there was some similarity between school and

home experience. The children who were finding their attempts rewarding were most keen to find opportunities for practice, while the others needed encouragement and further requirement to try. A few obviously felt saddened and discouraged, but even they were helped by the consciousness of moving on, however painstakingly, from line to line, page to page, and book to book. But one obvious feature of school experience which would be lacking in most homes and might even cause anxiety to teachers in some cases, was the eager competitiveness of the children. Not only were they keen to improve their own performance, many were also trying to race their friends through the scheme, and they expressed their likes and dislikes to each other. Learning to read in school was a public and shared activity.

During the time the children were observed some learned very rapidly. This could best be seen in the longitudinal study of the north Leeds children, some of whom were reading at a level at least two years in advance of their age norm. Of these, one or two were doing so on entering school; one little boy described very fully how he learned to read when he was three years old and how he had been growing more competent ever since. Other children could read nothing, except perhaps their own names, when first tested; and of these, while some learned rapidly, others made scarcely any progress. A notable qualitative difference was observed between those children who plodded faithfully through their readers but found difficulty in recognising words outside the scheme, and those who more readily managed to read more widely, albeit at a simple level.

Invariably, accounts of children's reading report that amongst the poor readers there are more boys than girls. This was also the case in both the north and south Leeds samples where much of the difference between scores for boys and girls was due to a bunching of boys at the lower end of the scale. They did not appear to suffer any particular handicap except a low level of interest which, as they became more aware of their relative lack of progress, was in some cases developing into a positive dislike of reading.

LINGUISTIC UNITS AND LEARNING TO READ

While children are learning to read they find that written symbols are referred to as letters, words and sentences. They have to learn to use these terms, part of the technical vocabulary of written language, in order to understand their reference, to attend to the appropriate symbols, and to both ask and respond to questions about them. Fairly recent studies by Reid (1966) and Downing (1970) showed that children of five to six years may have a very partial and insecure comprehension of such terms, and Downing discussed this in terms of their difficulty in acquiring abstract concepts. Investigation with the north Leeds children gave an opportunity to trace the development of comprehension and to compare it with general vocabulary skill (Francis, 1973).

One of the questions posed to the children was, 'Can you tell me a letter—any letter you know?' After they had answered they were asked, 'What do we use letters for?' The procedure was then repeated using the concepts *word* and *sentence*. After the questions about sentences they were asked how they knew when they came to the end of a sentence, both when reading and when listening to someone talking. At the first testing (at 5 years 9 months), correct examples of names of letters were given more frequently (31) than correct examples of words (22) or sentences (13), and from the second to fourth testings letters were supplied very well. Early confusions with numbers, names and words, or inability to respond, almost vanished at the last testing. At the second and third testings words were supplied as well as letters had been at the first, but not until the fourth testing (at 7 years 3 months) were virtually all the children able to give examples. Confusions in the early testings were predominantly with numbers or names, and were therefore partially within the area of the concept. Sentences were not reasonably well supplied until the fourth testing. There was a high proportion of nil responses when the children were younger, but very little confusion with any other concept.

When the questions were posed there had been no presentation of written material in the previous testing, nor any questions about reading experience. Only immediate recall had been attempted. There were of course, record forms being filled in by the author, but these did not seem to influence the children's responses as much as did their school experience. When asked about the use of letters, words and sentences, almost no replies indicated an awareness of the use of words or sentences in spoken language; the outstanding feature was almost universal reference to spelling, reading and writing. Answers to the question about use of letters ranged from undiscriminating 'Writing' and 'Helping us to read', to 'Writing words' 'Making words' and 'Spelling'. Discriminating answers to the question about words were 'Names' and 'Making sentences'; while for use of sentences 'For making stories', 'Poems', 'Writing letters (postal)', and 'Writing news' were proposed. There was, with grasp of the concept *sentence*, an increasing awareness of the relationships between letters, words and sentences. The additional question about recognition of the end of a sentence yielded prompt replies like 'full stop' or 'end of line' in the case of reading, but the question was puzzling in relation to spoken language. A few children ventured uncertain replies like 'Pause' or 'You stop'.

A further test of grasp of the concepts was to present the children with a card on which were printed two examples of each, so that every instance, whether letter, word or sentence, lay within its own outlined portion of the card, and the six were randomly arranged. The children were then asked to point to a letter 'all by itself inside a space'. They were then asked to do the same for a word and a sentence. If children pointed to a word or sentence when a letter was required, or to a sentence when a word was wanted, they were asked if they meant all of the writing in the space, and if they revised their answer the revision was accepted. Actually this happened very rarely. The results of the recognition test showed much confusion between concepts at the first testing, but by the second testing letters were most accurately recognised, and sentences were least accurately defined. By the fourth testing all items were recognised with almost complete accuracy. The recognition test therefore tended to support the finding from the supply test, that the concepts *letter, word* and *sentence* were acquired in that order, and that their acquisition was closely related to learning to read.

It was possible to sum the scores of individual children for correct responses to all the tests, then to rank order them, and so to correlate skill with the technical vocabulary of reading with general vocabulary skill, as measured by the Stanford–Binet scale at the final testing, and with reading skill at the same age. The highest correlation was between reading skill and technical vocabulary, and when general vocabulary skill was statistically controlled by using a partial correlation technique there still remained a considerable correlation, indicating that factors independent of a general ability to master concepts were involved in learning the technical vocabulary, and that these were closely related to learning to read. In other words, the children did not have to wait for the development of some general ability to deal with abstract concepts in order to use the technical vocabulary of reading and therefore respond to instruction. They learned the vocabulary in the course of learning to read. What is more they also acquired some novel ideas about spoken language. Most note-worthy was the thought that there were pauses between words in spoken forms, a factually incorrect notion, but one of some psycho-logical significance in relation to language competence. The whole process of learning to read had, in fact, made the children aware of spoken language in a new way. They had of necessity, in res-ponse to school instruction, to reflect on it and analyse it. Children who were unable to do this had difficulty in reading. Vygotsky (1962) commented on this kind of difficulty in some depth. This is not to say that such an analytic approach is necessary for learn-ing to read—some younger children begin to learn without it—but any instruction that utilises a technical vocabulary induces and depends on such an approach.

While the concepts *word* and *sentence* may be applied to analy-sis of both spoken and written language, there are further units which are of linguistic importance but which do not enter into the technical vocabulary of reading. These are the suffixes used for such purposes as marking plural forms and various tenses of verbs. Because it was thought that children's ability to identify these in spoken and written forms might throw some further light on the relationship between their mastery of the skills of listening and reading, discrimination tests were given to the north Leeds children. Three suffixes were used, the plural *s*, the past tense *ed*, and the participle *ing*. In each case three words were presented to the children, two carrying the suffix and one without, and the or-der of presentation was varied. Thus, for example, *cats, mops, girl;* and *ran, walked, jumped;* and *sticking, glue, pasting,* were some of the sets of three used in the tests. The children were first asked to listen carefully to each set of words and to choose two that sounded the same in some way. After their choice they were asked to explain it, and if the basis was inappropriate they were asked to listen again and find another way in which two of the words sounded alike, emphasis being laid on *sound*. If no appropriate reply was then given a nil score was recorded. After the auditory task the same task was presented visually, the words being printed on cards in sets of three, and the children being asked to choose two that looked the same in some way and to explain their choice. The visual task was given after the auditory to prevent facilitation of the latter by the former when the children were able to recognise the words. Careful analysis of the distributions of chosen pairs according to their position as presented in the three words revealed no bias towards the selection of any particular pair according to position.

The auditory and visual modes yielded rather different results, auditory discrimination being consistently more difficult. This seemed in part due to the contrast between comparison of three memorised items and of three open to visual inspection. Sometimes in the auditory task children identified the suffix but attached it to the wrong word. If, for example, *sticking* and *glueing* was offered instead of *sticking* and *pasting* and the reason given was that they had *ing* in common, then the response was regarded as correct. The visual task was scored correct only when the children matched the complete suffix; lengthy scanning culminating in identification of separate letters was not thought to indicate adequate discrimination. In both visual and auditory modes the suffix *s* was identified earlier and better than either *ing* or *ed*. Recognition of the visual *s* improved from 25 to 49 instances out of a possible 50 over the four testings, while the auditory mode yielded a range of 5 to 35. The corresponding figures for *ing* were 15 to 40 and 5 to 30, while for *ed* they were 4 to 41 and 1 to 26.

Difficulty in the auditory task did not only lie with memory, however, for there was a marked tendency to attend to meaning rather than form, and this happened however distant or close the semantic content of the words chosen. The children attempted to construct relations where none was readily apparent. At first the hunt for meaning was not possible with the visual display, for the children could not read all the words, but even at the later testings when reading was more advanced they still attended to form rather than meaning, thus noting the similar suffixes. A curious feature of the later auditory testing was that sometimes identification seemed to proceed via a visual coding, for in the case of *logs* and *beds,* for example, the children reported a common letter *s*, not a voiced plural marker sounding like a letter *z*. Considering how well the children used the suffixes in their speech, having done so probably to some extent since they were two or three years old, it was interesting to find that they did not identify them well in the auditory discrimination task until they were seven years old. Yet the finding was entirely consistent with that of Bruce (1964), who used a different task to show that children were not able to analyse heard words into component consonant and vowel patterns until they had reached a mental age of seven years. Thus not only does acquaintance with the technical vocabulary of teaching reading lead children to adopt an analytic attitude to spoken language, but the task of deciphering written words comes more readily than that of analysis of heard words, and indeed seems further to promote a reflective and analytic approach to speech.

SENTENCE STRUCTURE AND READING

Although children encounter individual words in signs and notices from an early age, and some kinds of instruction in reading emphasise alphabetic or word recognition methods, when they start using a complete reading scheme they are committed to attempting to read sentences. Fries (1962) pointed out that since 1870 some approaches to reading have emphasised a sentence method. Underlying these is a notion that the sentence is the unit of expression of thought, and sentence reading is therefore more interesting and comprehensible to children; so whether reading begins or ends with sentences it may be helpful to know how they are understood by novice readers.

Lefevre (1962) and Stern and Gould (1966) thought that children drew on their knowledge of language structure in speech to help them interpret written sentences, and they therefore advocated teaching methods that exploited the intonation and stress patterns and the grammatical structures of simple sentences, but they did so without exploring three very important questions. First, they did not find out how soon children are able to span sufficient print with enough accuracy to be able to make use of grammatical structure. Second, they did not know whether children in fact interpreted sentences via some sort of knowledge of grammar. And third, they did not know how far children were aware, or might be made aware, of the syntax of speech. The author felt that these questions were worth exploring, and therefore introduced further tests to the north Leeds children (Francis, 1972a). These were a sentence-matching and a sentence-splitting task. The former was designed to test ability to read and comprehend simple sentences, and the latter was intended to explore awareness of structure in both spoken and written forms.

The first test was based on the fact that the syntax, but not the basic reference, of a simple active sentence may be altered by changing to interrogative, negative and passive forms. But two sentences of identical grammatical structure might bear very different reference. Thus the test sentence *Who made the hat?* might be matched with the active form *Ann made the hat* if the similarity of reference is appreciated, while it might be matched with *Who made the dress?* if reference is ignored and similarity of syntax is observed. For each testing four sets of three sentences were constructed, using two kinds of question, a negative and a passive form as the test sentence. In each case the children were presented with the test sentence printed on a card and with two other sentences printed on a separate card. These two were the active declarative form of the test item (choice 1) and another sentence of the same grammatical form as the test item but with different meaning (choice 2). The children were instructed to place the test sentence by each of the others in turn and then to say which one was most like it and why. They were then asked to read aloud what they could of all three sentences.

The children enjoyed the task but were not always able to give reasons for their choices at the first testing, yet only one or two choices were unsubstantiated thereafter. In the case of the passive form, children overwhelmingly matched passive with passive and there was no sign of change with testing. Only a very few children recognised the identity of meaning of the passive and active forms. In the case of the negative the early matching was predominantly syntactical, but thereafter there was a roughly even choice between the declarative and negative versions. Some of the children who explained that the reference of the negative and declarative was the same were yet unwilling to match them because effectively negation changed meaning. In the case of the interrogatives there was a definite trend with each testing towards more matching on a basis of identity of reference. The overall picture, then, was of some shift from choice 2 to choice 1 as the children became older, but the shift was more marked for questions than for negatives and passives.

The way the children read and matched the sentences gave some indication of the reasons for this pattern. At first a left-to-right approach had been learned, but the children adopted a careful step-by-step strategy, pointing with their fingers to letters and words in turn. They matched without recognising many words and often without comprehension. But they saw similarity of early words and therefore matched the *Who* and *is* of question forms and the logical object of the passive (which was the same in both the test and the matched items). In the case of negatives all three items began with the same three words, as in *The boy is not standing; The boy is standing* and *The boy is not walking.* The children had therefore to read well into the sentences to find the divergent points and this seemed at least partly to explain their more equal choices. It was only when comfortable sentence reading was achieved that the matching shifted to a semantic rather than a syntactic basis. This was shown by finding the average word recognition scores for the children for the different patterns of choice made. Table 5.1 summarises the findings. Ability to read well enough to compare whole sentences depended on reading the content words well enough to realise semantic relation. Thus reasons for making choice 2 tended to be based on recognition of early similarity of sentence forms, whereas reasons for choice 1 lay in an appreciation of semantic content. Very few answers conveyed a recognition of grammatical form, but when they did the question and answer relation was seen, the negative change of meaning was appreciated and the passive/active identity was explained. No-one said, for example, 'They are both questions'. The matching of similar grammatical forms was based on perceptual similarity.

It was concluded that children depended on ability to span enough words to make sense of the sentence before they could appreciate anything of its structure, and that for many children this was only achieved with confidence by the age of seven. Moreover, when they were able to comprehend the sentences, it was not grammatical structure but semantic content which provided the basis of their somewhat tentative reading.

It is not easy to find ways of testing children's awareness of structure in speech or writing. Effectively one wishes to know whether there is any feeling for phrase structure—any recognition, for example, of the distinction between subject and predicate phrases. Yet children of five to seven years lack the vocabulary that might be used in direct questioning, and indeed the acquisition of the appropriate terminology presents problems even to adolescents and adults, as both teachers and grammarians know

TABLE 5.1

Word recognition and choice in sentence-matching task

| Choices | Average word recognition score (max. 21) at ages: | | |
Ratio Meaning based (1) : Pattern based (2)	6 years 3 months	6 years 9 months	7 years 3 months
4 : 0	12·3	20·0	20·8
3 : 1	18·3	18·0	20·5
2 : 2	8·8	16·7	19·7
1 : 3	9·1	11·3	16·3
0 : 4	5·0	11·2	16·9

well! Indirect methods of exploration might well reveal a phrase structuring of sentences, as the sentence recall tasks tended to do, but they tell us nothing of what children are aware. The problem was tackled by the author in a direct and somewhat naïve manner, but pilot study work had indicated that the task was one which the children could perform and that it also yielded interesting results. Moreover it could be used for both spoken and written sentences.

The children were asked to listen carefully to a sentence. After hearing it they were asked to repeat it, but to stop before the end, when they found it easiest to stop. They were told that any stopping place would do, there was no right or wrong answer but we wanted to find out what felt most comfortable to them. Training examples were given, demonstrating the freedom to stop at any point, and when necessary test sentences were repeated to the children. Nine sentences of different phrase structuring, and ranging from three to seven words in length, were used. Sometimes some children found it impossible to subdivide particular sentences, but on the whole they responded confidently. The written sentences were printed on separate cards and given to the children one at a time at the fourth testing when they were seven years old. For each, the child was asked to point to the writing that he read or looked at first. A training card was used to help convey the instructions, and children were shown how to cover the parts of the sentence they did not attend to first by covering them with a blank card. This helped to make their decisions firmer and clearer to observe. After responding the children were asked to try to read the whole sentence, and it was found that children who claimed to span several words or whole sentences could in fact read them pretty well.

When children tended to stop consistently after a particular word position, after the first word for example, they were asked if they knew they had done so. In the spoken form of the task only one child showed a first position preference, and two stopped after the penultimate word. Not one of these three was aware of having done so; but in the written form 12 children explained that they always attended to the first word alone, while one child claimed always to span two. At the fourth testing all of the 50 children attempted to split all the spoken sentences; but, because three children could not manage all of them and because those with fixed span strategies were excluded, the sample size for the written form was 35 for eight of the sentences and 34 for the ninth. Given that the children might equally well have stopped at any word position, expected frequencies for each were calculated on the basis of the number of words in the sentence and number of children making an attempt. The observed and expected frequencies could then be compared, and for both the oral and written tasks statistically significant differences were found (Francis, 1972a). The most obvious difference between the tasks lay in the difficulty of avoiding complete spanning of very short sentences in reading, compared with the relative ease of considering a stopping in the spoken form. Apart from this difference the findings were very similar, though there seemed to be little interaction between the modes. For each sentence only 10 to 15 children made the same choice in both modes, a number which held no significance in view of the shortness of most of the sentences. The most favoured dividing points were after the second and third words, but the actual choice was related to sentence structure. Fewer separations than expected were made after modifiers, auxiliaries and adverbs, while more than expected were made after pronouns, nouns, verbs and the negative *not*. A strong preference for the end of the subject noun phrase—whatever its length—was shown, but this was exceeded by a tendency to go on into the predicate, halting either after the emphatic *did not* or after the main verb.

It was thought possible that the group analysis might be a summation of important strategies, some children consistently splitting sentences after the subject noun phrase and others after the verb. But for the spoken sentences only nine children showed enough consistency to make at least three similar choices, and of these five preferred the subject noun phrase and four the main verb. In the case of written sentences, only four children showed such consistency, two after the subject phrase and two after the verb. Only two children were at all consistent in both modes, one after the subject phrase and one after the verb. Thus there was no evidence of really consistent grammatical splitting at either point. On the other hand the sum picture did cover a range of responses to structural and functional cues, some of which were position in relation to sentence length, noun phrase identification, noun–verb relation, emphasis and negation. There was no indication of a clear tendency to honour the primary noun phrase/verb phrase distinction which is basic to much syntactic analysis.

What then can be said in answer to the three questions these matching and intuitive splitting tasks were designed to probe? First, that even when acquainted with a sentence reading approach the children did not seem able to span enough of the sentence to make any consideration of its structural features useful until they were about seven years old. Whatever young children do when presented with different sentence patterns for instructional purposes they do not attend to the whole sentence frames. Secondly, interpretation of sentences tended to rest predominantly on content words, for when these were read the semantic structure of the sentence was grasped, or at least guessed. Even in early reading children seem to be doing what adults tend to do—read for content, and correct errors when the interpretation seems discordant (Schlesinger, 1968). In this context it is worth noting that McKinnon (1959), in a study of children's reading, reported more confident progress when materials were designed not so much to utilise formal structure as to ensure that 'guessing and checking' paid off most of the time. Thirdly, while the sentence splitting task indicated that children did have a feeling for the subdivision of sentences, this did not reflect an awareness of grammatical categories so much as a feeling for functional units and relations, whose relationship to grammatical structure was far from simple.

WRITING, READING AND SPEECH

Literacy is not only a matter of reading, and the north Leeds children were encouraged to write while they were learning to read. They learned to write their names, write labels to pictures and objects, and to copy individual letters. It may well have been that they learned the concepts *letter, word* and *sentence* as much from reading their own writing and the models they were given to copy, as from reading without writing. As they became more competent they built up their own vocabulary books, and referred to these in their 'free' writing.

When first tested at five years nine months, the children were asked to copy a set of six words printed on a card. Only four failed to copy at all and seven failed to complete the six words. In 39 completed lists there were only 11 disorientated letters (including both left-to-right and top-to-bottom inversion) and 17 other errors and omissions, while the quality of writing in at least 22 cases was judged to be firm and regular. It seemed that most of the children had little perceptual-motor handicap in writing. Only four were observed to be consistently left-handed in this and later tests, five showed some variability, while the remaining 41 seemed to be definitely right-handed. Two of the left-handed and two of the uncertain children proved to be good readers and writers while the other two and three respectively were not good. Handedness by itself did not seem to affect performance.

From the second to fourth testings the children were required to write what they could of the story they had retold. In free writing the quality of handwriting was not at first as good as in copying, but it steadily improved. Letter disorientations were few, the maximum number and frequency occurring on the third occasion with 47 errors in 2,140 words, but no child had a consistently high proportion of such errors. Spelling errors, on the other hand, were much more common with an average of one mis-spelled word in every six. There was a tendency for very common words to be better spelled and a parallel tendency for less familiar words to be used with an attempt at some sort of phonic spelling. This was to be expected, and only later experience of reading, or producing correct forms accurately, would modify this trend. Poor spelling may have inhibited some writers, for there was a small but positive correlation between amount and accuracy of writing. On the other hand some children made very courageous efforts to write good stories liberally peppered with errors. This was particularly true of one boy, a poor reader, whose writing could only be decoded by knowing what he might be writing about, from repetitions within his account and from a partial phonic coding. His handwriting was firm, with clearly distinguishable letter forms and words; and one could only conclude that he had developed a very idiosyncratic code which did not help him much with ordinary reading and made it difficult for others to read his writing. A later inquiry as to his reading ability at nine years, however, revealed progress that had taken him out of the poor reader category. The other children's stories presented little difficulty, and where there was uncertainty it tended to be in the efforts of poor writers whose work contributed little to the total.

There was a virtual doubling (from the second to the fourth testings) in the amount written and on each occasion the amount compared with that of the spoken story six months earlier. It may well have been the case that a second telling would have shown a reduction in amount comparable with the writing, for continued reproduction is known to result in reduction. There was also a difference in degree of complexity of sentence structure as compared with speech. Whereas in storytelling the children were moving on from the two-unit level, in writing they were only beginning to go beyond the simple sentence. Some children, however, were able to produce quite complex sentences, occasionally combining four or more sentence units in one complex form, and in the case of one or two very shy children their writing was more complex than their speech.

While most of the complex sentence patterns produced in writing were like those in the children's speech, one interesting difference emerged, namely that the written forms showed a stronger tendency to begin a sentence with a subordinate unit. It was strange that this should be the case when the spoken form had intervened between the model and the written account. Possibly even at this immature level of writing some evidence is seen of different decision procedures between writing, when the first part of the sentence remains evident, and speech in which it may more easily be lost.

Two important questions were raised earlier about the relationship between spoken and written language, asking how speech might facilitate learning to read and what effect literacy might have on language competence. They are not unrelated and it is probably easier to approach them via the first.

Since the north Leeds children had been tested in a variety of skills it was possible to compare the relationships between them by calculating the various intercorrelations. Using Kendall rank-order coefficients, most noticeable were, first, the lack of significant correlation between speech structure and both reading and the associated discrimination skills, and, second, the contrasting higher correlations with writing and vocabulary skills. It was as though speech and reading were very different in nature, but writing combined the language skills of speech with the auditory and visual discrimination skills of reading.

That some children had begun to learn to read a year or two before entering school suggested that early reading was not hampered by a relatively simple level of speech development, and the lack of correlation between speech complexity and reading ability in the early school years reinforced this view. The extreme simplicity of early reading material would make it highly improbable that the same content in spoken form would be incomprehensible to pre-school children if encountered in relevant situations. But not only is a relatively immature level of speech competence adequate for early reading, the studies of deaf and aphasic children suggest that productive speech is not a necessary prerequisite at all, though comprehension of events and some ability to communicate about them are indispensable. Yet historically and in the case of the vast majority of individuals, learning to speak precedes learning to read and write. Written language bears a very clear relationship to spoken—not so much in the details of correspondence between written symbols and the sounds of speech as in the fact that what can be talked about can be written about. This is not always clear to children. Downing (1970) suggested that at five to six years they have difficulty in understanding the nature and purpose of reading although they recognise the act of reading. He thought, as did Vygotsky (1962), this might be due to a failure to realise the abstract nature of language.

The young child learns to speak as he learns all other forms of action, and his use of language is embedded in the ongoing situation. But written language is abstracted from the course of events. What is written about must be created by the author or the reader, not from his participation in it but from his understanding of it. Possibly children who are acquainted with storytelling and having to give an account of events are better placed than others to grasp this. But more is required than understanding the separation of communication from the events referred to; the form of communication becomes the object of attention, and it must be understood that one can not only talk about events but one can also talk about the means of reporting them. One can talk about the elements and structures of language. There are, then, two aspects to understanding the nature of written language. One is to grasp that it can be used, like speech, as a means of conveying information abstracted from the time and place of an event, and the other is to see that it is possible to talk about words or utterances themselves, to abstract them from ongoing use and to reflect upon them. In teaching children to read we usually require that they understand both, but when children learn by listening to a model, practising, correcting and being corrected, they lean more heavily on the former. Perhaps this has something to do with the way some children start learning to read at a very early age. Leaning on the latter is less easy and we have seen in the study of the north Leeds children that in spite of a good command of spoken language they did not readily come to understand the instructional terms of reading, being unused to reflecting on the forms of their speech.

The instructional process also requires attention to other levels of correspondence between spoken and written language, whether or not they are essential prerequisites of reading. In spite of its deficiencies, the English alphabet is basically phonemic. Like phonemes, many letters can be perceived to act as single differentiating elements distinguishing between words. There is also a rough correspondence between spoken and written words and between utterances and sentences. Recognition of these levels of correspondence has led to the elaboration of different methods of introducing children to reading. Fries (1962) described the long history of use of various methods and how undue emphasis on one at the expense of another has always led to dissatisfaction and change. 'Look and say' methods emphasise the correlation between written words and their spoken forms, while phonic methods identify letters and attempt to correlate them with the constituent sounds of spoken words. Chall (1967) undertook a survey of research, and found that, while word recognition approaches were more interesting and led to quicker early learning, the load on memory soon became heavy, and a phonic approach then gave better results; but suiting the approach to the child was more important than choosing between methods. Yet even an eclectic approach, with attention to individuals, such as was practised in the north Leeds school, still leaves the possibility of children failing to demonstrate their readiness and their needs. Some of the dissatisfaction with the teaching of reading lies not in the methods but in the conditions and practice of teaching. Interest in method still waxes strong, however, and recent work in linguistics has led to suggestions that it might be possible to make more use of correlates between speech and writing, for in both cases there are more complex and reliable patterns of organisations within and between words than the single and variable letter-sound correlations.

The complexity of the speech code has been pointed out by Liberman *et al.* (1967) who have shown how perceived words cannot be identified on the basis of simple serial recognition of phonemes, for, depending on context, the same acoustic pattern may be perceived as different phonemes, and the same phoneme may cover considerable variation of acoustic signal. The perceptual process is one of judgement of sound within syllable context. Ladefoged and Broadbent (1957) showed, too, how the perception of syllables varied with the sound patterns of the sentence context. Young children spend much time learning to perceive and construct these patterns within patterns, differentiating between vowel and consonant elements in the context of syllabic features such as stress and shape (Waterson, 1970) and learning these in the context of utterance patterns. Even babies of six months have been shown to vocalise with the stress and intonation patterns characteristic of their native tongue (Weir, 1966). Thus learning to use structured spoken language involves the increasing differentiation of perceptual patterns in nested, interdependent levels, and there is no simple one-to-one correspondence between acoustic information and perceived units. Similar structuring in visual perception has been studied since the era of Gestalt psychology, and it is possible then that correspondence between spoken and written language might more effectively be made at a high-level order of structure than the phoneme or letter. These last do not correspond closely because both, being the smallest differentiated elements, show a moderate level of variability. But Hockett (1960) and Venezky (1962) have shown that within consonant or vowel groupings correspondences are much more reliable, a few rules of combination accounting for much variation. Gibson *et al.* (1962) showed how letter groupings could be relatively invariant in pronunciation, and also functional in the sense that they were easily pronounced by native speakers. A further paper reported that the spellings of pronounceable trigrams were learned more readily than unpronounceable versions by children who could read familiar words of the same three letters. For example *deb* might be learned better than *ebd* by children who could read *bed* (Gibson *et al.*, 1963). They concluded that generalisation from identification of letter groupings promoted reading efficiency, and that, although good readers tended to do this anyway with increasing exposure to written language, perhaps learning to read might be aided by an appropriate presentation of material. Effectively they suggested that children's attention be drawn to functional higher-level units. Unfortunately, however, children are sometimes confused by the presentation of inaccurate or over-simplified information of this kind. It may be that, as in speech, they do well if left to discover the patterning themselves.

The findings reported in this study raised questions as to the children's ability to profit from instructional methods based on auditory-visual correspondences, at least before they were seven years old. It was only then that they were able to identify functional patterns in the auditory mode; and they appeared to become aware of patterning only with the development of an analytic approach induced by the requirements of reading and writing. (It is interesting that Downing and Latham (1969) considered that possibly the principle advantage of i.t.a. was that it induced greater understanding of the structure of English.) The approach to reading was heavily influenced by the perceived unity of individual letters, for in sentence matching tasks five year old children painstakingly matched letter by letter. But even before they could read the children then moved on to matching by words, perceiving these as unitary within the sentence. Then they began to see groups of letters within words, identifying suffixes as perceptual units even before they could do so auditorily. When they began to read they grasped significance from the content words, using their order and meaning to estimate the meaning of the whole sentence. Thus 'function' words were not always read, yet their presence was anticipated from the inferred meaning of the sentence. They were not really needed as abstracted elements of speech until the children wished to write. While reading skill did not correlate with speech, writing did, and was moreover often 'phonemic' in its spelling errors.

The way children read also threw doubt on the possible usefulness of instructional methods making use of the syntactic correspondence between spoken and written English. The idea that it might be useful rests on the notion that children derive understanding of sentences via some implicit knowledge of grammar, but the young readers first found some meaning from scanning for a few words and then imposed a sentence form on the written material, expecting it to conform to their interpretations. This is in accord with adult practice. Schlesinger (1968) showed how a semantic process of decoding written language was indicated by experimental work on adult reading. Much syntactic information seemed to be redundant once the semantic relations within the sentence were established. Comprehension did not rest on awareness of form unless some error of judgement had been made and correction of the reading was felt to be necessary.

The doubt as to whether children might utilise the structure of their speech as an aid to reading was reinforced by the lack of correlation between speech complexity and reading ability. One might expect some shared factor to show up if there were grounds for believing that one skill might facilitate acquisition of the other. Loban (1963) and Strickland (1962) found a similar lack of correlation at the same stages of reading development, though their indices of complexity were slightly different. They did find an increasingly significant correlation however at more advanced levels and suggested that the more demanding texts required a higher level of speech skill. This might well be so, especially if more demands were being made on cognitive ability and immediate memory.

But Fries (1962) and Lefevre (1962) have made strong claims for incorporating in reading instruction some methods that depend on young children's implicit knowledge of phonology and grammar. To these claims four points can be made. Firstly, until children can understand the abstracted nature of language symbols they will find the task impossible. Secondly, awareness of formal structure in speech is not a necessary concomitant of good speech production. Thirdly, Fries' argument for phonemic approaches requires the recognition that appropriate perceptual units must be identified in written forms, and that training in ability to make use of auditory coding skill is required. In view of the complexity of the auditory and visual codes perhaps the best form of training is based on steady practice and accumulation of experience in matching written to spoken forms in sentence contexts. Learning to read and write takes time spent in active search for both regular and irregular forms, just as does learning to listen and talk. As with the early stages of talking, errors of discovery are to be expected and even enjoyed when they lead to incongruity. Attempts to hasten learning by avoiding error may actually impede it in some cases, and the great danger of formal teaching and guidance towards awareness of regularities is that 'model' errors can so easily be made and these can only lead to confusion and doubt. Fourthly, Lefevre's argument for the use of syntactic information seems unnecessary in that most of the important structural features are common to both speech and writing and therefore automatically used if required; but since there appears, from this and other studies, to be some doubt as to the nature of structural encoding and decoding in their speech, it might be misguided to try to make young children aware of its syntactic structure as an aid to learning to read. Moreover if too much attention is paid to constructing reading material based on sentence frames deemed appropriate to the learning task, there is a considerable risk of producing a rather artificial and stilted English. Some school reading books already suffer from such design, and the children can be highly critical. Perhaps, as in speech, it is better that they grope for meaning and search for regularities in interesting material, than that they have them thrust upon them in a form that runs the risk of being essentially boring. Extremely well produced children's books are available nowadays in which size of print, illustrations, sentence variety and story content all appeal to the child who is learning to read.

It will have become apparent that learning to read and write has a considerable effect on children's perceptions of spoken language. By the age of seven years they are able to isolate spoken forms, reflect upon their form and make judgements about them, and so it becomes possible for them to begin to treat them as grammarians do. Perhaps some instructional methods are more likely to produce embryo linguists than good readers! Yet the difficulty of teaching formal grammatical analysis to children even at adolescence is notorious. It would seem that whatever sort of language competence young children possess it is very different from the linguistic competence, or knowledge of a language, that is evinced by linguists making judgements about acceptable and non-acceptable forms, and attempting to formulate descriptive theories of syntax. It does not help to say that the child's is implicit and the grammarian's explicit, for the untrained adult with implicit competence resembles the linguist but not the child in his ability to make judgements of grammatical acceptability. Moreover there is a fundamental difference in nature between the kind of knowledge that lies behind the skill explored in Chapter 4 and the sort of linguistic competence described by Chomsky. In this the untutored adult may well be more like the child. What sort of competence, then, can be attributed to the child? In earlier chapters this question was asked about very young children. In the next chapter it will be explored with the help of the north Leeds schoolchildren, and the question of the relationship between competence and acquisition will be further examined in the final chapter.

6 Linguistic Competence?

ASPECTS OF SURFACE STRUCTURE

The reader will recall that analysis of children's speech structuring led to some doubt as to whether any linguistic competence in the Chomskyan sense could be thought to underlly such ability. In discussing early attempts to describe the syntax of child speech, Chomsky himself pointed out how necessary it was to use a variety of sources of information for inference about the nature of language ability (Chomsky, 1964). He suggested 'rather devious kinds' of observation and the exploration of both comprehension and production. Unfortunately it is not at all easy to do this with very young children, but with schoolchildren it is much more feasible. One of the aims of the author's investigation into the language abilities of five to seven year olds was to move beyond the description of systematic production to an exploration of what linguistic competence could possibly mean in relation to their skills.

Such an investigation required the co-operation of the children in tasks which seemed to verge on games, but in which they were required either to make decisions about language forms or to supply missing items. Two tasks which had a bearing on the question of competence have already been described with reference to learning to read. The ability to recognise suffixes to spoken words in a comparison task was shown to develop rather late, though children acquire the correct use of these *in situation-appropriate utterances* from the age of three years onwards. It was also found that although children produced a wide variety of sentences, they did not intuitively split simple examples into *subject* and *predicate* phrases. Their responses were, in a sense, more sophisticated than this, and possibly based on reactions which bore no relation to the intuitions of grammarians.

Essentially, to explore the concept of *linguistic competence* as a basis for language skill, one must try to find empirically whether children are at all sensitive to the categories and relations of grammatical analysis, remembering that they may not be aware of such sensitivity but rather that their responses might reveal it. Moreover one must try to compare structuring ability when speech is used in an appropriate supporting context with that when one is essentially playing language games with no situational or contextual support. Part of the acute division between Chomsky and Skinner related to a failure to make this contrast clear. As MacCorquodale (1970) pointed out, Chomsky's competent speaker may be able to produce grammatical sentences but there is no guarantee that he will have anything appropriate, or indeed anything to say. Skinner's speaker, on the other hand, would tend to produce relevant, but not necessarily novel or grammatical, remarks. If an account of acquisition might include a better account of language learning than Skinner was able to produce, a better integration of structure and function, then an ability to deal with novel language might be seen to rest more on learning in context than on inherent linguistic competence.

The tests to be reported and discussed in this chapter fall into two groups. In the first, ability to deal with familiar and novel forms in different contexts and the bases of children's choices of words in different tasks were examined to determine how adequately a presumed knowledge of syntax might account for them. Such tasks, however, only probed categories and rules that could be described in terms of surface structure, so in the second group the question of deep structure was explored. The tasks were given to the north Leeds children during the testings already reported in the previous two chapters.

An aspect of grammatical structure in English that has already been explored in various ways in this book is the use of verb tense and noun number markers as integral parts of words. Competent use of suffixes is often taken to imply rule-governed behaviour in the sense that a grammatical rule is observed that will be applied in all relevant sentence contexts. The question of how the child appreciates the relevant context is not explored; but it seems possible that different reactions might be obtained in speech where understanding is aided by what is actually perceived in the situation of use, and in speech abstracted from such use and unsupported by any perceived or remembered reference. How do children respond in these different cases?

We know that three year old children begin to use suffixes correctly in their everyday speech, and their ability to extend this skill to novel words has been explored. This has always necessitated the use of non-linguistic support, however. The Berko-type (1958) tests are the best known of the means used; and in these the children were first shown pictures, and the experimenter spoke about them to introduce a nonsense syllable as a novel word. Then he posed a leading question which the children usually completed using a marked version of the new word. The nonsense syllables were apparently quite readily accepted in relation to the pictures, and the introductory sentences were attended to as referring to objects, actions and perceptible qualities of objects. For example the children were first shown a picture of an object faintly resembling an animal and told that it was a *bik*. They were then shown a picture of two such creatures, the experimenter saying, 'Now there are two of them. These are two ——'. A maintained intonation level signalled to the children that they were expected to complete the sentence, and they usually supplied *biks*. The experimenter's use of language was in no essential way different from that of a mother talking to a child about a picture book; and how the child arrived at the plural form remained a mystery. It was some form of analogic extension of previous experience, but how far it might be described as linguistic was not clear. The same kind of task without pictorial or equivalent support does not seem possible with small children.

It is, however, possible with schoolchildren, and it seemed to the author that how they responded to the task both with familiar and novel words was worth exploring. The children were asked to complete what the experimenter said. In the case of the plural noun suffix the form was:

'I found another book, so now I have two. Two——'.
For the verb *ing* suffix it was:
'What am I doing if I jump? I am——',
and for the *ed* suffix it was:
'Every day Mary washes. Yesterday she ——'.

With both familiar and nonsense syllable words the responses were made more readily to the plural noun form, but this may have been due to differences in the cueing potential of the sentence frames. The differences in responses between familiar and nonsense words were independent of this, however, and they proved to be interesting. The familiar plural noun form was supplied so well at the first testing, (all the children giving a correct response except for a very shy child from whom nothing was then forthcoming) that it was not subsequently required. The unfamiliar, however, was not supplied so well. The syllables *reg, jod, jat,* and *deg* were used, and over all the testings between five and seven years an average of 84% of correct responses was achieved. There was no consistent trend. The familiar verbs with *ing* were *jump, talk, write* and *wave.* At the first testing 72% were correct, but thereafter 90% or more correct replies were given. For the unfamiliar words the nonsense syllables *bong, dob, zob* and *jid* were used, and for the first three testings only about 50% of replies were correct, but the figures rose to over 80% at the final testing. Before this about 25% of the children did not respond at all, while the other 25% simply supplied the syllable without the required suffix. For the past tense marker the familiar words *wash, talk, walk* and *knit* were used with an average 80% correct response rate, while the unfamiliar *tib, sig, bup* and *nop* yielded only 50% correct for the first three testings and 70% for the last. This was very similar to the findings for the *ing* suffix, and the same lack of supply of a suffix at all was the chief reason for incorrect answers. In the case of irregular familiar past tense markers to the verbs *run, sing* and *write,* only a 50% level of correct responses was achieved. The principle faults were the adoption of the regular marker instead of a vowel change, or the omission of a marker.

These results yielded sufficient in the way of reliable differences between skill with familiar and novel words to suggest that the children needed more than the cues they could obtain from the sentence frames to enable them to extend their 'marking' skill to unfamiliar words. Judging by the much better results obtained by Berko (1958) for younger children and by Anisfeld and Tucker (1967) using Berko-type tests with school children, the required cues are something to help them identify the nature of the referent object or action. It is possible that children extend marking rules, not by making linguistic analogues, but by identifying similarities between situations in which familiar expressions are used and those in which novel ones occur. Linguistic analogy would only be possible when sufficient skill had been obtained in using language without concomitant situational involvement.

Another task given to the north Leeds children explored their skill in interpreting novel words in sentence contexts. This time

they were asked to supply a 'real' word instead of the word that
was not a 'real' one to make given sentences sensible. Examples
were first given to illustrate the task, and to show that a choice
of words might be available, but that any word that made
the sentence sensible was acceptable. Thus *I googed the bus*
could be *I caught the bus* or *I stopped the bus*. At all testings sentences of the following forms were used,

> Jane is motting
> Peter motted the shoes
> Mary likes mots
> I found some mot
> The baby played mottily
> This is a mot ball
> I shut the mot

In addition, at the last testing another three were tried,

> We saw those mots
> Some mot was dropped on the floor
> Mary is motting the cake

It is immediately apparent that a sensible outcome might not
retain the grammatical form implied by the formal cue given in
the sentence. Thus, ignoring the *ing* suffix one might supply *Jane
is happy* for the first example. The children were required, however, to restrict their substitutes to one word, so that phrases or
clauses were not often supplied. It was thought that if the children
were sensitive to grammatical form they would offer substitutes
of the same grammatical class as the nonsense syllable and with
the same marker. To put it another way, in searching for an
appropriate word they would be involved in a process of identifying the required form class and then scanning their memories
for a suitable word entered under this label. They would, of
course, not be conscious of such a process, but in order to find a
'sensible' item would need to attend to the semantic constraints
imposed by the other words in the sentence. If, however, they did
not attend primarily to the grammatical cues but instead constructed a sensible whole from the array of words in the sentence,
they might well produce a response grammatically unlike that
cued. In order to satisfy the requirement to complete the given

sentence sensibly, however, the response would be a grammatical sentence, for the children had a good command of simple English sentences in that for the most part, when they knew what they wanted to say, they could command appropriate syntax.

No child failed to respond correctly to at least some of the items on each occasion, and all made sufficient response to show that they understood the nature of the task.

Responses which were both semantically and grammatically acceptable, given all the cues in the sentence, were scored as correct, while those which were sensible but not in accordance with the cues were classed as permissible. The percentage frequency of correct responses to the first seven sentence frames increased from 51 at the first testing at 5 years 9 months to 81 at the final trial at 7 years 3 months. Meanwhile the proportions of permissible and incorrect or nil responses both steadily dropped so that it seemed that there was a steady increase in attention paid to grammatical cues attached to novel words in a sentence context. This finding suggested that the children primarily sought to make a sensible remark in a form that was familiar or habitual to them as conveying that sort of sense, and that they were more inclined to attend in detail to the grammatical form of the novel words as they approached the age of seven.

The percentage of correct responses varied between items in a consistent manner and analysis of responses revealed that adjectives and adverbs were supplied less well than nouns and verbs, but within form classes variation was due to differences in the range of permissible responses as cued by the rest of the sentence. This was clearly illustrated with the addition of the three extra sentence frames at the last testing. The plural noun *mots* occurred in *Mary likes mots* and in *We saw those mots*. In the latter frame *those* cued the plural form even if the *s* in *mots* went unnoticed, whereas in the first frame if the plural *s* were ignored there was no cue to distinguish between possible count and mass nouns and even between those and verb phrases. A comparison between the responses to the two sentences showed that the former yielded 72% correct responses while the latter gave 96%. Similar differences were found when comparing *I found some mot,* where both mass and plural count nouns were supplied and *Some mot was dropped on the floor* where the singular verb sufficed to restrict the choice to mass nouns. When *Jane is motting* was compared with *Mary is motting the cake* the former allowed adjective as well as verb responses, but the presence of the direct object noun phrase in the latter restricted choice to a verb. It was apparent, then, that the complex of semantic and formal features in the familiar part of the sentences was attended to, but that the grammatical markers attached to novel words were not often noticed, even at seven years of age. In order to test whether their absence made any difference, parallel but unmarked forms of the sentences containing *motting, motted, mots* and *mottily* were used. In each case there was no difference between marked and unmarked versions in the percentage of correct and of permissible responses, suggesting even more strongly that in fact the suffixes had not been noticed.

The results of the two tests of ability to use suffixes with novel words in sentence contexts, but without any situational means of identifying the use of the novel word, indicated that the children did not readily extend their suffix marking skills in production, nor did they readily notice the markers in comprehension. The sense of a sentence was their primary consideration, and its form was dependent more on familiar ways of expressing this sense rather than on abstract rules which could be applied to the use of novel words.

How then would the children react to a jumbled sentence, which if correctly ordered would be sensible? Would they recognise the possible sense? Would they be able to extract the subject noun phrase as that which was predicated in some way? Would they be able to allocate words to appropriate form classes? In other words might they possess some linguistic knowledge that would enable them to formulate the sentence correctly? These are important questions, and much experiment might be conceived from them, but only a simple test was tried with the Leeds children. The jumbled sentences had to be short, for immediate recall of random items ranged from four to seven, so five-word forms were used. The children only tackled one item at each testing and it was presented as follows. The experimenter said that there would be something wrong with what she was about to say, and the children were asked to find out what was wrong. The scrambled sentence was then spoken, and repeated if required. After the children had given a response they were asked if they could put the sentence right, and again it was repeated for them. Sentences used were *Fish these fresh like cats, Crumbs these bread like birds* and *Milk those cold want boys*. It was found that children responded more readily to the request to put the sentences right than to the question of what was wrong, and the most useful way of analysing the responses was to consider both together. Explicit mention of order error was not as common as correct reordering of words functioning as subject, verb and object, but even when both responses were considered together only 22% of children achieved recognition of the error at the first testing and only about 50% at each of the other three. Those few who were explicit about reordering seemed to recognise that it was possible to identify words in sentences by their relative positions, but the others seemed to attend to sense rather than form. Often those who reordered correctly explained that the error was 'It's not sensible' or 'Fish couldn't like cats', or 'Crumbs don't like birds'. Similarly those who did not correctly rephrase the sentence tended to focus on one word and then make a sensible remark about it, although other words were ignored. It was interesting to observe that the 'correct' subject noun phrase was chosen in about 60% of those responses that attempted a correction, but that whereas *birds* were preferred to *crumbs* more often than *cats* to *fish,* as might be expected if there was a tendency to select an agent as subject and to use an active form of sentence, *boys* was not so easily distinguished in relation to *milk.* Instead there was a tendency to contruct a new remark based on *milk* as an imperative form of the verb and introducing *cows.* Such a choice was less often made with *fish* and was not made with *crumbs,* as though the plural marker excluded the imperative interpretation. But *fish, crumbs* and *milk* were all chosen as sentence subjects and predicated with new constructions which ignored the rest of the given array. Thus the children's responses revealed two major strategies, neither of which suggested that they were able to construct sentences according to grammatical rules, but that they had built up expectations of ordering words according to the truth value of the relations between them and that they had a strong tendency to expect a sentence to begin with a logical subject or with an imperative form of the verb. Thus a word might even be allocated to a different form class from that which would be a necessary consequence of an analysis of all the grammatical cues in the array.

After considering the ways children performed the tasks described so far in this chapter, it would seem to be rash to credit the children with any intuitive knowledge of the structure of language as an independent system. Although they were perfectly well able to comprehend and produce quite complex sentences employing familiar vocabulary, and were able to understand and use speech effectively in a variety of situations including both ongoing and recalled or imagined happenings, they were only beginning to extend their grammatical skill to novel words in sentence contexts or to use it in sentence reconstruction. Their early knowledge was not the kind which could be applied to language 'data' without benefit of comprehension of the logical and functional relations between the words used, relations which reflected the understanding of everyday events to which the use of language is tied, and in the context of which modes of expression are learned. But how do children categorise their experience and their words?

At any particular stage of acquisition the child's language might be described in terms of the extent to which he appears to have elaborated the grammar, and on this view it must be assumed that his words fall into whatever grammatical categories are adopted in his native tongue, and that such groupings or associations become part of the organisation of words in his memory. In speaking of the grammar of English the form classes of noun, verb, adjective and adverb are deemed appropriate for the language of children from the time they utter two- or three-word remarks. Indeed Brown (1957) attempted to show that young children did indeed categorise in this way by checking that they associated nonsense syllables marked as count nouns, mass nouns, verbs and adjectives with appropriate illustrations in pictures. He could not, however, check whether the children would associate words within form classes independently of a situation of use. That children can use two words as count nouns in their everyday reference does not necessarily mean that they recognise any class similarity or indeed that they store them in the same mental file.

The results of word association tests suggest that children do not readily link words within form classes in their early years. Woodrow and Lowell (1916) observed that they made associations which were frequently found as consecutive or contiguous words in speech, whereas adults' associations tended to be of the same form class and often to show similarity or contrast of meaning. Thus children tended to respond to *dark* with *night* and to *deep* with *hole* whereas adults more often gave *light* and *shallow* respectively. Brown and Berko (1960) classified associations by form class, and concluded that whereas adults' tended to be homogeneous, children's were heterogeneous. They interpreted the shift from one to the other, which is most marked between seven and ten years of age, as being due to grammatical learning. Ervin (1961) re-emphasised the distinction between the contiguity in speech of children's associations and the similarity of position in sentence context of adults'. She considered that children's (syntagmatic) associations were based on frequent co-occurrence, but that extended experience of such associations would lead to response competition such that an increase in paradigmatic associations might occur. Presumably the frequent association of *deep* and *hole* and of *shallow* and *hole* might lead to indecision about responding with either *hole* or *shallow* when presented with *deep*. But this is not entirely satisfactory, because no explanation of how the paradigmatic response might 'win' is forthcoming, and unexpressed assumptions are made about how words become available for recall. There is some suggestion of a selection process. Entwisle (1966) emphasised that within the class of paradigmatic responses there were semantic and functional bases of grouping which could not be ignored.

McNeill (1966b) felt that explanation in terms of grammatical learning was inappropriate, because he, as was pointed out in earlier chapters, took the view that children had virtually mastered the grammar of their native tongue by the age of four or five years. He felt, however, that learning of semantic class systems might account for the shift, such learning increasing the likelihood of responses consisting of synonyms and antonyms. Thus the adjectives and verbs that might early be associated with nouns would come to be the basis of identifying features which distinguish one class of words from another—as do 'animal', 'vegetable' and 'mineral' in the popular *Twenty Questions* game.

Similar problems are presented however by both the syntax- and the semantics-learning theories. Neither gives any account of what actually might happen in the formation of associations since both depend on data obtained from tasks which do nothing to reveal this. Moreover both adopt classifications which are identified by adults in terms of abstract features. Form class is defined by relative position (privilege of occurrence) in sentence contexts while semantic class is defined by such features as, for example, animate, human and male. Whether either frame of reference is suitable for accounting for processes of association as distinct from outcomes is debatable. Lippman's (1971) study threw some light on the question, for in addition to testing the value of a semantic feature description she also asked children to identify similarities between words. She found that when making paradigmatic associations based on similarity the younger children grouped together words which referred to objects with similar perceptual or functional features or to qualities that could be attributed to the same object, whereas older children mentioned the class membership of nouns or the similarity or opposition of meaning of adjectives. One understands this to mean that a younger child might associate *cat* and *dog* because both have tails, and *big* and *little* because a flower can be big or little, but an older child would say the first pair are both animals while the second are opposites.

In order to examine more fully what kind of classifications children might make, and whether indeed they appeared to show any tendency to recognise form class similarity, the author devised two tasks to present to the north Leeds children (Francis, 1972b). The first was a matching task in which the children were asked to listen carefully to a set of three words, two of which were of the same form class and the other was not. Each set was presented in an order such that the most frequent sequences in everyday speech were avoided. The words were simple, familiar, and each was as nearly as possible only to be found in one form class in English usage. The children were told that two of the words were of the same kind while the other was different, and were asked to choose the words they thought were alike. After their choice they were asked to give their reasons. Each set of words fulfilled one of three different conditions. In the first, the unrelated condition, the words were not easily associated either across or between form classes as in *sing, table* and *car*. The second, the across-form-class condition, the odd word was easily associated with either of the form class pair, as in *cup, mouse* and *small*, whereas in the third, the related condition, there was an additional association between the words of the same form class, as in *house, school* and *new*. Noun pairs were grouped with either adjectives or verbs, adjective pairs with nouns, and verb pairs with nouns. Only one child felt unable to attempt the task; the others seemed both to understand what they were required to do and to enjoy attempting to do it. Of all pairings made by the children 86% were supported with explanations. These could be classified as those which recognised equivalence of some sort such as 'They mean the same' or *'Boy* and *tree* because a boy grows and a tree grows'; those which recognised a complementary relation in a sentence, such as *'Boy* and *grow,* because a boy grows'; those which allowed some perceptual similarity between referents, and, lastly, invalid comparisons. Equivalence was necessarily associated with paradigmatic responses, but complementarity in a sentence might be either paradigmatic or syntagmatic. The proportions of perceptual and invalid matchings were small, most responses being backed by explanations involving equivalence or complementarity. There was no evidence in any set of words that the order of presentation systematically affected the children's choices.

In the unrelated condition the task was felt to be difficult and there was a high proportion of failures to come to a decision. The proportion of syntagmatic to paradigmatic responses also suggested a large element of chance decision making backed up by *post hoc* explanation. Equivalence was rare, and was expressed by presenting both words in the same form class in the same sentence, as in *'Come* and *chew* because you can come and you can chew,' and *'Pretty* and *white,* because flowers can be white and pretty'. Paradigmatic pairing without recognition of equivalence was explained either by some form-class change, which strictly speaking implied a syntagmatic association, as in *'White* and *pretty,* because white is a pretty colour', or by stretching the bounds of semantic acceptability as in *'Boat* and *roof,* because a boat can have a roof'. These explanations—efforts to combine the words meaningfully in a sentence—entailed the complementary associated with syntagmatic pairings. These too, in the unrelated condition, required some ingenuity and the children were very adept at trying to find sentences which contained such pairs as *chew* and *hat* and *grass* and *white*.

The second condition produced more responses, though few of these were paradigmatic. The children fastened on to the possibility of relating nouns with suitable adjectives or verbs and often justified their choices simply with phrases as in *'Mouse* and *small*—a small mouse, or *'Bread* and *eat*—eat bread'. They were expressing phrase relations rather than complete sentences. Their paradigmatic pairings were interesting in that the reasoning behind them was quite complex, as in *'Cup* and *mouse,* because you can have a small cup and a small mouse'. Both possible syntagmatic relations were realised and combined. A non-equivalent example, using complementarity, was '*Cup* and *mouse,* because the cup could have cheese in for the mouse'.

In the third condition the responses came even more readily and they included significantly more paradigmatic pairings, these being based on equivalence reasons such as 'They mean the same' or 'They're both buildings'. The differences in frequency of response in the various categories in the three conditions were statistically significant, and similar results were obtained at the three prior testings, though the proportion of nil responses was higher at the younger age levels.

It was concluded that the children readily made syntagmatic associations on a basis of familiarity with relations expressed in phrase sequences, and that they also easily made paradigmatic associations based on the perception of features underlying semantic classifications. But they also readily made paradigmatic associations based on possible phrase relations within a sentence, and these were essentially very little different from syntagmatic pairings. Further they were sometimes able to make paradigmatic pairings based on an appreciation of the similarity of two syntagmatic associations—a complex operation. The matching task thus tended to confirm the kind of associations made by children in simple word association tasks and to support Lippman's findings, though more was discovered about the bases of association. Yet the task was different from simple association in that it was not 'free'—the children had to make choices from given words, and this induced a different mental set. A task which left the children free to supply a word but which nevertheless threw some light on the basis of their orientation was perhaps nearer to simple association. This was the second task given to the north Leeds children—directed association.

In this simple exercise the children were given not one word with which to associate but a pair of words of the same form class. There were two conditions of pairing. In the first the words were judged to be semantically unrelated as with *sandal, window* and *eat, sing;* while in the second they were related in categories familiar to the children as in *chair, carpet* and *walk, jump.* Twenty undergraduate students allocated the pairs of words to the two conditions, all of them agreeing about the noun pairs used, 19 agreeing about the verb pairs, and 17 about the adjectives. The latter was not surprising in that the basis of pairing was that the related adjectives should be applicable to the same noun—this being the kind of adjective association most commonly made by young children, but less commonly made by adults. All the children were able to give associations and the overall response rate was high, though the unrelated nouns and verbs yielded marginally fewer responses than the related, and the co-occurring adjectives also tended to be a slight stumbling block. The unrelated noun and verb pairs included rather more syntagmatic associations than in the related condition, but predominantly they were of the same form class. The significant difference between the two conditions was that, in the unrelated, associations tended to be made within the same semantic class as one of the pairs, while in the related they were frequently within the same class as both items in the pair. In the case of the adjective pairs the co-occurring pairs tended to elicit a suitable noun—a syntagmatic response—but otherwise in both conditions an adjective was produced, often closely related to one of the presented pair. The set towards form class similarity did seem to tap a mental filing system, although it was obviously based largely on categories related to the features by which we identify semantic classes, but which are in fact perceived or used aspects of the directly encountered environment.

The outstanding features of all approaches to the basis of children's classification of words are their constant anchoring in the experience from which usage is derived, and the frequent inclination to relate words as they have been experienced in the ordinary run of speech. Children do not refer to words as words but as cues to what they know about their world. It scarcely makes sense to speak of either form or semantic class knowledge, for what they know is something of the ways in which words can be related in phrases, and sequences of phrases, in everyday use. Pre-school children do not find it easy to make associations to simple words in isolation (Entwisle, Forsyth and Muuss, 1964). When they do respond they tend to make 'clang' associations, i.e. words that sound similar, or they produce a full sentence incorporating the word. Huttenlocher (1964) showed that they found it difficult to separate two-word groups and reverse the words, though they found the task easier in the early school years. Such findings suggest an early classification of words in a system of phrases or simple propositions, which is broken down when cross-classification becomes possible. Miller (1969) suggested, after a detailed examination of associations, that words might be stored in the form of topics and predicates, such that forms like *A taxi is a car* and *A brush has bristles* would be a better basis for paradigmatic association than syntactic or semantic class knowledge. The explanations given by the Leeds children in the matching task would tend to support this, but they would suggest that predicates containing other verbs than *have* and *be* must be allowed, so that a topic noun might be associated with another noun in any predicate phrase. There is no reason to suppose that adults make associations on any other basis, for it allows all the associations previously described as based on form or semantic class, and also allows that associations which reflect common relations or definitions will be most frequent. The shift towards more paradigmatic associations as children mature requires some explanation beyond supposed form or semantic class learning. A hint of a possible hypothesis is obtained from the explanations of the Leeds children. Those children who added to the possibilities of making paradigmatic associations by relating two syntagmatic ones supplied a clue. If one takes two propositions of the form X r Z and Y r Z which independently relate X and Y to Z in the same manner, then even if X and Y have not been related in the experience of the proposer he may well come to associate X with Y. Thus a child may come to know that a nail is sharp and that a pin is similarly sharp and thus come to associate *nail* and *pin* not only independently with sharp, but also with each other. This will not in fact make the paradigmatic association any stronger than the syntagmatic but simply increase the overall chances of making paradigmatic associations, which is precisely what is implied by the term syntagmatic–paradigmatic shift. The explanation of shift then rests in the ability to combine propositions and form a simple judgement from both, a task which is cognitively more complex than the skills of the young child will allow. Such operations are implicit in the formation of complex sentences as described in Chapter 4 and in the formation of judgements about conservation of physical properties as described by Piaget (1952) and by Bruner and his colleagues (1966). The ability to make such judgements does not become widespread in children until school age, and increases markedly from the ages of seven to ten years.

Even with simple picture classification tasks—grouping two out of three items—the north Leeds children improved their performance between five and seven years. But while the bases of classification were similar in picture and word tasks, skill with language data was markedly the poorer. Moreover, such skill as was tested correlated significantly with literacy, but not with speech complexity. These findings suggested that whatever was being tested was related to general intelligence and to knowledge derived from learning to read, and did not bear much relation to the innately based linguistic competence discussed by Chomsky.

DEEP AND SURFACE STRUCTURE

The aspects of linguistic competence hitherto explored, knowledge of word classes and rules of grammatical marking, could quite fairly be said to relate to the surface structure of sentences, whereas much has been made by both Chomsky and McNeill of a hypothesised deep structure. Chomsky was concerned to account for the sort of knowledge that allows a native speaker to discern two sentence meanings in one surface form, as in *Racing cars can be dangerous* and two possible sentence forms for the same meaning as in *John hit the ball* and *The ball was hit by John*. Linguistic competence must include not only knowledge allowing categorisation and rule following at the surface level, but also at the deep structure level, and consequently of the transformations that relate them. McNeill hypothesised that the young child's knowledge was essentially of deep structure relations. The latter possibility was discussed in earlier chapters, where it was held that, in so far as we are able to understand what the young child says, the forms he adopts give one no special reason for hypothesising any knowledge other than what he can glean from the actual forms of the language he hears in use and the responses he receives to his own constructions. The schoolchild, however, has a greater grasp of language and it is possible to test his comprehension of surface forms more adequately. Is he aware, then, that the same thing may be said in different ways or that one sentence may have alternative meanings? Under what conditions does he either comprehend or produce alternative forms?

That difficulty in comprehension does not always rest with the vocabulary has been shown by Menyuk (1969) and Carol Chomsky (1971). The latter explored, amongst other kinds of sentence, the form *The doll is easy (or hard) to see,* finding that up to the age of ten years or so children tended to treat *doll* as the subject of the verb *see*. In other words the form was treated like the comparable surface structure *The boy is ready to go*. It looked as though the children's competence did not extend to differentiating between the possibilities. It is debatable, however, how far this can be said to indicate any deficit in competence beyond the inability to appreciate that *The doll is easy to see* rests on a particular and restricted use of *easy*.

The same might also be said about other contrasts used, like *John told Mary to fasten the cage* with *John promised Mary to fasten the cage* and *John told Mary what to do* with *John asked Mary what to do*. The children tended to regard *Mary* as the logical subject of *fasten* and *do* in all cases. It will be noticed that the difficulty in interpretation was to recognise exceptions to a general rule that the logical subject of a verb immediately precedes it. Unfortunately Chomsky's use of toys to enable the discrimination tasks to be performed easily might have reinforced a tendency to adhere to the general rule, for the children's shift of attention accompanying the spoken sentences would leave them looking at the last named referent as they listened to the second verb. Nevertheless Chomsky clearly showed that at some stage between six and ten years the children developed an ability to discriminate the exceptions from the rule.

It is possible however, to use sentences with less particular usage to test children's competence, for the problem of locating the logical subject is presented by the passive form of sentences. But the passive is particularly interesting in that not only is it possible to explore whether both the active and passive surface structures are similarly interpreted, but the passive itself may be differently interpreted, in that the phrase *by + agent* might be taken to be a locative phrase, *by* being interpreted as *beside*.

The actual free production of the full passive form by children tends to come quite late, such studies as have been made noting its occurrence towards the age of seven years. Imitation may be achieved earlier; and Turner and Rommetveit (1967), with 48 children at each of five age levels from four to nine years, found that correct imitation preceded comprehension, which in turn preceded production. From five years virtually all imitations were correct, but depending on the kind of passive form only 55% (reversible) and 85% (non-reversible) of the comprehension tasks were correct, while 50% (reversible) and 75% (non-reversible) of the production tasks were fully achieved. Reversible passives are more difficult because the logical subject (agent) and object can be interchanged without making nonsense of the

N

sentence. Thus it is easier to be in error in identifying the logical subject.

It will be recalled that in Chapter 4 it was reported that the north Leeds children made errors in the recall of passive sentences, almost all of which were non-reversible. About 5% of responses consisted of attempts to give the active form (which implied comprehension) and about 30% omitted the agent phrase. The task of recalling a simple 12-word sentence was different from the Turner and Rommetveit task of recalling two five- or six-word sentences together, and this possibly explains the poorer imitation performance of the north Leeds children.

Comprehension and production of passive forms was tested with the north Leeds children with reversible passives only, except that at the third and fourth testings non-reversible passives were introduced in the comprehension test to explore the possibility of alternative construing of the agent phrase as locative. In the Turner and Rommetveit study comprehension was tested by asking the children which sentence of a pair of active and passive forms went with a given picture. The question was framed to elicit a simple affirmative or negative response. The production task was similar except that, after hearing both forms, the child was required to produce the correct version. The north Leeds study did not use the same tasks. To test comprehension the children were asked to listen carefully to a sentence such as *Mary was chased by John*. They were then asked *Was Mary chasing John?* When the children replied that she was not, they sometimes did more than give a simple *no*, saying rather, 'No, John was chasing Mary'. They did not repeat the passive form. Thus they indicated that they were aware that the two sentences meant the same. However, only eight of the 50 children responded consistently in this way. (It may be recalled that in one of the reading tests only a very small number of children recognised the active–passive equivalence). At each testing a further 20 children on average also supplied a correct answer, thus the percentage responding correctly to comprehension of the reversible passive was very much the same as that in Turner and Rommetveit's study, though the tasks were very different. The Leeds study, however, did not suggest much stability in individual's responses. To the non-reversible passives, such as *The ball was dropped by Tom,* about 70% of north Leeds children indicated correct (passive) comprehension, and five children interpreted the agent phrase as a locative, none doing it consistently. Thus a few children found it possible to interpret the same form in two different ways, though they gave no sign of being aware of this.

To elicit production of the passive, the north Leeds children were presented with two pictures of people, animals or vehicles so that, when they were placed side by side, one appeared to be following the other. Thus pictures of a boy and a girl were shown and the arrangement described correctly as *The girl is being chased by the boy*. Then the pictures were reversed so that the girl appeared to be chasing the boy and the child was asked *What is happening now?* If the passive response was not elicited a second question was posed—*What is happening? The boy is   ?* If this failed to elicit the full response, a final question—*The boy is being   ?* was posed. At five years only a few children produced the full passive, but during the seventh year about 40% did so. This figure is rather lower than Turner and Rommetveit's 50% for reversible passives, but the tasks were rather different and the results are not very dissimilar. When the logical object was given as an introducer more children produced the full passive, there being as many as a further 40% at seven years, but others produced an agentless passive or a different active form. The final cueing of object plus passive auxiliary raised the proportion of full passives to 90% or more at all but the first testing, when it was still only about 25%, but even on that occasion it did significantly boost the number of passive responses without the agent. These results suggested that the passive form was very difficult to elicit at five years, but that by seven years of age more children were able to produce it and did so more readily.

In summary, it did not seem that the children were ready to see that the active and passive forms of sentences were equivalent in meaning, and that it took them a long time to become accustomed to the idea. This may have been partly due to limited exposure to full passives in everyday experience, but it should be remembered that the logical object given as an introducer did not have any great effect until seven years. Prior to that there was a strong tendency to make it the subject of a different sentence. For example if the correct passive form was *The boy is being chased by the girl* the child might well say *The boy is running,* and even if the agentless passive was supplied one felt that *The boy* was actually being treated as the principal focus of attention and there was no mental preparedness to consider the logical subject. Pragmatic aspects of the use of the sentences seemed to dominate and be much more important than grammatical structure. Something of the sort may also have lain behind the very small proportion of interpretations of the non-reversible agent phrase as a locative. Given equal chances of interpreting *The ball was dropped by Tom* as a passive with agent or a passive with locative one would have expected a higher proportion of locative versions, although the questioning might have weighed in favour of the passive. In fact there was a strong tendency to make Tom the actor, even in incorrect responses which suggested, for example, that Tom did not drop the ball, but threw it! It is possible that children accord a high priority to human agents as the logical subjects of sentences.

It would seem then that not until well into their school years do children come to be able to allot different interpretations to the same surface form and to recognise the equivalence of meaning of some alternative forms. In learning to do so their interpretations rest strongly on pragmatic considerations and there is no strong reason to hypothesise any knowledge of a deep structure related to surface structure by transformation rules. Children do, however, have the prior knowledge that one word may have two or more meanings and that two words may have much the same meaning. They recognise the rough equivalence of different phrases in use as, for example, *by himself* and *on his own*. There is a mental preparedness to find similar features about longer chunks of language; though, after all, to find any regularities in these requires exposure to less frequent forms in use. It must, of necessity, take the child time to become familiar with them. Since the usual examples given by linguists of ambiguous and equivalent sentences require the relation of at least two sentence units in one complex form it is not surprising that young schoolchildren are not readily aware of alternative possibilities. Rather older children reveal awareness, particularly in their laughter when ambiguity is amusing. This is most often the case when they recognise a mismatch between intended and achieved meaning in their own construction errors. A report, 'Mummy, we saw Orion walking home from the bus-stop' was immediately followed by a burst of laughter from the nine year old amateur astronomer. At this age, too, headlines like DOCKS—WILSON STEPS IN and NASSER FLIES BACK TO FRONT are regarded as prize sources of mirth. When children are capable of thinking about sentence differences like this they are also able to learn directly the rules of expression of semantic relations, that one surface pattern has two meanings and that one meaning may have two representations. Do we really need to attribute to such children any abstract knowledge of a supposed grammatical deep structure?

7 Form and Function in Children's Speech

A CRITIQUE OF THE NOTION OF LINGUISTIC COMPETENCE

It is hoped that this book has conveyed to the reader not only something of the intricate and fascinating development of children's speech, but also something of the problem of accounting for a very special kind of human behaviour. Speaking and listening with comprehension are vital aspects of man's existence, but are extremely complex forms of action. If speech were just a small collection of relatively unrelated signals, then the account might not be too difficult; but since when we speak we share with others the adoption of a particular kind of systematic arrangement of the signs we use, yet are not aware that we do so nor conscious of having been instructed, an account is not easy, and we feel it important to try to explain how children come to acquire such an ability.

The distinction between systematic structuring and a special linguistic competence made throughout the book has been necessary for two reasons. First, while an inferred ability to construct and comprehend speech in a systematic way can be described in terms of conformity to and deviancy from the structuring of adult speech, we should remember that such a description does not itself account for the constructive ability; the relationship between a grammar and an ability to construct the speech from which it can be drawn has not been fully explored. Second, some linguists and some psychologists have proposed that a particular kind of grammar, a generative transformational grammar, is a description of the kind of ability required. This linguistic competence, or knowledge of the kind of formal categories and relations involved, is, according to them, the basic knowledge given to all men that enables them to construct the particular forms of their own native languages when they encounter them. Given this competence, children would begin to identify the basic category relations of their language at an early age and would essentially only have to learn transformations to achieve mastery of the possible sentences in the language. How otherwise, ask its proponents such as Chomsky (1965) and McNeill (1970), could they possibly learn to speak so well in their early years, when the speech they hear is so fragmented, so distorted a version of the language? They need some prior knowledge.

The hypothesis is attractive for several reasons. First, there is the guarantee that children exposed to the same native tongue will ultimately acquire it, and not a variety of distorted and fragmentary versions. Second, a child will acquire whatever language he is exposed to, provided that it is a natural language, and all children will do so in the same sort of way, so that worldwide general similarities in development will be found, as indeed they are. Third, it is possible, because of the very simple yet non-random nature of early speech, to argue, as McNeill has done, that children make basic categorisations and speak 'deep structure' in spite of hearing 'surface structure'; and there is no way to reach a knowledge of deep structure from surface structure without knowing a generative grammar. Fourth, children do seem to learn regular transformation rules in that they systematically develop mastery of the category markings from which these are inferred. The development of negative and interrogative forms discussed in Chapter 3 illustrates this.

But the exploration of language skills reported in this book yielded findings that could not be accounted for by the linguistic competence hypothesis. Given that there was evidence of enough systematic patterning to infer aspects of such a competence, the phrase-structuring of early remarks was more limited than would have been expected, both in terms of content and variation in order. Moreover the assumptions on which inferences of knowledge of transformation rules are usually made were called in question. Although relevant regular patterning was identified, it was such that no certain claims for a basic sentence deep structure knowledge could be made, and supposed deletions and reorderings were seen as possible consequences of linear integration of a limited number of phrase patterns. Reported observations and experiments also suggested that children's production and comprehension were embedded in larger behavioural units than the remarks themselves, and that the integrating feature was not the abstract concept of a sentence but the relationship of words to the total structure of the event of which they were a part. The further exploration of skills of older children showed their remarks to be much better described in terms of sentences, for they were rarely incomplete, were for the most part grammatically acceptable, and were at times quite complex. But the very same children seemed to have little skill in making formal judgements about linguistic data, especially when unsupported by extra-linguistic information. The kinds of judgements they did make were better explained in terms of semantic and pragmatic features of language than in terms of syntax. Indeed it seemed that any formal knowledge they might have was not in any sense a prior endowment, but a consequence of learning an analytic approach to language as a result of reflection on both spoken and written forms. Learning to read seemed to exert a powerful influence in this respect and to help set the children on the road to becoming linguists!

Empirical investigation thus revealed inadequacies in the linguistic competence hypothesis as a basis for accounting for the kind of speech children actually produce, and led to a questioning of the appropriateness of entertaining the notion of a kind of abstract knowledge as an explanation of language acquisition. Dissatisfaction with the idea that a grammatical competence is essential for relating the sounds of speech to its meaning has been expressed strongly in recent literature. Morton (1966) criticised such a performance model, elaborated by Wales and Marshall (1966), on the grounds that a direct link between sound patterning and meaning was necessary. Katz and Postal (1964) and Fodor and Garrett (1967) have tried to amend such models to give a more satisfactory account of such features of performance as guessing and checking, making sense of a sentence as it is produced rather than after it has been heard, and modifying a sentence as it is produced. But while dissatisfaction has been shown, nevertheless the model has been felt to be the only account of how speakers and hearers evaluate and adhere to the structures appropriate to their tongue. Accounts of language acquisition in which such a performance model is implicitly incorporated regard some kind of innate language generating device as the only basis for learning, and evaluation procedures as the only means. Such a view has been the outcome of linguists' frustration in trying to discover the grammars of newly encountered languages. There is no foolproof procedure nor guarantee of success. Nor is it even possible to say of a grammar 'This is the best description of the structure of that language'. Instead one can only hope to formulate descriptions that can be compared in such a way that one account is thought to be a more adequate description than the other. Chomsky (1957) made this abundantly clear, rejecting discovery and decision procedures and advocating evaluation. His theory of grammar allowed such procedures to be undertaken fairly effectively, and he therefore thought that in acquiring a language a child must be equipped like a linguist with the necessary toolset, a knowledge of possible grammatical structuring. This inevitably meant that the only way open to learn involved the construction of a grammatical form and its testing against heard speech. If the form could take the data it was appropriate for that language, unless or until experience of further data showed an alternative to be better. This was, of course, a hypothesis-testing model of learning such as is shown in Figure 7.1; but, while it might well apply to how linguists attempt to learn about other languages, it is not well suited to children's learning.

In the first case it requires that the learner be informed that what he regards as a test instance is correct or incorrect. Now this is a greater requirement of the adult speaker than is the lesser requirement, already dismissed by Chomsky as ridiculous, that adults should speak grammatically. Effectively it means that they should somehow tell their children which of their adult remarks are linguistically acceptable and which are not! This would seem to be about the most improbable parental behaviour imaginable. Moreover a subsidiary requirement would be that somehow the child should request the information; and yet that would be well beyond his powers until he was already giving evidence of having acquired considerable speech. A lesser requirement would be that the adults told the child whether his own productions were or were not acceptable. But this meets three major objections. There seems to be unanimity in the literature that parents do not act in this way. Second, it would mean that the child learned from his own productions, only comprehending adult speech in their light; yet comprehension often precedes production and is not identical with it, and those who are unfortunately mute are able to acquire the comprehension of language (Lenneberg, 1967). The third objection is that, especially in the early stages, the child's remark is so 'telegraphic' that the parent has no basis for judging grammaticality.

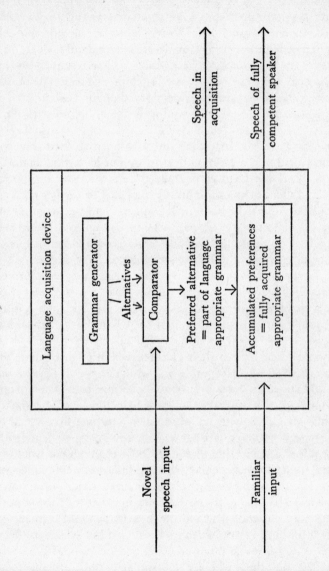

Figure 7.1

An evaluation model of language acquisition

A second major reason for doubting the suitability of the model for first language acquisition is that it requires comparison procedures. The child has somehow to assess whether one categorisation or relation rule is better than another in face of the speech he hears, for his supposed language acquisition device generates alternative structures for testing. Thus, for example, he may have to test such alternatives as negation before sentence and negation within sentence, yet in no sphere of activity does the young child appear able to deal with alternatives together. While he is considering one he forgets the other, or at the most he refuses to treat two possibilities as alternatives and wants them simultaneously! In this respect he might be said to have a 'one track mind'.

There are other major difficulties about the hypothesis-testing model, this time at the theoretical level. A knowledge of grammar supposes the potential to codify in terms of grammatical categories and relations, but these are abstractions, derived by adults thinking about spoken language long after they have become accustomed to knowing that they can break up the stream of speech sounds into meaningful words, and long after they have been aware that they are capable of abstract thought. Linguists have first worked from words to grammar. How is it conceivable to work the other way with no vocabulary? How indeed does the child know what constitutes language data?

The very nature of the model of innate competence with learning by hypothesis testing ensures that it can only be evaluated on theoretical grounds. It is not possible to explore experimentally any supposed innate ideas, and their advocates are surprisingly vague about their nature. Nor is it possible to find out whether a child learns by hypothesis testing for it is not possible to know without means of communication what hypotheses he might entertain. One can infer expectancies from non-verbal behaviour, but not predictions, for these take a propositional form. One wonders why the notion was ever put forward. Was it due, perhaps, to an error in thinking, a confusion between different kinds of theory similar to the error of considering mind and body as terms of the same semantic category? Descriptions of structure made in abstract terms, invented by scientists as category labels for classes of actual observations, may supply useful shorthand statements about possible regularities of orderings of these data, but they cannot account for the occurrence of such patterning. The latter can, however, be explained in two ways, either as the outcome of the behaviour of the scientist in producing the description, or as the outcome of prior events leading up to the array of instances sampled in observation. Explanations of the structure of remarks in a language must be sought then not in laws relating abstract descriptive categories but in an analysis of the structure of the behaviour of which they are the outcome. Knowledge of what kinds of patterning are achieved is the outcome of the linguist's activities; it cannot logically be attributed to the child (Francis, 1970). There is too great a jump from the explicit knowledge of the grammarian to his own tacit knowledge as a speaker or listener and also to that of the child. One is tempted to extend Occam's admonition against the unnecessary multiplication of explanatory entities to add another against the inappropriate transfer of an entity from one kind of account to another of a different status.

TOWARDS A THEORY OF CONSTRUCTIVE LEARNING

If one argues that the only kind of tacit knowledge the child might possess is that built up in the development of skilled behaviour, knowledge how to construct functional and significant action patterns, it can be seen that the question of prior knowledge is still important; but if one posits some kind of competence that can in principle be acquired under the known conditions of childhood then one does not need to base an account of acquisition on some sort of given or innate knowledge. Instead the account can be based on a combination of aspects of skill, dependent on the biological potential of the child and on analysis of his experience. Lenneberg's (1967) account of the biological foundations of language points to features of the organisation of the perception and articulation of speech which go far to explain many universal features of the pattern of development of children's talking, and in this respect surely one can speak of man's innate and unique potential or ability, for no other species has such a well developed basis for coded communication unless it be the dolphin.

But an account of universal features of speech perception and articulation, while showing astonishing capacities for coding, does not explain the verbal structuring of remarks. Is it possible that some special feature of the human brain predetermines the form of language in a manner analogous to that described in abstract terms by Chomsky? Is there some parallel to the 'innate conception of language that makes language possible' (Chomsky, 1968, p.120). Although doubt has been cast on the proposed possession of knowledge of abstract features of language, yet it remains possible that the actual patterning may be unlike that of any other form of behaviour and may be in some way innately determined.

Lenneberg considered aspects of this question and examined other kinds of behaviour which suggested that the ability to transform both perceptual and motor structures in this way was a characteristic of human performance, and that no special language transformation ability need be posited. For example we systematically transform our view of a brick, which can never cover more than three faces, into a solid rectangular structure having six faces. We see the edge view of a plate and make a mental transformation to a circular face. We imagine two bricks, and then their conjunction into one. In all these cases a geometrical structure is transformed into another by systematic mapping, which could be expressed in the application of mathematical rules in the same way as sentence structure transformations can be described in terms of linguistic rules. The nature of the general human ability involved in transformation must rest largely on the organisational potential of the brain, though obviously its application to such spheres of activity as perception, action, thought and language must vary with the demands made by the tasks on memory and prior experience.

Examining a particular kind of construction thought to be most important for language, namely embedding, one can see parallels in other forms of behaviour. Observing a child carrying one brick at a time to place each on a growing tower one can discern units of behaviour which bear similarity to each other, and which are separable into discrete meaningful actions. Thus one can suggest *initial act + purpose*, e.g. *Grasp brick, to place on tower*. This purpose can be further broken down to *movement + final act*, e.g. *Carry, place on tower*. Such a description is reminiscent of *sentence → noun phrase + verb phrase*, and *verb phrase → verb + noun phrase*. Moreover, if the child should suddenly grasp two bricks before moving to place them on the tower one would have an example of conjunction with embedding in the initial part of the sequence.

Similarly if the child were pasting coloured triangles onto a page one at a time, and had previously obtained them by cutting squares diagonally in half one might observe two kinds of action, *Take square, cut into triangles,* and *Take triangle, paste onto page.* Then if he were to take up a free square, cut it into triangles and then paste these onto the page one might infer either *Take square, cut into triangles and paste onto page,* or *Take triangles cut from square, paste onto page,* representing either a conjunction or a qualification, each with embedding. Note that the isomorphism between sentence and action structure is achieved primarily because both forms ultimately represent a description of intentional behaviour which can be planned in either discrete or combined units. These examples make it clear that the kind of transformations described in linguistic theory are not unique to language. Moreover it is apparent that small children may display organising skill in the construction of other action sequences that only later becomes evident in the structure of their remarks. Prior competence in the case of transformation seems to be evident, but it need not be thought of as having a language specific or abstract nature. Rather it is a consequence of the possession of the kind of brain that makes intentional behaviour possible and allows sequences to be engaged in together, so that not only may one follow another, but one may also interrupt another without preventing its completion. Undoubtedly much of man's brain must be involved in one way or another in the organisation of verbal behaviour, but what is known of special language function is difficult to relate to accounts of acquisition. That we cannot explain brain anatomy and function well enough to correlate them with mental processes is shown clearly by von Bonin (1962). How much the steady evolution of a speaking creature has resulted in the kind of brain man now possesses, and how much the child inherits special capacity, or only the potential to develop it for himself as learning progresses, is debatable on the present evidence. It seems there is both a predisposition to use the brain for language function, but also a measure of adaptability which shows particularly in the face of damage, especially in the young child (Lenneberg, 1967).

If there is a general disposition of the central nervous system to encode, transform and plan the reception and production of information for effective action, it is possible to propose models of language performance and acquisition which do not incorporate a special grammatical competence as a prior requirement. Schlesinger (1971a) made an important contribution to accounts of performance in pointing out the need to explain how the child produces a remark that is not only linguistically but also situationally appropriate. Something of the speaker's intentions are encoded in forming it. Of most interest are the elements of experience the speaker wishes to incorporate and the relations between them that he wishes to express. The intended semantic structural relations would be comparable with the deep structure grammatical relations of the incorporated grammar models, and Schlesinger therefore argued that it is much more economical to suggest that the speaker does not use a grammatical competence to form his remark, but instead links meaning to surface forms through learned *realisation rules,* which will have features of transformation rules. These will have been acquired slowly as the child learns to adopt the conventional forms of expression of his native language. Much of the basic structural experience that is encoded is inevitably universal, though some of that, too, is conventional and will be particularly linked to local forms of expression.

Schlesinger illustrated his argument by using examples of children's two-word utterances culled from the observations of Braine, Brown and his colleagues, and Miller and Ervin. He was able to show that these expressed particular relations such as agent-action *Bambi go,* and action-object *see sock,* agent-object *Eve (is having) lunch,* and that the children were adopting realisation rules for ordering the functional categories to express the relation. He also noted that the qualifier–object relation was apparently expressed in either order. He went on to suggest that the combination of two-word order rules would lead to remarks of three or more words whose structure could be described in terms of a sentence with a hierarchical phrase structure, and, further, that transformation rules could be learned and used in a second stage of the production process, after the phrase structure realisation rules. Such an account would require that in comprehension the listener depended on his knowledge of rules that allowed him to find from the uttered form cues to both basic and transformational realisation rules in order to interpret the speaker's expressed intentions.

Given some degree of ambiguity in the expression, or ignorance in the listener, there is nothing except contextual cues to prevent mistakes. This is precisely what happens in everyday life. Encountering the sentence *Shooting criminals can be dangerous* I know from previous experience that active verbs with *ing* can be used to express an action or can be used to qualify some person or object by describing its state of activity. Therefore I have two possible interpretations, and only the context of use can set me to choose one rather than the other. I do not need to make a grammatical analysis beyond this level of knowing how surface cues may be used. Similarly I have learned that *The dog chased the cat* and *The cat was chased by the dog* express the same agent-action-object relations. The young child on the other hand may only have the active realisation rules and therefore when faced with the second sentence is likely to misinterpret it. Findings that this is indeed the case have been reported by Fraser, Bellugi and Brown (1963) who discovered that three year olds systematically associated sentences like *The boy is pushed by the girl* with pictures which showed the equivalent of the boy pushing the girl. Turner and Rommetveit (1967) summarised findings pointing in this direction, and in their own experiments found that children of four years of age showed considerable differences in their ability to comprehend and produce various active and passive sentences correctly. In some sentences it is possible to reverse the subject and object and still produce a sensible remark as in *The boy pushed the girl,* but in others it is not, as in *The boy pushed the barrow.* The former can therefore be described as reversible, whether in active or passive form, whereas the latter is non-reversible. Turner and Rommetveit found that children systematically dealt with active forms more correctly than with passive, and with non-reversible better than with reversible, and that they were not at ease with all forms until the age of eight or nine years. The findings suggested a readiness to use an agent-object ordering in realisation rules but an increasing willingness to accept a re-ordering (transformation) if the agent-object order did not match the relevant word order. Thus, at first, lack of transformation realisation rules tended to result in misinterpretation of all passives, especially perhaps in a 'testing' rather than a 'natural' setting when normal expectancies might have been shelved, but as they grew older the children felt unable to accept their own interpretations of non-reversible forms and mentally transformed the sentences, recognising that with certain cues it was possible to adopt an object-agent order. The tendency not to transform persisted longer when agent and object were reversible and the interpretation had to be checked not only against mental acceptance but also against the evidence from pictures or whatever was the basis of reference. Turner and Rommetveit were at first surprised that sometimes children regarded reversed non-reversible active sentences like *The pony rides the girl* as acceptable, but they found on investigation that the children's strong tendency to interpret the first position noun as agent led to a loose interpretation of the verb to yield an acceptable meaning. Thus they interpreted it as *The pony gives a ride to the girl*. Such findings lend a cautionary note to interpretations of children's performance in experimental situations. While the experimenter may expect the child to make an unbiased judgement, the child may be doing what comes naturally to him, namely struggling to impose sense on information, however improbable that information might seem. He is biased to expect forms of language to be appropriate, and is therefore easily misled.

The discussion of Jonathan's speech led to inferences about his performance that were in accord with Schlesinger's model. The description of categorising, ordering and marking strategies can be seen as one way of attempting to describe the learning of realisation rules. But the account went a step further than Schlesinger's in that it was doubted whether it was appropriate to speak at all of the learning of grammatical categories and relations in the process of adopting conventional forms of expression, for there was no simple relationship between the functional categories and relations of child speech and the formal categories and relations of syntax (a condition that also necessarily obtains in adult speech). The grammatical relation of subject-predicate covered both the agent-action and object-comment. Moreover the categories *noun* and *noun phrase* covered a wide variety of functions. Thus a personal name was clearly used for an addressee, an agent and a possessor of an object, and as such might take different relative positions in the left-to-right structuring of a remark. A word for a person or an animal might be positioned as agent before certain kinds of active verbs, and unlike a word for an inanimate object might warrant the pronoun *he* or *she*. A word for an inanimate object might not be found in the agent position before certain active verbs like *want* and *sleep* and *see*, but was very likely to be found after some active or operative verb as the direct object of some agent's action. Yet it could well be found before the verb phrase that predicted it in some way, or fulfilling a locative function after a direct object.

Bloom (1970) had noted the necessity of imputing some sort

o

of case-grammar to the child to account for such variety of functional relations, but still thought in terms of the child possessing implicit knowledge of a case-grammar deep structure. Thus she did not go as far as Schlesinger in suggesting that some notion of grammatical deep structure was superfluous in a model of language acquisition. Had she done so she would have been released from feeling bound to consider incomplete utterances as being reductions from a more complete deep structure based on the grammatical unit of *sentence*. She could have treated two-word utterances as straightforwardly expressive of a functional relation the child wished to point out or use, irrespective of how it might rest in a hypothetical sentence structure.* Schlesinger himself did not explore the implications of his suggestions that realisation rules were learned in order to relate sets of semantic relations to surface forms of utterances. He found no necessity however to use the concept *sentence,* which was basic to McNeill's (1970) account of acquisition.

A possible performance model based on the foregoing considerations is shown in Figure 7.2, where it is shown that the apropriate use of language depends on planning and interpretation in relation both to the total situation in which it is used and to the learned skills derived from past experience of construing the sense of heard speech in action. An acquisition model would have to account for this past learning within the performance model itself by including a discovery procedure whereby newly encountered regularities are stored in memory. This would require an elaboration of the attention, perception, interpretation and memory parts of the model to extend beyond allowing incoming data to be used on a basis of prior dispositions and knowledge and to allow some of it to be newly recognised and stored. Such an elaboration is sketched in Figure 7.3. A major advantage of such a model is that it makes no difference in principle whether perceived and learned regularities are such as would be described by linguists as phonological, syntactic or semantic. Aspects of any will be encountered as soon as the hearer recognises something of a sound pattern functioning as a meaningful vocal action. A disadvantage is that it is not apparent how the linguistic regularities that come to be adopted are those and only those of language. It is contended, however, that this book has already questioned the

---

* In a later work Bloom (1973) has moved in this direction. See Bibliography.

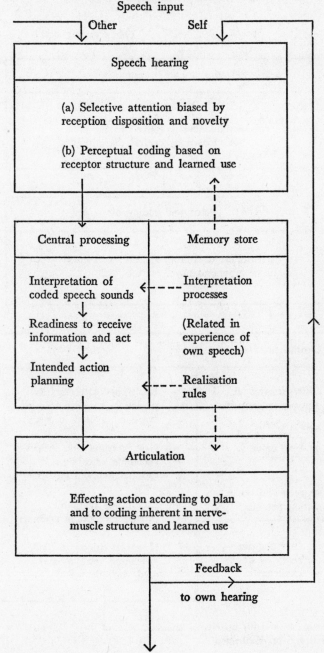

Figure 7.2

A model of speech performance

Speech input

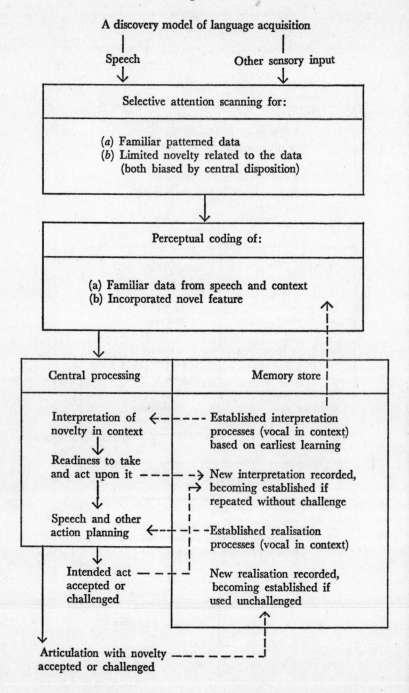

Figure 7.3

A discovery model of language acquisition

legitimacy of attributing over-precise knowledge to the native speaker and learner sufficiently for the reader to be willing to explore the possible explanations of systematic and appropriate acquisition advocated by those who regard it as a process of learning.

To suggest that any one process might be either necessary or sufficient would be folly in the face of the complexity of the task. Suggestions as to the contributions of conditioning, imitation, reinforcement, practice, feedback information, expansion and learning by analogy, have been explored in Chapter 2, where it was seen that both experimental and observational evidence suggested that all might play a part in various ways, but that not one particular mechanism could be shown to be necessarily used in natural language learning. The only requirements seem to be that the child should not suffer severe mental handicap and should be able to share his experience of life with at least one person who is willing and able to communicate with him as he attempts to use his vocalisations and make sense of the spoken forms he hears.

Some important requirements of learning processes should be considered, however. First there should be those that relate the form and function of speech data in such a way that sensible interpretations are made. In this respect those accounts of learning that associate speech sounds reliably with some aspects of meaning have something to offer. Although it is not satisfactory as it stands, the basic paradigm of classical conditioning is not entirely inappropriate as a description of the acquisition of the first words. (For various accounts of classical conditioning in acquisition the reader might consult Mowrer (1958), Stemmer (1971) and Staats (1968, 1971).) Essentially it requires that the child hears the sound patterning of the word at the same time as he is attending to relevant aspects of the circumstances in which it is used, so that he comes to reliably associate the sound pattern with attention to those aspects. As it is frequently described the paradigm simply relates a seen object to a felt emotion or image which is then associated with the heard word. But this is too simple, and although Stemmer, for example, laid great stress upon the fact that neither the object nor the word are perceived identically on each occasion, and allowed a degree of perceived similarity in the child's experience, this was a long way from the more complex accounts of Waterson on the sound patterns of early words and Piaget on the structure of early object schemata. Yet a combination of all these three approaches would be a very powerful explanatory account of early word comprehension. It is perhaps important to make the point at this stage that if a conditioning paradigm is adopted the unconditional response associated with a heard word is not as simple as a knee jerk or salivation, but is nevertheless an activity pattern. It is the child's perceptual-motor activity, as it is organised at the time of hearing the word. The meaning that accumulates in memory is compounded from all instances, so that common aspects are strongest, but there is no simple association of a word with an object referent. The child will respond appropriately to the word because he has learned something of its use, though his usage may not be quite what adults expect or intend! A final important point to make is that, as in conditioning experiments, the learning process only takes place if the unconditional response (child's activity pattern) is reliably related to the unconditional stimulus (referent) as a knee jerk is to a hammer blow, and if conditions are such that the association can be reliably made with the conditioning stimulus (spoken word). In experiments this is achieved by deliberate exclusion of other stimulation. In children's word learning it can only be achieved when the child's attention is directed in such a way that other stimulation is effectively excluded. Parents are very good directors of attention! It does not seem that this kind of learning is important for long, however, for children seem to become aware of the process in such a way that they can deliberately make associations after only one experience and then act as though comprehension is immediate. Their vocabulary grows more rapidly, though further experience refines their interpretations as revealed in their responses.

Stemmer argued that it is because children learn the functional meaning of words that they are able to comprehend sentences that they have never previously heard. He claimed that the child who had comprehended *Mummy holds the train,* and also knew *Daddy* was functionally similar to *Mummy* (as persons) and *train* to *ball* (as toys), would be able to comprehend the novel sentence *Daddy holds the ball*. This argument presupposed an ability to classify heard words according to a categorisation of the kinds of experience with which they were associated, and here it is revealing that young children appear to categorise words appropriately if given clues as to their function. Brown (1957) found them able to respond as though they used noun, verb and adjective categories when given new words (nonsense syllables) to represent objects, actions or qualities that were shown in simple pictures. It is even more interesting that so many early words fulfil more than one function, yet this seems no problem to the child. It is not easy to select monosyllabic words with only one possible meaning from a list of words commonly found in the vocabulary of young children. While a given written form might have more than one meaning, there is also frequently a homonym to confuse the picture as in *ball* and *bawl*. Moreover the different meanings of a word might establish it as either a noun or a verb, as is the case with *throw* and *bat*. It is difficult to see how children could learn their language if they were only equipped with the ability to make some kind of formal comparisons as distinct from the ability to relate spoken acts to the structure of events as they perceive them. Stemmer did not press the argument any further, and the question of comprehension of more complex discriminations and structures was not raised. Yet in principle it would seem likely that the comprehension shown by the two to three year old could be explained in these terms and that functional similarity might be the basis for learning realisation rules.

Explanation of learning the regularities of language is a second major requirement. Braine (1971) attempted to describe how the child might learn the structuring of remarks, though he based his model on an assumed ability to recognise words. He postulated a rule-discovery procedure which depended on three major operations : scanning, storing and recognising. First, heard remarks were to be scanned for pattern properties. These were then passed on to a first-stage memory store, and to subsequent stages of storage as they were reinforced by new instances, until finally they were confirmed enough to be stored permanently. If, however, they were not reinforced they were subject to decay. Thus 'deviant' properties would be lost and the most frequent patterns most strongly learned. As patterns became confirmed this 'knowledge' could automatically be used to facilitate the scanning process by incorporating a recognition procedure which would allow well learned patterning to be scanned quickly and novel features to be noticed so that they, too, were learned.

These suggestions have essentially been included in the discovery model in Figure 7.3 and several points about it are worth mentioning. First, they can apply to both word-sound and word-order learning, so that any structural feature of the heard remark is open to an appropriate scanner, and the understanding of words and of remark patterns can proceed together. This is what in fact happens in early acquisition. Second, the input is any adult remark or fragment of that remark as heard by the child, thus scanning will proceed in the temporal order of the utterance of a remark, but may sample only certain aspects, notably those already known and those that additionally catch the attention. The relations between units of speech are therefore likely to be mapped to the order in which they are perceived. Third, the scanner is soon able to identify appropriate units of heard speech.

At first only word-sound patterns are likely to be processed, as exemplified by Lewis and Waterson, but, with a few of these in store, the pattern of any adult remark that is noticed as containing more than one will also be stored, and the child will begin to show comprehension of more of the adult's speech. A requirement only hinted at by Braine would be that, with each scanning, 'meaning' from experience of the situation would be imposed and at intermediate storage levels partial comprehension would be evinced, while at permanent levels more certain interpretation would take place. The whole process would be subject to recognition of the functional value of the perceived parts of the heard remark. Thus no pattern would actually be stored as *word* or *word + word*. At first direct storage of fragments like *Daddy (is) com(ing), Mummy (is) com(ing), Daddy('s) car, Daddy (is reading his) book,* etc., would be likely, but each would be nested in other stored knowledge of the context. This would ensure the development of some sort of categorisation such that *Daddy* and *Mummy* would be interpreted as persons who could do such things as *come,* and *Daddy* would also be a person who possessed things, and could act on objects. With such a learning process perceived sound patterns would be conveyers of spoken information, and both word patterns and between-word discriminations would be learned hand in hand. There would be no temptation in viewing learning in this way to conceive of separately acquired systems of phonology, syntax and semantics. Nor would it be necessary to imply that interpretation or production rested on a mental filing system of words which could readily evoke others from the same functional category. Unless the context of use called out two such items, a heard word would be more likely to call up another from a different, but functionally related category, for the earliest storage of associations would be of those encountered in use.

Essentially learning would amount to the storing of possible orderings of functional categories expressing their relations as they are perceived and comprehended in adult speech. While this would tend to reflect the orders and frequencies of use in material speech in particular, the possibility of storing other orders was not ruled out. In English one would predict that it would be very likely that the child would acquire comprehension rules of the *agent + action, agent + object, operation + object, possessor + object, indicator + object, qualifier + object* and *object + qualifier* types. Note that the latter two allow essentially the same relation in reverse. This is because sentences the child hears are very likely to include both forms, as in *That boy's naughty* and *That's a naughty boy*. Eventually, as pattern recognition of two-word forms became well learned and attention could be given to longer spans of adult speech, it would be likely that some reorganisation of stored patterns would occur. Thus the combination of *agent + object* and *operation + object* would yield *agent + operation + object,* being the only rule that combined both the others while retaining both category order and category relations. Realisation rules derived in this way would, of course, be associated with expectancies in child behaviour. The more a rule were confirmed the stronger would be his reliance on interpretation made in conformity with it. Yet interestingly enough there is also an inbuilt readiness to accept possibilities that the heard order of words may map two different relations, and that two different heard orders may map very similar relations. The child 'knows' that *Daddy + car* may be interpreted as *Daddy's car* or *Daddy is in the car* or *Daddy wants the car,* and he also knows that *(That's) Daddy's car* and *(The) car (is) Daddy's* are functionally almost equivalent. There is thus from the start a readiness to utilise the phrasing of heard remarks to impose meaning by direct mapping and by alternative or transformation rules.

It is not difficult to see that Braine was able to account for the gradual expansion of comprehension to include features of full phrases in the surface order of a sentence. This was essentially accomplished by arguing that well established learning of some categories and relations allowed the scanner more scope for identifying further elements in the heard remark. One would wish to add to Braine's account the requirement that the child was in a position to grasp the functional relations involved in the acquisition of such new elements as articles, auxiliaries and tense markers.

The account would essentially suggest that the child acquired the various patterns independently, rather than in any particularly systematic way. Yet for each new marker, given that its function were grasped, only a few instances would be required to confirm its use, and, given the relative frequency of these items in adult speech, rapid acquisition could be expected. One would expect some difficulty with irregular forms, but in time they too would be confirmed. There is no rejection device in Braine's model, so all the instances are treated as positive examples of speech, apparent alternatives being learned together unless one drops out through lack of support. This would seem to agree very well with what can be discerned of children's expectancies that they will be dealt appropriate and meaningful examples.

It might be objected at this point that the child might well have acquired some functional knowledge of language and understood some of its regularities of form, but this is no account of the acquisition of syntax. This is not how the child learns grammatical creativity and what are and are not acceptable forms in his language. One can only answer, 'Quite so!' The three year old shows very little evidence of understanding beyond the level of systematically interpreting the ordered functional categories and markers of relatively simple utterances, with a best guess and check (or not, as the case may be) when he encounters novel items. What is more, if one treats him to non-examples of vocabulary, as in nonsense syllable experiments, he happily obliges by treating them as new words. And if one treats him to non-examples of grammatical remarks he simply regards them as further positive instances, storing them temporarily as unconfirmed examples and making the best sense he can out of them. He might not even perceive them as different from well learned instances!

Little has been said of other learning processes that have from time to time been suggested for natural language acquisition. This is primarily because they tend to reinforce production rather than comprehension, and the latter has been taken to be the more true indicator of competence, particularly in the case of evaluation models of acquisition. Nevertheless if one takes the discovery model seriously then certain processes, while perhaps not necessary, may well contribute to acquisition, if only because in a very important way the child's own remarks relate within himself his comprehension of productions made in a context whose meaning he knows.

Some relevant ways of learning to talk rather than comprehend were discussed in Chapter 2. Practice increases the heard input for the child, so his productions reinforce his learning. If practice includes the use of realisation rules on items not previously so associated, it will enlarge his knowledge. Weir (1962) was inclined to this view of practice after studying her child's crib monologue, and Jonathan's ways of organising his remarks in relation to his activity suggested that this was an important part of reinforcing and developing learning of both remark structure and the organisation of remark sequences or themes. Whereas practice may be indulged both in monologue and dialogue, a related process, imitation, is a kind of social interaction. Its most significant use would seem to be to extend knowledge by confirming additional, previously unnoticed elements of the input in situations where they are perceived to be possibly functional. This would allow sufficient learning for the likelihood of functional association to take place in later hearing. Imitation is particuarly useful in the acquisition of the sound patterns of words and remarks, but it seems to be more effective though less perfect if initiated by the child as a means of discovery, than if required out of context by parents or experimenters. Perhaps the most important method of learning that could be involved in production is the feedback information obtained from adults. Whereas in comprehension there is no clear learning what is not allowed in the patterning of utterances, the possibility always exists in production. At first, realisation rules that yield inappropriate phrase orders tend to be corrected. Thus in English an object-action-agent order would tend to elicit an adult correction because the truth value would not be thought correct. Later, when the child is past three years old there is more correction of errors in marking and agreement rules. Thus, production, simply because it lays open to communal inspection the child's learning of the realisation rules of the community, is an important feature of language learning.

Beyond this early level of learning the acquisition of abstract vocabulary and relational terms serves to emphasise the importance of seeing language learning set not only in the child's experience of the use of speech but also in his developing powers of thought. In the sense in which *abstract* is being used here one is thinking of words for which there is no direct mapping from experience in the world to use of the word. The transition in the

Stanford–Binet vocabulary scale from words such as *orange, envelope* and *puddle,* to *haste* and *skill* illustrates what is meant. The first three quoted can be defined by reference to actual objects, and even by pointing if necessary, but the latter two require a verbal definition which, if it is to refer to observables, must require a complex sentence that accounts for word derivation implicitly or explicitly in terms of human thinking. It was suggested in Chapter 4 that phrases such as *in his hurry* might require description involving transformation rules for the conversion of verb to noun forms, and it can now be seen that such rules, while not accounting for the actual acquisition of the ability to use these forms, nevertheless indicate that something more than concrete thinking is required. The mapping from non-verbal knowledge to speech is more complex, and both the knowledge and the speech require fuller specification. It is, of course, when this level of knowledge is reached that language becomes an even more efficient coding of thought, facilitating thinking in that complex thoughts can be expressed in economical phrases. But probably everyone has experienced at some time the feeling that an expression is incomprehensible, and has required a fuller exposition in terms of words more directly related to the observables of experience.

It is appropriate at this point to emphasise again a point that was made in the introductory chapter, namely that interest in the functions of speech must inevitably lead to a close relationship in research between the studies of language and thought. The reader who is particularly interested is referred not only to the work mentioned there but also to that of Sinclair de Zwart (1969), who explored the growth of comprehension of terms of comparison in relation to the development of thought in children of five to seven years; to that of Donaldson and Balfour (1968), who found children of three to four years confusing the use of *less* and *more,* and to that of Clark (1971), who studied children's problems in understanding and using the terms *before* and *after.* A paper by Macnamara (1972) gives a very full discussion of the cognitive basis of language learning in younger children.

But mapping the sense of experience into speech rests in effective communication, and the importance of early communication patterns in infancy cannot be over-emphasised. It was clear in Chapter 2 that pre-verbal experience laid the foundations for the incorporation of utterances as meaningful acts into these patterns, that shared verbal experience was rooted in shared non-verbal. Schaffer (1971) has emphasised the patterning involved in early social interaction, paying particular attention to the infant's demonstrated capacities and the mother's sensitivity to these at any particular age. He has pointed out how the infant's gain in control of the timing of his actions allows the development of true 'dialogue' in play. Gregory (1973), Gray (1973) and others under the guidance of Newson (1973) have explored in some detail the emergence of various patterns of infant action in play with mothers, who quite naturally demonstrate intuitive combinations of guidance and understanding responsiveness to infants' strategies. Both Newson and Schaffer were impressed by the 'quite massive' amount of guidance given to infants in the course of ordinary care, leading them to behave in quite detailed ways according to the conventions of the parent community. Pre-verbal experience of the learning of shared expectancies and patterning would seem to contribute considerably to the prior knowledge needed by children in order to learn to talk, but it has been entirely ignored by many whose concern to account for language acquisition has led them to see the language itself as the only source of information about speech construction.

It is because language is learned in the context of effective social interaction that the emphasis in the first chapters on the interpretation of children's remarks prior to their description was made so strongly. Nothing can be said about children's learning unless what has been learned can be specified, and in the case of speech it is particularly clear that such a specification rests on interpretation. Even to label an utterance as a word is an interpretative act. To go further is quite clearly so. Interpretation, however is a complex activity which does not rest only on the form of an utterance, and certainly is not accounted for by an abstract knowledge of a deep grammatical structure. It rests in part on additional situational information and in part on prior knowledge of the speaker's speech habits. Implication is also involved, for more than is verbally represented may be construed with justification. This is not only true of ambiguous remarks; it is true of much of what we say, and in particular of our understanding of the fragmentary remarks of young children. We may supplement from our experience, but in so doing we need not infer that the children present deleted forms, merely that what they say is for them appropriate. Mutual understanding at any level of communication does not necessarily imply identity of intention and interpretation, and therefore a common deep structure, but a sufficient knowledge of how each makes the form of language function. Two recent approaches to functional analysis which have attempted a finer examination than previous work are those of Halliday (1971) and Wells (1973). Halliday recognised different major functions such as the instrumental, regulatory and social interactional in the speech of a nineteen month old child, and saw, within these, subordinate aspects of function such as the kinds of objective sought, the kinds of performance required, and the kinds of social relationship expressed or needed. Wells adopted a detailed classification of remarks of children between one and four years, examples of such categories being expressions of a state of affairs, of change in an object, of an agent causing change, of an instrument causing change and of both an agent and an instrument being involved in change. Each category could be subdivided into expressions of existence of a state of affairs, of equation, of attribution of some characteristic, of experience, of location, of possession and of benefaction. This scheme bars even finer sub-categorisation and is very like the kind of analysis proposed earlier in this book as the outcome of the study of Jonathan's speech. Wells has begun to use it and is finding developmental trends in the adoption and use of various expressions.

The use of functional explanations of the forms of behaviour has often been avoided lest it should seem that the consequence of an event is being described as its cause, like saying that a bird has wings because it flies. Yet such a fear is groundless if one is explaining the forms of man-made systems. The shape of a house is determined predominantly by the functions it is intended to serve, by the artistry of the designer and only marginally by the physical properties of the materials. Similarly the forms of language are determined predominantly by their function. Instead of seeking explanations in terms of external influences on a passively reacting child by looking at conditioning processes, or in terms of internal abstract characteristics of man, pre-programming him biologically or mentally like some hapless Sputnik or Apollo, it is necessary to do full justice to his creative and constructive potential as a planner and thinker working in conjunction with his fellows.

Undoubtedly the critic who seeks a neat and adequate account of how children come to be competent speakers of their native tongue will find too many loose ends in this discussion of explanation in terms of learning. But it is possible that he might have been persuaded that the various forms of the hypothesis of innate competence also look ragged and inadequate, if not downright inappropriate. Perhaps, too, he will at least agree that, in the pursuit of knowledge of how children acquire language, examination of the constructive nature of how they make forms of speech function to some purpose is a worthwhile activity. Both the children who were mentioned at the beginning of this book spoke truly. One was referring to the outcome of all the construction done during almost ten years of life, while the other was referring to an awareness that information had been gleaned from observation and communication with others. The reader will be happy to know that, unlike Chomsky and Skinner, they did not fall out. They started asking questions, for their remarks were not the final word but only a beginning.

Appendix A
Samples of Jonathan's Speech

(I=imperative N=negative, Q=interrogative)

1. MONOLOGUE AT 2 YEARS 7 MONTHS, PLAYING WITH CHESSMEN, A CAR AND A WOODEN TRAIN

Remark	Adult equivalent	Notes
Man gone a bye-byes	The man has gone to bye-byes	
Play chessmens	I am playing with chessmen	
Look a train going	Look, a train is going (I)	
Look big full	Look, a big truck-full (I)	Full of chessmen
Two goings in dere	Two are going in there	Putting two in another truck
Train-train going	The train is going	
Man go waket up	The man is going to waken up	
Train-train going	The train is going	
It going like this	It is going like this	
Who's done dis a car?	Who has done this to the car? (Q)	Examining car which has a piece broken off
Bloke?	Is it broken? (Q)	
A bloke on a car	A 'break' is on the car	
Car-car on a train	The car is on the train	Having placed it
Pull my train	I am pulling my train	
Who done dis a my train?	Who has done this to my train? (Q)	Finding a piece of wool on train
Come off again	It has come off again	
Train-train going	The train is going	
Where's a box?	Where's the box?	Reaching for it
Put it in a box	I am putting it in the box	

2. SOCIAL MONOLOGUE AT 2 YEARS 7 MONTHS, PLAYING WITH MODELLING CLAY IN PARALLEL

Remark	*Adult equivalent*	*Notes*
Watch this Wilwe	Watch this, Hilary (I)	
Two going downs	Two are going down	Two clay balls down a slope
I got a lulu Wilwe	I've got a lulu, Hilary	Lulu is clay ball
I can't make a lulu	I can't make a lulu (N)	
Hey! Wilwe make a lulu	Hey! Hilary has made a lulu	Commenting on her achievement
Watch dis Wilwe	Watch this Hilary (I)	
Lots an lots an lots	Lots and lots and lots	Looking at pile of clay
Dere's sun over dere	There's the sun over there	Looking through the window
Play modelling-play	Play modelling-play (I)	Telling self to play again
Car-car go	The car is going	Pushing empty lorry
Car-car go	The car is going	
On dere	On there	Loading lorry with clay balls
Look at me make, Wilwe	Look at what I am making, Hilary (I)	
I do lots more modelling-play	I am doing a lot more modelling-play	
Put my lulu on dere	I am putting my lulu on there	
Lots an lots an lots	Lots and lots and lots	
Gone up dere	It has gone up there	Second layer of load
Lots an lots a modelling-plays	Lots and lots of modelling-play	
Mine din-dom	Mine has gone	Pile used up
Look a me made	Look what I've made (I)	

3. DIALOGUE AT 2 YEARS 7 MONTHS, SORTING TOYS, SHARED ACTIVITY

Remark	*Adult equivalent*	*Notes*
Dere's a green	There's a green one	Green brick
Dat's mine	That's mine	
No	No (N)	
Dat's your baby	That's your baby	Doll
Dis	This	
Dis mine	This is mine	
Dat your box	That's your box	
It's yours	It's yours	

Remark	Adult equivalent	Notes
It's your box	It's your box	
Dere's a horsie	There's a horsie	In picture-book
I been on a horsie, Wilwe	I've been on a horsie, Hilary	Reference to rocking-horse, moving towards
I going on a horsie	I'm going on a horsie	it in next room but changing mind
Going round and round, faster faster	It's going round and round, faster and faster	Playing with top
What's dat?	What's that? (Q)	
It's mine	It's mine	
Dat Andrew's	That's Andrew's	
Play rollies Wilwe	Let's play rollies, Hilary (I)	Playing with circular pouffe
I go round a corner	I'm going round a corner	

4. MONOLOGUE AT 2 YEARS 10 MONTHS, PLAYING WITH TOY CARS, ALONE

Remark	Adult equivalent	Notes
Dese car-cars not in the sea	These cars are not in the sea (N)	Pretending carpet is sea
They're on a boat	They're on a boat	Boat is toy cot
See car-car turning wheels	See, the car has turning wheels (I)	
I know where's a car-car	I know where there's a car	Looking for another
Car-car go in a water-splash	The car is going in a wave	Intention
Ready, steady, go!	Ready, steady, go! (I)	Pushes car
Dat one is in a water-splash	That one is in a wave	
Dat racing-car not wet	That racing-car is not wet (N)	Another car
Dis was my box with crayons in	This was my box with crayons in it	Finding crayon box on floor
I draw a J	I drew a J	Recall
And a red one	And a red one	Noting a crayon
Open dis boot	Open this boot (I)	Returning to car instructing self
That will go down	That will go down	Car down slope
Put that roadway up dere	Put that roadway up there (I)	Self-instruction
Dat police-car will go this way	That police-car will go this way	Intends to move car

5. SOCIAL MONOLOGUE AT 2 YEARS 10 MONTHS, PARALLEL PLAY, EACH WITH OWN CHESSMEN

Remark	Adult equivalent	Notes
Yes, I find it	Yes, I'll find it	Searching for a chess piece
It's in the lounge	It's in the lounge	
It's under here	It's under here	
I have this one	I'm having this one	
Where's the black king?	Where's the black king? (Q)	
A king again	A king again	Another king
The king a witch	The king is a witch	
Another coming down	Another is coming down	Inclined box lid
Dey not Keren's chessmen	They are not Keren's chessmen (N)	Witch play copied from Keren
Dey mine chessmen in dere	They are mine, the chessmen in there	
See baby coming up	See a baby coming up (I)	Baby is a pawn
See horsie coming up	See a horsie coming up (I)	Horsie is a knight
Dat one	That one	Hilary provides toy cots to share
My baby go in dat one	My baby is going in that one	
Put dis on dere	I am putting this on there	Filling cot with chessmen
I got your cot	I've got your cot	
I dropped one	I've dropped one	Tilts cot, one falls
Dey not falling	They are not falling (N)	
See-saw	See-saw	Tilting cot
One fall down	One fell down	Another falls
Ah! Dere's a black king	Ah! There's a black king	
Ah! Dere it is	Ah! There it is	
See it skidding Hilary	See it skidding, Hilary (I)	
And another black one	And another black one	More falling
See dose coming	See those coming (I)	
And another one	And another one	
Two babies coming	Two babies are coming	Here Hilary changes her game
See dat	See that (I)	
I going to get all of them	I'm going to get all of them	
See king coming	See the king coming (I)	

Remark	Adult equivalent	Notes
I not playing that chessmen	I'm not playing that game (N)	Decides to change game
I not playing with my chessmens	I'm not playing with my chessmen (N)	
No I not	No, I'm not (N)	

6. DIALOGUE AT 2 YEARS 10 MONTHS, SHARING PLAY, CARING FOR BABY DOLL

Remark	Adult equivalent	Notes
I haven't got any soups	I haven't got any soups (N)	Pots of soup
I got some soups	I've got some soups	Pretending soup is in
I got some more soups	I've got some more soups	toy tea-pots
Where's a baby?	Where's the baby? (Q)	Searching for doll under covers
I can't see him	I can't see him (N)	
Dere's baby	There's baby	
You got soup on hair	You've got soup on your hair	Talking to doll
I go upstairs	I'll go upstairs	Intention
I get some more soups	I'll get some more soups	
I want a white cup	I want a white cup	
He's not crying now	He's not crying now (N)	
Baby won't put a legs down	Baby won't put his legs down (N)	
Put hands down	I am putting his hands down	
Baby not crying	Baby's not crying (N)	
Gone fast asleep	He's gone fast asleep	
Dere's anuver cover	There's another cover	
He's not crying now	He's not crying now (N)	
Dere's eyes	There are his eyes	Examining doll's eyes—Hilary
I can't spoil them	I can't spoil them (N)	remonstrates
I better have anuver cup	I had better have another cup	
Lots and lots of cups	Lots and lots of cups	
I fetch anuver one	I've fetched another one	Action complete
I like dat baby	I like that baby	
You like dat baby, Hilary	You like that baby, Hilary	
Hey! Baby dressed	Hey! Baby's dressed	
Baby cold	Baby's cold	
She want to go to bed	She wants to go to bed	Change of pronoun

Remark	Adult equivalent	Notes
See he haven't got teeth in there	See, he hasn't got teeth in there (I, N)	Examining mouth
Put his leggies down	I am putting his leggies down	
Baby has got toe-toes	Baby has got toe-toes	
Where's anuver cover?	Where's another cover? (Q)	Putting doll to sleep again, and demonstrating tucking in
I put dis like dat, Hilary	I am putting this like that, Hilary	

Appendix B
The Model Stories

(1). Busybody was always knitting. She knitted in the shops, she knitted in the street, and some people even said she knitted in the bath.

One day as Busybody walked along the High Street knitting busily, she saw something very strange. A boot was hanging out of Teddy's window on a piece of string. Busybody stopped and stared at the boot, but she couldn't think what it was doing there. It worried her so much that she just had to find out why it was there.

'I'll ask Teddy,' she said, and she banged very hard on his front door.

Now because Teddy happened to be having a bath, he didn't answer the door, but that didn't stop Busybody. She opened the door and walked right in. She was so anxious to find out about the boot that she didn't notice when she dropped her knitting on the doorstep. Now Busybody kept her ball of wool in her pocket when she was knitting, and when she walked into Teddy's house she left a trail of wool behind her. She could hear Teddy singing in his bath while she went straight upstairs and crept into his bedroom where the boot was hanging out of the window. But the boot couldn't tell her anything.

Then Teddy came out of the bathroom, tripped over the trail of wool and fell downstairs. Busybody ran towards him.

'I wanted to know why that boot is hanging out of your window' she said.

Teddy was very angry. He picked himself up. 'I dropped it in the bath, so I hung it out to dry' he snapped, as he rubbed his elbow and nose. 'And mind your own business.'

Busybody ran out of the house without even saying she was sorry. But when she saw her knitting it was all undone and the wool was tangled. She must have wished she hadn't been such a busybody.

(2) One day Kanga met Jumbo, the elephant, in the High Street of Cuddly Town. Usually Jumbo was very cheerful, but this morning he looked so unhappy that Kanga felt quite worried about him.

'What's the matter, Jumbo?' she asked.
Jumbo sniffed,
'I've got to have a tooth out,' he said.

Nobody likes having teeth out, of course, and Kanga knew that. But if you have magic teeth it's rather exciting, and that's what she told him.

'I know someone who always says his teeth are magic', she said, 'because when he has one out he puts it under his pillow at night, and next morning it has turned into a sixpence.'

Jumbo's face brightened when Kanga told him that.

'How do you know if your teeth are magic?' he asked.

Kanga smiled and said, 'You just have to try it and see.'

Jumbo felt very excited as he hurried into the dentist's and he asked for the tooth as soon as it was out. He carried it home in his pocket, wishing it was time for bed.

He waited all day long for bedtime, and as soon as he had eaten his tea he ran upstairs and got into bed. Then he put the tooth under his pillow, just as Kanga had told him.

A little later Kanga called to see if Jumbo had remembered his tooth. She went upstairs, but he was fast asleep. The tooth was under his pillow when she looked, so she crept downstairs and out of the house as quietly as a mouse.

The very first thing Jumbo did when he woke the next morning was to look under his pillow. There wasn't a sign of his tooth, but exactly where he had put it was a bright, shiny sixpence. He was so pleased he went straight to Kanga's house to tell her all about it.

(3). Wonky, the donkey, was always late. He never seemed to get anywhere in time. When Teddy asked him to his birthday party Wonky felt very worried about it because he thought he would be late and get there just as the party was ending.

'I won't be late,' Wonky told himself, and he tied a knot in his tail to remind himself to be early. But he worried so much that he couldn't sleep very well and he woke up late in the morning. He was surprised when he saw the clock. It was nine o'clock. He was supposed to start work at six o'clock, pulling the milk-cart for the milkman. Now he was sure to be late all day; he would be late getting to work and then late going to the party.

He jumped out of bed and ran downstairs and out of the house like an express train. The milkman couldn't understand what was the matter with Wonky. He rushed round Cuddly Town like a racehorse, and he broke so many bottles that they had to go back for another load.

When he had finished work it was so late that Wonky didn't think he would go to the party. He thought he couldn't be in time for it. But he did go. First he ran home and brushed his face and untied the knot in his tail. Then he ran down the road and knocked on Teddy's door.

'I have come to the party', he panted, when Teddy opened the door. Teddy stared at him, so hard that Wonky was sure the party must have ended, but then Teddy began to laugh.

'You're too early, Wonky', he said. 'The party is tomorrow.'

Wonky did feel silly. He had worried so much about being late that he had forgotten when the party was.

(4). Koo lived in a soft, furry pocket underneath Kanga's pinafore. It was warm in Kanga's pocket, and every night Koo climbed into it and went to sleep curled up in a little ball.

But one night when Koo climbed into Kanga's pocket to go to bed he took some biscuits with him. Now Koo knew very well he wasn't allowed to take biscuits to bed, but Kanga was reading the newspaper when he climbed into her pocket, so he thought she wouldn't notice.

Koo had a lovely time eating the biscuits. He crunched and munched them for nearly an hour, and it wasn't until he'd eaten the very last one that he realised that Kanga's pocket was almost full of crumbs. In fact, there wasn't really room for Koo at all.

'Crumbs,' said Koo. 'What shall I do?' He couldn't throw them out of the pocket or Kanga would see them, so he had to leave them where they were. He tried to curl up in a little ball as usual, but he couldn't do that because there wasn't room.

So he just sat on top of the crumbs with his feet and his head sticking out in the cold. He felt very unhappy because his nose and toes were very cold, and he was so uncomfortable sitting on the crumbs that he couldn't sleep at all.

Koo stayed awake all night, and in the morning he had caught a cold. He sneezed and sneezed, and every time he sneezed he blew a shower of crumbs into Kanga's face. An that's what woke her in the end.

She was cross when she saw all the crumbs that were in Koo's bed. They had an awful job cleaning the pocket, and Kanga had to stand on her head in the bath for nearly half an hour while Koo brushed the crumbs out. Of course, Koo was very sorry about the crumbs, and he promised he would never eat biscuits in bed again.

Analysis of stories

Story	No. of words	No. of sentences	No. of unit sentences
1	334	28	65
2	315	29	67
3	314	27	65
4	341	29	68
mean	326	28	66

References

ANISFELD, M. and TUCKER, G. R. (1967), 'English pluralisation rules of six-year-old children.' *Child Development,* **38**, 1201–1217.

ANNETT, J. (1969), *Feedback and Human Behaviour.* Penguin, Harmondsworth.

BANNISTER, D. and FRANSELLA, F. (1971), *Inquiring Man.* Penguin, Harmondsworth.

BARTLETT, F. C. (1932), *Remembering.* Cambridge University Press, Cambridge.

BERGER, K. (1967), 'The most common words used in conversations.' *Journal of Communication Disorders,* **1**, 201–214.

BERKO, J. (1958), 'The child's learning of English morphology.' *Word,* **14**, 150–177.

BERLYNE, D. E. and FROMMER, F. D. (1966), 'Some determinants of the incidence and content of children's questions.' *Child Development,* **37**, 177–189.

BERNSTEIN, B. (1972), 'Social class, language and socialisation.' In P.P. Giglioli (ed.), *Language and Social Context.* Penguin, Harmondsworth.

BLOOM, L. (1970), *Language Development: Form and Function in Emergent Grammars,* M.I.T. Press, Cambridge, Mass.

BOWER, T. G. R. and PATERSON, J. G. (1972), 'Stages in the development of the object concept.' *Cognition,* **1**, 47–55.

BOWERMAN, M. F. (1969), 'The pivot-open distinction.' Unpublished paper. Harvard University.

BRAINE, M. D. S. (1963a), 'The ontogeny of English phrase structure: the first phase.' *Language,* **39**, 1–13.

BRAINE, M. D. S. (1963b), 'On learning the grammatical order of words.' *Psychological Review,* **70**, 323–348.

BRAINE, M. D. S. (1970), 'The acquisition of language in infant and child.' In C. Reed (ed.), *The Learning of Language: Essays in honor of David H. Russell.* Appleton-Century-Crofts, New York.

BRAINE, M. D. S. (1971), 'On two types of models of the internalisation of grammars.' In D. I. Slobin (ed.), *The Ontogenesis of Grammar.* Academic Press, New York.

BROADBENT, D. E. (1970), 'In defence of empirical psychology.' *Bulletin of the British Psychological Society,* **23**, 87–96.

BRODBECK, A. J. and IRWIN, O. C. (1946), 'The speech behavior of infants without families.' *Child Development,* **17**, 145–156.

BROWN, R. W. (1957), 'Linguistic determinism and the part of speech.' *Journal of Abnormal and Social Psychology,* **55**, 1–5.

BROWN, R. W. (1968), 'The development of *wh* questions in child speech.' *Journal of Verbal Learning and Verbal Behavior,* **7**, 279–290.

BROWN, R. and BELLUGI, U. (1964), 'Three processes in the child's acquisition of syntax.' In E. H. Lenneberg (ed.), *New Directions in the Study of Language.* M.I.T. Press, Cambridge, Mass.

BROWN, R. W. and BERKO, J. (1960), 'Word association and the acquisition of grammar.' *Child Development,* **31**, 1–14.

BROWN, R., CAZDEN, C. B. and BELLUGI, U. (1969), 'The child's grammar from I to III.' In J. P. Hill (ed.), *1967 Minnesota Symposia on Child Psychology.* University of Minnesota Press, Minneapolis.

BROWN, R. W. and FRASER, C. (1963), 'The acquisition of syntax.' In C. N. Cofer and B. S. Musgrave (eds.), *Verbal Behaviour and Learning.* McGraw-Hill, New York.

BROWN, R. and HANLON, C. (1970), 'Derivational complexity and order of acquisition in child speech.' In J. R. Hayes (ed.), *Cognition and the Development of Language.* Wiley, New York.

BRUCE, D. J. (1964), 'The analysis of word sounds by young children.' *British Journal of Educational Psychology,* **34**, 158–170.

BRUNER, J. S. (1964), 'The course of cognitive growth.' *American Psychologist, 19,* 1–15.

BRUNER, J. S., OLVER, R. R. and GREENFIELD, P. M. (1966), *Studies in Cognitive Growth.* Wiley, New York.

BURROUGHS, G. E. R. (1957), 'A study of vocabulary of young children.' *Educational Monograph No. 1, University of Birmingham Institute of Education.* Oliver & Boyd, Edinburgh.

CAZDEN, C. B. (1972), *Child Language and Education.* Holt, Rinehart & Winston, New York.

CHALL, J. S. (1967), *Learning to Read: the Great Debate.* McGraw-Hill, New York.

CHOMSKY, C. (1971), *The Acquisition of Syntax in Children from 5 to 10.* M.I.T. Press, Cambridge, Mass.

CHOMSKY, N. (1957), *Syntactic Structures.* Mouton, The Hague.

CHOMSKY, N. (1959), 'Review of B. F. Skinner's *"Verbal Behavior".*' *Language,* **35**, 26–58.

CHOMSKY, N. (1964), 'Formal discussion of Miller, W. and Ervin, S. The development of grammar in child language.' In U. Bellugi and R. Brown (eds.), *The Acquisition of Language.* Monograph of the Society for Research in Child Development, **29**, 1.

CHOMSKY, N. (1965), *Aspects of the Theory of Syntax.* M.I.T. Press, Cambridge, Mass.

CHOMSKY, N. (1968), *Language and Mind.* Harcourt Brace Jovanovich, New York.

CLARK, E. V. (1971), 'On the acquisition of the meaning of *before* and *after.*' *Journal of Verbal Learning and Verbal Behavior,* **10**, 266–275.

COWE, E. G. (1967), 'A study of kindergarten activities for language development.' Unpublished doctoral dissertation, School of Education, Columbia University.

DARWIN, C. (1872), *The Expression of the Emotions in Man and Animals.* Murray, London.

DARWIN, C. (1877), 'A biographical sketch of an infant.' *Mind,* **2**, 292–294.

DAVIE, R., BUTLER, N. and GOLDSTEIN, H. (1972), *From Birth to Seven: The second report of the National Child Development Study (1958 cohort).* Longman, London.

DE LAGUNA, G. A. (1927), *Speech: Its Function and Development.* Yale University Press, New Haven.

DEVILLE, G. (1891), 'Notes sur le développement du langage.' *Revue de Linguistique et de Philologie Comparée,* **24**, 10–42, 128–143, 242–257, 300–320.

DONALDSON, M. and BALFOUR, G. (1968), 'Less is more: a study of language comprehension in children.' *British Journal of Psychology,* **59**, 461–471.

DOWNING, J. (1970), 'Children's concepts of language in learning to read.' *Educational Research,* **12**, 106–112.

DOWNING, J. and LATHAM, W. (1969), 'A follow-up of children in the first i.t.a. experiment.' *British Journal of Educational Psychology,* **39**, 303–305.

ENTWISLE, D. R. (1966), 'Form class and children's word associations.' *Journal of Verbal Learning and Verbal Behavior,* **5**, 558–565.

ENTWISLE, D. R., FORSYTH, D. F. and MUUSS, R. (1964), 'The syntagmatic-paradigmatic shift in children's word associations.' *Journal of Verbal Learning and Verbal Behavior,* **3**, 19–29.

ERVIN, S. M. (1961), 'Changes with age in the verbal determinants of word association.' *American Journal of Psychology,* **74**, 361–372.

ERVIN, S. M. (1964), 'Imitation and structural change in children's language.' In E. H. Lenneberg (ed.), *New Directions in the Study of Language.* M.I.T. Press, Cambridge, Mass.

FILLMORE, C. J. (1968), 'The case for case.' In E. Bach and R. T. Harms (eds.), *Universals in Linguistic Theory.* Holt, Rinehart & Winston, London.

FODOR, J. A. and GARRETT, M. (1967), 'Some syntactic determinants of sentential complexity.' *Perception and Psychophysics,* 2, 289–296.

FRANCIS, H. (1969), 'Structure in the speech of a $2\frac{1}{2}$-year-old.' *British Journal of Educational Psychology,* **39**, 291–302.

FRANCIS, H. (1970) 'Linguistic competence and natural language.' *La Linguistique,* **6**, 47–51.

FRANCIS, H. (1972a), 'Sentence structure and learning to read.' *British Journal of Educational Psychology,* **42**, 113–119.

FRANCIS, H. (1972b), 'Toward an explanation of the syntagmatic-paradigmatic shift.' *Child Development,* **43**, 949–958.

FRANCIS, H. (1973), 'Children's experience of reading and notions of units in language.' *British Journal of Educational Psychology,* **43**, 17–23.

FRANCIS, H. (1974a), 'Social class ,reference and context.' *Language and Speech,* **17**, 193–198.

FRANCIS, H. (1974b), 'Social background, speech and learning to read.' *British Journal of Educational Psychology,* **44**, 290–299.

FRASER, C., BELLUGI, U. and BROWN, R. W. (1963), 'Control of grammar in imitation, comprehension and production.' *Journal of Verbal Learning and Verbal Behavior*, **2**, 121–135.

FRIES, C. C. (1962), *Linguistics and Reading*. Holt, Rinehart & Winston, New York.

GIBSON, E. J., OSSER, H. and PICK, A. D. (1963), 'A study of the development of grapheme-phoneme correspondences.' *Journal of Verbal Learning and Verbal Behavior*, **2**, 142–146.

GIBSON, E. J., PICK, A. D., OSSER, H. and HAMMOND, M. (1962), 'The role of grapheme-phoneme correspondence in the perception of words.' *American Journal of Psychology*, **75**, 554–570.

GRAY, H. (1973), 'Communication and reaching for objects.' Paper presented at the annual conference of the Developmental Psychology Section of the British Psychological Society, Nottingham.

GREENBERG, J. H. (1963), 'Some universals of grammar, with particular reference to the order of meaningful elements.' In J. H. Greenberg (ed.), *Universals of Language*. M.I.T. Press, Cambridge, Mass.

GREGORY, S. (1973), 'Learning to discriminate: the learning of meanings.' Paper presented at the annual conference of the Developmental Psychology Section of the British Psychological Society, Nottingham.

GUILLAUME, P. (1926), *Imitation in Children*. (1971 translation of 1968 edition). University of Chicago Press, Chicago.

HALLIDAY, M. A. K. (1971), 'The functional basis of language.' In B. Bernstein (ed.), *Class, Codes and Control: applied studies towards a sociology of language*. Routledge & Kegan Paul, London.

HAWKINS, P. R. (1969), 'Social class, the nominal group and reference.' *Language and Speech*, **12**, 125–135.

HEISENBERG, W. (1958), *Physics and Philosophy*. Harper & Row, N.Y.

HERRIOT, P. (1969), 'The comprehension of tense by young children.' *Child Development*, **40**, 103–110.

HOCKETT, C. F. (1960), 'Analysis of English Spelling.' Mimeographed paper, Cornell University, Ithaca, New York.

HUTTENLOCHER, J. (1964), 'Children's language: word-phrase relationship.' *Science*, **143**, 264–265.

IRWIN, O. C. (1948), 'Infant speech.' *Journal of Speech and Hearing Disorders*, **13**, 224–225, 320–326.

ISAACS, S. (1930), *Intellectual Growth in Young Children*. Routledge, London.

JAKOBSON, R. and HALLE, M. (1956), *Fundamentals of Language*. Mouton, The Hague.

JESPERSON, O. (1922), *Language: Its Nature, Development and Origin*. Allen & Unwin, London.

KATZ, J. J. (1971), 'The philosophical relevance of linguistic theory.' In J. R. Searle (ed.), *The Philosophy of Language*. Oxford University Press, London.

KATZ, J. J. and POSTAL, P. M. (1964), *An Integrated Theory of Linguistic Descriptions*. M.I.T. Press, Cambridge, Mass.

KLIMA, E. S. and BELLUGI, U. (1966), 'Syntactic regularities in the speech of children.' In J. Lyons and R. J. Wales (eds.), *Psycholinguistic Papers*. University Press, Edinburgh.

LADEFOGED, P. and BROADBENT, D. E. (1957), 'Information conveyed by vowels.' *Journal of the Acoustical Society of America*, **29**, 98–104.

LEFEVRE, C. A. (1962), *Linguistics and the Teaching of Reading*. McGraw-Hill, New York.

LENNEBERG, E. H. (1967), *The Biological Foundations of Language*. Wiley, New York.

LEOPOLD, W. F. (1953), 'Patterning in children's language learning.' *Language Learning*, **5**, 1–14.

LEWIS, M. M. (1936), *Infant Speech*. Routledge & Kegan Paul, London.

LEWIS, M. M. (1963), *Language, Thought and Personality in Infancy and Childhood*. Harrap, London.

LIBERMAN, A. M., COOPER, F. S., SHANKWEILER, D. P. and STUDDERT-KENNEDY, M. (1967), 'Perception of the speech code.' *Psychological Review*, **74**, 431–461.

LIPPMAN, M. Z. (1971), 'Correlates of contrast word associations: developmental trends.' *Journal of Verbal Learning and Verbal Behavior*, **10**, 392–399.

LOBAN, W. (1963), *The Language of Elementary School Children*. National Council of Teachers of English, Champaign, Ill.

LURIA, A. R. (1961), *The Role of Speech in the Regulation of Normal and Abnormal Behaviour*. Pergamon, London.

LURIA, A. R. and YUDOVICH, F. I. (1959), *Speech and the Development of Mental Processes in the Child*. Staples Press, London.

McCARTHY, D. A. (1930), *The Language Development of the Pre-School Child*. University of Minnesota Press, Minneapolis.

MacCORQUODALE, K. (1970), 'On Chomsky's review of Skinner's "Verbal Behavior".' *Journal of the Experimental Analysis of Behavior*, **13**, 83–99.

McKINNON, A. R. (1959), *How Do Children Learn to Read?* Copp Clark, Vancouver.

MACNAMARA, J. (1972), 'Cognitive basis of language learning in infants.' *Psychological Review*, **79**, 1–13.

McNEILL, D. (1966a), 'Developmental psycholinguistics.' In F. Smith and G. A Miller (eds.), *The Genesis of Language*. M.I.T. Press, Cambridge, Mass.

McNEILL, D. (1966b), 'A study of word association.' *Journal of Verbal Learning and Verbal Behavior*, **5**, 548–557.

McNEILL, D. (1970), *The Acquisition of Language: the study of developmental psycholinguistics*. Harper Row, New York.

MENYUK, P. (1963), 'Syntactic structures in the language of children.' *Child Development*, **34**, 407–422.

MENYUK, P. (1969), *Sentences Children Use*. M.I.T. Press, Cambridge, Mass.

MILLER, G. A. (1969), 'The organisation of lexical memory: are word associations sufficient?' In G. A. Talland and N. C. Waugh (eds.), *The Pathology of Memory*. Academic Press, New York.

MILLER, G. A., GALANTER, E. and PRIBRAM, K. H. (1960), *Plans and the Structure of Behavior*. Holt, Rinehart and Winston, London.

MILLER, W. and ERVIN, S. (1964), 'The development of grammar in child language.' In U. Bellugi and R. Brown (eds.), *The Acquisition of Language*. Monograph of the Society for Research in Child Development, **29**, No. 1. University of Chicago Press, Chicago.

MORTON, J. (1966), 'Comment in discussion of Wales, R. J. and Marshall, J. C., The organisation of linguistic performance.' In J. Lyons and R. J. Wales (eds.), *Psycholinguistic Papers*. Edinburgh University Press, Edinburgh.

MOWRER, O. H. (1958), 'Hearing and speaking.' *Journal of Speech and Hearing Disorders*, **23**, 143–152.

NEWSON, J. (1973), 'Towards a theory of infant understanding.' Paper presented at the annual conference of the Developmental Psychology Section of the British Psychological Society, Nottingham.

OLVER, R. R. and HORNSBY, J. R. (1966), 'On equivalence.' In J. S. Bruner *et al.* (eds.), *Studies in Cognitive Growth*. Wiley, New York.

OPPENHEIMER, R. (1956), 'Analogy in science.' *American Psychologist*, **11**, 127–135.

PIAGET, J. (1926), *The Language and Thought of the Child*. Routledge & Kegan Paul, London.

PIAGET, J. (1928), *Judgement and Reasoning in the Child*. Routledge & Kegan Paul, London.

PIAGET, J. (1951), *Play, Dreams and Imitation in Childhood*. Routledge & Kegan Paul, London.

PIAGET, J. (1952), *The Child's Conception of Number*. Routledge & Kegan Paul, London.

PIAGET, J. and INHELDER, B. (1966, *The Psychology of the Child*. Routledge & Kegan Paul, London.

REID, J. F. (1966), 'Learning to think about reading.' *Educational Research*, **9**, 56–62.

RHEINGOLD, H. L., GEWIRTZ, J. L. and ROSS, H. W. (1959), 'Social conditioning of vocalisations in the infant.' *Journal of Comparative and Physiological Psychology*, **52**, 68–73.

SCHAFFER, H. R. (1971), *The Growth of Sociability*, Penguin, Harmondsworth,

SCHLESINGER, I. M. (1968), *Sentence Structure and the Reading Process*. Mouton, The Hague.

SCHLESINGER, I. M. (1971a), 'Production of utterances and language acquisition.' In D. I. Slobin (ed.), *The Ontogenesis of Grammar*. Academic Press, New York.

SCHLESINGER, I. M. (1971b), 'The grammar of sign language and the problems of language universals.' In J. Morton (ed.), *Biological and Social Factors in Psycholinguistics*. Logos Press, London.

SIGISMUND, B. (1856), *Kind und Welt*. Brunswick.

SINCLAIR DE ZWART, H. (1967), *Acquisition du Langage et Développement de la Pensée*. Dunod, Paris.

SKINNER, B. F. (1957), *Verbal Behavior*. Appleton-Century-Crofts, New York.

SLOBIN, D. (1965), 'The role of imitation in early language learning.' Paper presented to the Society for Research in Child Development, Minneapolis.

SLOBIN, D. (1966), 'The acquisition of Russian as a native language.' In F. Smith and G. A. Miller (eds.), *The Genesis of Language*. M.I.T. Press, Cambridge, Mass.

SLOBIN, D. (1972), 'Early grammatical development in several languages, with special attention to Soviet research.' In T. G. Bever and W. Weksel (eds.), *The Structure and Psychology of Language*. Holt, Rinehart & Winston, New York.

SMITH, N. (1971), 'Puggles and lellow lollies.' *Listener*, 2nd Dec.

STAATS, A. W. (1968), *Learning, Language and Cognition*. Holt, Rinehart & Winston, New York.

STAATS, A. W. (1971), 'Linguistic-mentalistic theory versus an explanatory S–R learning theory of language development.' In D. I. Slobin (ed.), *The Ontogenesis of Grammar*. Academic Press, New York.

STEMMER, N. (1971), 'Some aspects of language acquisition.' In Y. Bar-Hillel (ed.), *Pragmatics of Natural Languages*. Reidel, Dordrecht.

STERN, C. and GOULD, T. S. (1966), *Children Discover Reading*. Harrap, London.

STERN, C and STERN, W. (1928). *Die Kindersprache*. 4th ed., Barth, Leipzig.

STERN, W. (1914), *Psychology of Early Childhood*. Translated by A. Barwell from the German, 1924. Allen & Unwin, London.

STRANDBERG, T. E. (1969), 'An evaluation of three stimulus media for evoking verbalisations from preschool children.' Unpublished master's thesis, Eastern Illinois University.

STRICKLAND, R. G. (1962), 'The language of elementary schoolchildren.' *Bulletin of the School of Education, Indiana University*, **38**, 1–131.

SULLY, J. (1896), *Studies of Childhood*. Longmans, London.

TAINE, H. (1877), 'Acquisition of language by children.' *Mind*, **2**, 252–259.

TEMPLIN, M. C. (1957), *Certain Language Skills in Children*. University of Minnesota Press, Minneapolis.

TURNER, E. A. and ROMMETVEIT, R. (1967), 'The acquisition of sentence voice and reversibility.' *Child Development*, **38**, 649–660.

VELTEN, H. V. (1943), 'The growth of phonemic and lexical patterns in infant language.' *Language*, **19**, 281–292.

VENEZKY, R. (1962), 'A computer program for deriving spelling-to-sound correlations.' Unpublished master's thesis, Cornell University, Ithaca, New York.

VON BONIN, G. (1962), 'Brain and mind.' In S. Koch (ed.), *Psychology: a study of a science. Vol. 4*. McGraw-Hill, New York.

VYGOTSKY, L. S. (1962), *Thought and Language*. M.I.T. Press, Cambridge, Mass.

WALES, R. J. and MARSHALL, J. C. (1966), 'The organisation of linguistic performance.' In J. Lyons and R. J. Wales (ed.), *Psycholinguistic Papers*. Edinburgh University Press, Edinburgh.

WATERSON, N. (1970), 'Some speech forms of an English child: a phonological study.' *Transactions of the Philological Society.*

WATERSON, N. (1971), 'Child phonology: a prosodic view.' *Journal of Linguistics,* **7**, 179–211.

WATTS, A. F. (1944), *The Language and Mental Development of Children.* Harrap, London.

WEIR, R. (1962), *Language in the Crib.* Mouton, The Hague.

WEIR, R. (1966). 'Some questions on the child's learning of phonology.' In F. Smith and G. A. Miller (eds.), *The Genesis of Language.* M.I.T. Press, Cambridge, Mass.

WELLS, G. (1973), 'A proposal for the analysis of samples of children's spontaneous speech.' Paper presented to the Linguistics Association, March 1973, in Hull.

WOODROW, H. and LOWELL, F. (1916), 'Children's association frequency tables.' *Psychological Monographs,* **22**, No. 97.

Bibliography

ADAMS, P. (1972), *Language in Thinking.* Penguin, Harmondsworth.
BAR-ADON, A. and LEOPOLD, W. F. (1971), *Child Language—a book of readings.* Prentice Hall, Englewood Cliffs.
BELLUGI, U. and BROWN, R. (1964), *The Acquisition of Language.* Monograph of the Society for Research in Child Development. University of Chicago Press, Chicago.
BLOOM, L. (1973), *One Word at a Time.* Mouton, The Hague.
BOWERMAN, M. (1973), *Early Syntactic Development.* The University Press, Cambridge.
BROWN, R. (1956), *Words and Things.* The Free Press, New York.
BROWN, R. W. (1973), *A First Language—the early stages.* Allen and Unwin, London.
DE CECCO, J. P. (1967), *The Psychology of Language, Thought and Instruction.* Holt, Rinehart & Winston, New York.
FERGUSON, C. A. and SLOBIN, D. I. (1973), *Studies of Child Language Development.* Holt, Rinehart & Winston, New York.
GIGLIOLI, P. P. (1972), *Language and Social Context,* Penguin, Harmondsworth.
HAYES, J. R. (1970), *Cognition and the Development of Language.* Wiley, New York.
HUXLEY, R. and INGRAM, E. (1971), *Language Acquisition—models and methods.* Academic Press, London, New York.
LYONS, J. and WALES, R. J. (1966), *Psycholinguistic Papers.* Edinburgh University Press, Edinburgh.
MORTON, J. (1971), *Biological and Social Factors in Psycholinguistics.* Logos Press, London.
OLDFIELD, R. C. and MARSHALL, J. C. (1968), *Language.* Penguin, Harmondsworth.
REED, C. (1970), *The Learning of Language—essays in honor of David H. Russell.* Appleton-Century-Crofts, New York.
SLOBIN, D. (1971), *The Ontogenesis of Grammar.* Academic Press, New York.
SMITH, F. (1973), *Psycholinguistics and Reading.* Holt, Rinehart & Winston, New York.
SMITH, F. and MILLER, G. A. (1966), *The Genesis of Language.* M.I.T. Press, Cambridge, Mass.

Subject Index